CHARMING
SMALL HOTEL
GUIDES

ITALY

Including : SICILY & SARDINIA

CHARMING SMALL HOTEL GUIDES

ITALY

Including : SICILY & SARDINIA

Edited by Chris Gill

300 Raritan Center Parkway,
CN 94, Edison, N.J. 08818

Published by   Hunter Publishing, Inc.,
               300 Raritan Center Parkway,
               Edison, NJ 08818
               Tel (908) 225 1900
               Fax (908) 417 0492

Conceived, designed and produced by
Duncan Petersen Publishing Ltd, 54 Milson Road,
London, W14 0LB
Edited by Fox + Partners, The Old Forge,
Norton St Philip, Bath BA3 6LW

Editor Chris Gill
Assistant editors Julia Letts, Amanda Crook
Principal inspectors Stuart Morris, Richard Gibbs,
Lindsay Hunt
Proofreader Joshua Dubin
Art director Mel Petersen

Typeset by Fox + Partners, Bath,
and PCS Typesetting, Frome
Originated by Reprocolor International S.R.I., Milan
Printed by G. Canale & C. SpA, Turin

ISBN 1-55650-561-2

Contents

Introduction

This guide to hotels in Italy is part of a series also covering Britain and Ireland, France, Spain, Germany and (for the first time this year) Austria. This volume has been completely revised and extended for 1993, with more pages, and a new style of short entry that has allowed us to include more full entries with photographs and a greater number of entries in total. The maps have been completely redrawn including much more detail, giving immediate access to the entries you want to consult.

The *Charming Small Hotel Guides* are different from other accommodation guides on the market. They are designed to satisfy what we believe to be the real needs of today's traveller; needs which have been served at best haphazardly by other guides. The most fundamental difference is suggested by the title: we aim to include only those hotels and guest-houses which offer notable character and warmth of welcome, and which are small enough to offer truly personal service, usually from the owner. In Italy, most of our recommendations have fewer than 30 rooms, and only a few have more than 40.

The guides are different in other ways, too. Their descriptive style is different, and they are compiled differently. Our entries employ, above all, words: they contain not one symbol. They are written by people with something to say, not a bureaucracy which has long since lost the ability to distinguish the praiseworthy from the mediocre. The editorial team is small and highly experienced at assessing and writing about hotels, at noticing all-important details. Although we place great emphasis on consistency, we have made use of reports from members of the public, and would welcome more of them (see page 11). Every entry aims to give a coherent and definite feel of what it is actually like to stay in that place.

These are features which will reveal their worth only as you use your *Charming Small Hotel Guide*. Its other advantages are more obvious: it contains colour photographs of around 125 of the most appealing entries; the entries are presented in clear geographical groups; and each entry is categorized by the type of accommodation (for example, country inn).

Introduction

Small Italian hotels

Small hotels have always had the special appeal that they can offer the traveller a personal welcome and personal attention, whereas larger places are necessarily more institutional. But the distinction has become particularly clear in Italy during recent years with the energetic restoration of historic buildings to create singular hotels. Of course, Italy's cities and towns have always had their share of *pensioni* which, at their best, are the stuff of a guide such as this; but you do need a guide like this to distinguish the seedy from the delightful.

The establishments described in this guide are simply the 350 or so small hotels, *pensioni* and bed-and-breakfast places that we believe most discriminating travellers would prefer to stay in, given the choice. Some undeniably pricey places are included – Italy is no longer a particularly cheap destination – but the majority of places in the guide offer double rooms for under L150,000.

Our ideal hotel has a peaceful, pretty setting; the building itself is either handsome or historic, or at least has a distinct character. The rooms are spacious, but on a human scale – not grand or intimidating. The decorations and furnishings are harmonious, comfortable and impeccably maintained, and include antique pieces that are meant to be used, not revered. The proprietors and staff are dedicated, thoughtful and sensitive in their pursuit of their guests' happiness – friendly and welcoming without being intrusive. Last but not least, the food, whether simple or ambitious, is fresh, interesting and carefully prepared. Elaborate facilities such as saunas or trouser-presses count for little in these guides, though we do generally list them.

Of course, not every hotel included here scores top marks on each of these counts. But it is surprising how many do respectably well on most fronts.

Introduction

How to find an entry

In this guide, the entries are arranged in geographical groups. First, the whole country is divided into 3 major sections; we start with Northern Italy and proceed to Central and finally Southern Italy. Within these sections, the entries are grouped into regions; some of these correspond to the administrative regions of the country (Tuscany and Emilia-Romagna, for example); some are combinations of these regions (Lazio and Abruzzi, for example); and some are broader (the North-West, for example).

Each regional section follows a set sequence:

- First comes an Area introduction – an overview of the hotel scene in that region, incorporating brief notes on hotels which have not justified a longer entry – hotels in cities which would otherwise not feature here at all, for example; where the section contains only one or two short entries, these are appended to this introduction.

- Then come the main, full-page entries for that state, arranged in alphabetical order by town.

- Finally come the shorter, quarter-page entries for that state, similarly arranged alphabetically.

To find a hotel in a particular area, simply browse through the headings at the top of the pages until you find that area – or use the maps following this introduction to locate the appropriate pages. The maps show not only the place-name under which each hotel appears, but also the page number of the entry.

To locate a specific hotel or a hotel in a specific place, use the indexes at the back, which list the entries alphabetically, first by name and then by place-name.

Introduction

How to read an entry
At the top of each entry is a coloured bar highlighting
the name of the town or village where the establishment
is located, along with a categorization which gives some
clue to its character. These categories are as far as
possible self-explanatory. The term 'villa' needs, perhaps,
some qualification: it is reserved for places with gardens
which have something of the air of a country house,
whether in a town or at the seaside.

Fact boxes
The fact box given for each hotel follows a standard
pattern which requires little explanation; but:

Under **Tel** we give the telephone number starting with
the area code used within Italy; when dialling from
another country, omit the initial nought of this code. We
now also give a **Fax** number; in some cases, to save space,
we omit the area code.

Under **Location** we give information on the setting of the
hotel and on its parking arrangements, as well as pointers
to help you find it.

Under **Food & drink** we list the meals available.

The basic **Prices** in this volume – unlike our volume on
Britain and Ireland – are **per room**.
    Normally, a range of prices is given, representing the
smallest and largest amounts you might pay in different
circumstances – typically, the minimum is the cost of the
cheapest single room in low season, while the maximum
is the cost of the dearest double in high season. If
breakfast is included we say so; if not, where possible we
give a price for breakfast, per person.
    After the room price, we give either the price for
dinner, bed and breakfast (DB&B), or for full board (FB
– that is, all meals included) or, instead, an indication of
the cost of individual meals. All of these prices are **per
person**. After all this basic information comes, where
space allows, a summary of reductions available for long
stays or for children.
    Prices include tax and service. Wherever possible we
have given prices for 1993, but for many hotels these
were not available; actual prices may therefore be higher
than those quoted, simply because of inflation. But bear
in mind also that the proprietors of hotels and
guest-houses may change their prices from one year to
another by much more than the rate of inflation. This is
particularly likely in Italy this year, because official

controls on pricing have recently been relaxed. Always check before making a booking.

Under **Rooms** we summarize the number and style of bedrooms available. Our lists of facilities in bedrooms cover only mechanical gadgets and not ornaments such as flowers or consumables such as toiletries or free drinks.

Under **Facilities** we list public rooms and then outdoor and sporting facilities which are either part of the hotel or immediately on hand; facilities in the vicinity of the hotel but not directly connected with it (for example, a nearby golf-course) are not listed, though they sometimes feature at the end of the main description in the **Nearby** section, which presents a selection of interesting things to see or do in the locality.

We use the following abbreviations for **Credit cards**:

AE	American Express
DC	Diners Club
MC	MasterCard (Access/Eurocard)
V	Visa (Barclaycard/Bank Americard/Carte Bleue etc)

The final entry in a fact box is normally the name of the proprietor(s); but where the hotel is run by a manager we give his or her name instead.

Unfamiliar terms
Some visitors, particularly from North America, may be mystified by some terms. 'Self-catering' means that cooking facilities such as a kitchenette or small kitchen are provided for making your own meals, as in a rental apartment. 'Bargain breaks' or 'breaks' of any kind mean off-season price reductions are available, usually for a stay of a specific or minimum period.

Reporting to the guides

Please write and tell us about your experiences of small hotels, guest-houses and inns, whether good or bad, whether listed in this edition or not. As well as hotels in Italy, we are interested in hotels in Britain and Ireland, France, Spain, Portugal, Austria, Switzerland, Germany and other European countries, and those in the eastern and western United States.

The address to write to is:

> Chris Gill,
> Editor,
> *Charming Small Hotel Guides,*
> The Old Forge,
> Norton St Philip,
> Bath, BA3 6LW,
> England.

Checklist

Please use a separate sheet of paper for each report; include your name, address and telephone number on each report.

Your reports will be received with particular pleasure if they are typed, and if they are organized under the following headings:

> Name of establishment
> Town or village it is in, or nearest
> Full address, including post code
> Telephone number
> Time and duration of visit
> The building and setting
> The public rooms
> The bedrooms and bathrooms
> Physical comfort (chairs, beds, heat, light, hot water)
> Standards of maintenance and housekeeping
> Atmosphere, welcome and service
> Food
> Value for money

We assume that in writing you have no objections to your views being published unpaid, either verbatim or in an edited version. Names of major outside contributors may be acknowledged in the guide.

If you would be interested in looking at hotels on a professional basis on behalf of the guides, please include on a separate sheet a short CV and a summary of your travel and hotel-going experience.

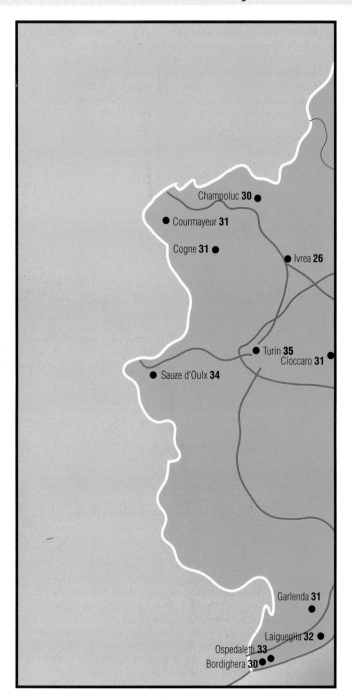

Champoluc **30** ●

● Courmayeur **31**

Cogne **31** ●

● Ivrea **26**

● Turin **35**
Cioccaro **31** ●

● Sauze d'Oulx **34**

Garlenda **31** ●

Laigueglia **32** ●
Ospedaletti **33**
Bordighera **30** ●●

Hotel location maps

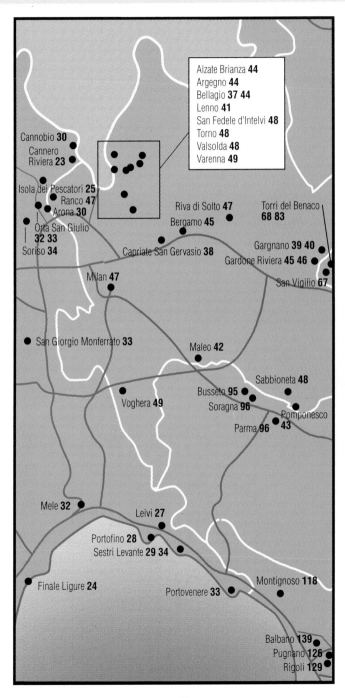

Alzate Brianza **44**
Argegno **44**
Bellagio **37 44**
Lenno **41**
San Fedele d'Intelvi **48**
Torno **48**
Valsolda **48**
Varenna **49**

Cannobio **30**
Cannero Riviera **23**
Isola dei Pescatori **25**
Ranco **47**
Arona **30**
Orta San Giulio **32 33**
Soriso **34**
Milan **47**
San Giorgio Monferrato **33**
Riva di Solto **47**
Bergamo **45**
Capriate San Gervasio **38**
Torri del Benaco **68 83**
Gargnano **39 40**
Gardone Riviera **45 46**
San Vigilio **67**
Maleo **42**
Sabbioneta **48**
Busseto **95**
Soragna **96**
Pomponesco **43**
Parma **96**
Voghera **49**
Mele **32**
Leivi **27**
Portofino **28**
Sestri Levante **29 34**
Finale Ligure **24**
Portovenere **33**
Montignoso **118**
Balbano **139**
Pugnano **126**
Rigoli **129**

13

Hotel location maps

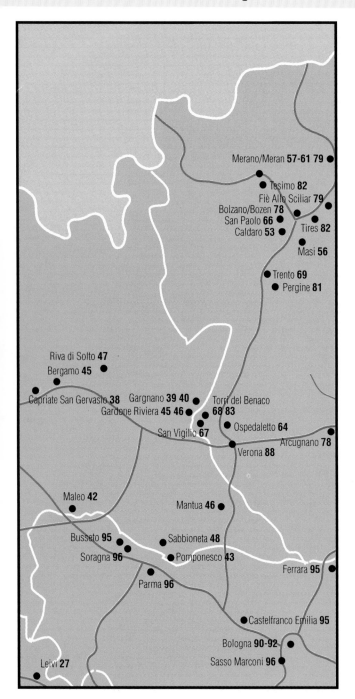

Merano/Meran **57-61 79**
Tesimo **82**
Fiè Allo Sciliar **79**
Bolzano/Bozen **78**
San Paolo **66**
Tires **82**
Caldaro **53**
Masi **56**
Trento **69**
Pergine **81**
Riva di Solto **47**
Bergamo **45**
Capriate San Gervasio **38**
Gargnano **39 40**
Torri del Benaco **68 83**
Gardone Riviera **45 46**
Ospedaletto **64**
San Vigilio **67**
Arcugnano **78**
Verona **88**
Maleo **42**
Mantua **46**
Busseto **95**
Sabbioneta **48**
Soragna **96**
Pomponesco **43**
Ferrara **95**
Parma **96**
Castelfranco Emilia **95**
Bologna **90-92**
Leivi **27**
Sasso Marconi **96**

14

Hotel location maps

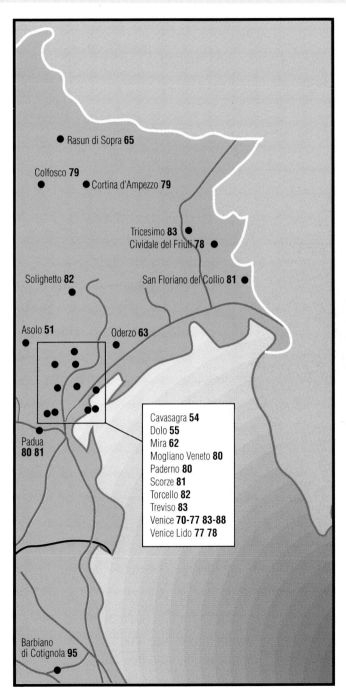

● Rasun di Sopra **65**

Colfosco **79**
●   ● Cortina d'Ampezzo **79**

Tricesimo **83** ●
Cividale del Friuli **78** ●

Solighetto **82**
●   San Floriano del Collio **81** ●

Asolo **51**   Oderzo **63**
●   ●

Padua
80 81

Cavasagra **54**
Dolo **55**
Mira **62**
Mogliano Veneto **80**
Paderno **80**
Scorze **81**
Torcello **82**
Treviso **83**
Venice **70-77 83-88**
Venice Lido **77 78**

Barbiano
di Cotignola **95**

Hotel location maps

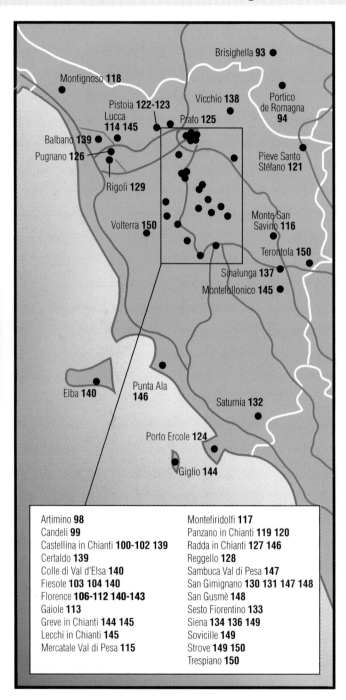

Brisighella **93**

Montignoso **118**

Vicchio **138**

Portico de Romagna **94**

Pistoia **122-123**
Lucca **114 145**

Prato **125**

Balbano **139**
Pugnano **126**

Pieve Santo Stéfano **121**

Rigoli **129**

Monte San Savino **116**

Volterra **150**

Terontola **150**

Sinalunga **137**

Montefollonico **145**

Punta Ala **146**

Saturnia **132**

Elba **140**

Porto Ercole **124**

Giglio **144**

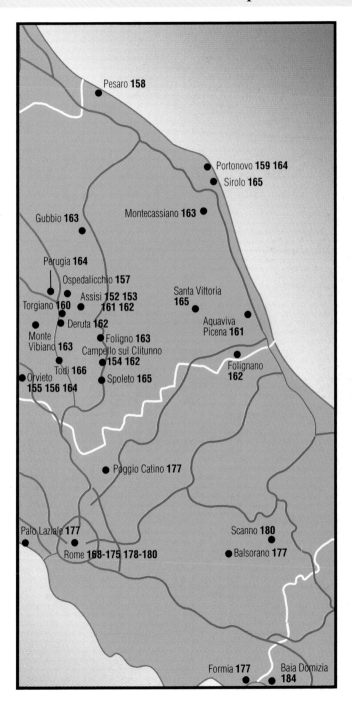

Pesaro **158**

Portonovo **159 164**

Sirolo **165**

Montecassiano **163**

Gubbio **163**

Perugia **164**

Ospedalicchio **157**

Assisi **152 153
161 162**

Torgiano **160**

Santa Vittoria
165

Aquaviva
Picena **161**

Deruta **162**

Monte
Vibiano **163**

Foligno **163**

Campello sul Clitunno
154 162

Folignano
162

Todi **166**

Orvieto
155 156 164

Spoleto **165**

Poggio Catino **177**

Palo Laziale **177**

Scanno **180**

Rome **168-175 178-180**

Balsorano **177**

Formia **177**

Baia Domizia
184

17

Hotel location maps

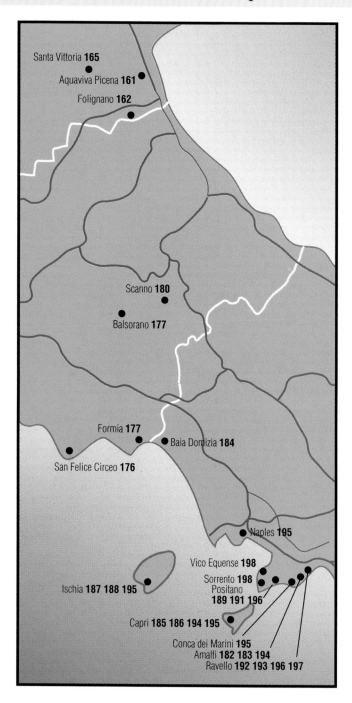

Santa Vittoria **165**
Aquaviva Picena **161**
Folignano **162**

Scanno **180**
Balsorano **177**

Formia **177**
Baia Domizia **184**
San Felice Circeo **176**

Naples **195**

Vico Equense **198**
Sorrento **198**
Positano
189 191 196
Ischia **187 188 195**

Capri **185 186 194 195**

Conca dei Marini **195**
Amalfi **182 183 194**
Ravello **192 193 196 197**

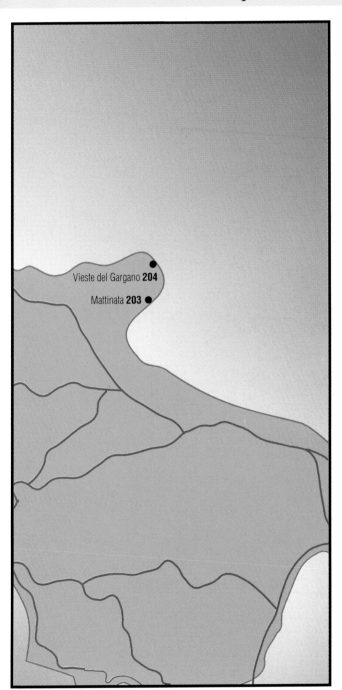

Hotel location maps

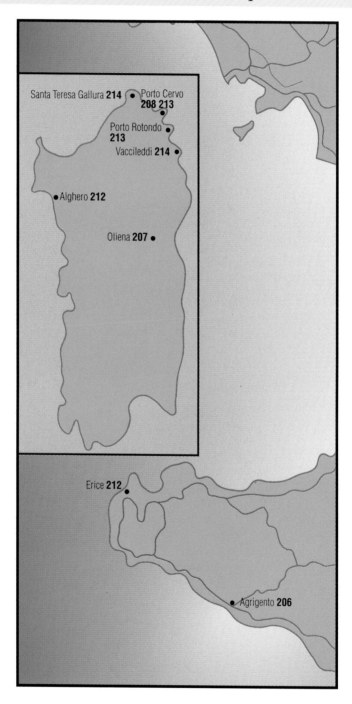

Santa Teresa Gallura **214**

Porto Cervo **208 213**

Porto Rotondo **213**

Vaccileddi **214**

●Alghero **212**

Oliena **207** ●

Erice **212**

● Agrigento **206**

Hotel location maps

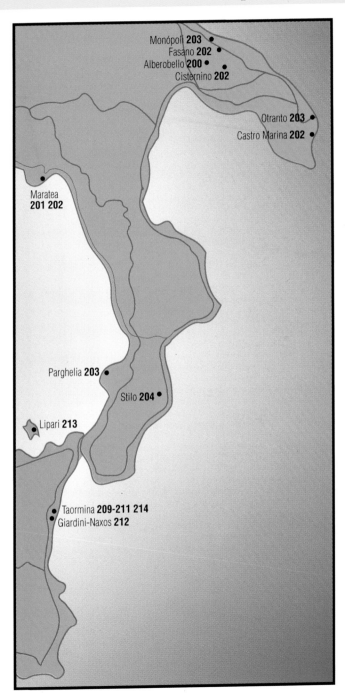

Monópoli **203**
Fasano **202**
Alberobello **200**
Cisternino **202**

Otranto **203**
Castro Marina **202**

Maratea
201 202

Parghelia **203**

Stilo **204**

Lipari **213**

Taormina **209-211 214**
Giardini-Naxos **212**

The north-west

Hotels in the north-west

North-west Italy offers three contrasting regions: the land 'at the foot of the mountains', Piedmont; the mountainous Valle d'Aosta; and the coastal Liguria.

Piedmont does, no doubt, have its attractions, but they do not impress themselves on many foreign visitors, who tend to hurry across this large region on their way to the recognized glories of Italy to the east and south.

To the traveller, as to the resident, the region is dominated by the city lying at its heart – Turin. Although we have found a couple of recommendable hotels within easy reach of Turin, and one on the fringes of the city itself (see below), we have not found hotels in the middle of the city which deserve to be picked out in these pages. But this does not mean that the city lacks comfortable hotels: there is certainly no shortage of swish, large impersonal places right in the heart of things. Of these, the most attractive (and not quite the most expensive) is the Jolly Hotel Ligure (Tel (011) 55641, fax 535438). Of the more modest places, the Genio (Tel (011) 650 5771, fax 8264) and the Victoria (Tel (011) 561 1909, fax 1806) are smartly modern, of moderate size and central – the former particularly handy for the station. Only a little further away from the middle is the cheaper Pied-montese (Tel (011) 669 8101, fax 057i) – ideal for travellers on a tight budget who do not wish to be confined to the suburbs. None of these cheaper hotels has a restaurant, but there are plenty of eating places in the central area.

To the north of Turin is the mainly French-speaking Valle d'Aosta, a steep-sided valley surrounded by the highest peaks in the Alps, and best known for its mountain scenery and winter sports facilities. Courmayeur, at the foot of Mont Blanc, and close to the road tunnel, is a popular ski-resort in winter but worth visiting in summer too. The Palace Bron (Tel (0165) 842545, fax 844015, 27 rooms) is a smart, well-equipped chalet hotel set in the pine forest above the town and offering glorious views of the surrounding mountains. For a less expensive but still comfortable stay, try the Del Viale (Tel (0165) 842227, fax 844513), the Bouton d'Or (Tel (0165) 846729, fax 842152), both in Courm-ayeur, or La Brenva (Tel (0165) 89285, fax 89301, 14 rooms) at Entrèves, the entry (or exit) point of the Mont Blanc Tunnel.

The third region is Liguria, a thin strip of mountainous coast-line dominated by the Italian Riviera, for which we offer several full recommendations on the following pages. If you want to visit Genoa – and there is much to see besides the modern docks and suburbs – you would do best to do so from a base on the Riviera itself.

This page acts as an introduction to the features and hotels of North-west Italy, and gives brief recommendations of reasonable hotels that for one reason or another have not made a full entry. The long entries for this region – covering the hotels we are most enthusiastic about – start on the next page. But do not neglect the shorter entries starting on page 30: these are all hotels that we would happily stay at.

The north-west

Lakeside hotel, Cannero Riviera

Cannero

Cannero is one of the quietest resorts on Lake Maggiore and its most desirable hotels lie right on the shore. Only the ferry landing-stage and a quiet dead-end road separate the Cannero from the waters of Maggiore.

The building was once a monastery, though only an old stone column, a couple of vaulted passageways and a quiet courtyard suggest it is anything other than a modern hotel. The emphasis is on comfort and relaxation and the atmosphere is very friendly, thanks largely to the smiling Signora Gallinotto. Downstairs, big windows and terraces make the most of the setting. The restaurant focuses on the lake, with an outdoor terrace running alongside.

The bedrooms are light and well cared for, and have adequate bathrooms. There are gorgeous views of lake and mountains from the front rooms, though many guests are just as happy overlooking the pool at the back – which, if anything, is quieter. By day this provides a delightfully peaceful spot to take a dip or lounge under yellow and white parasols.

Nearby Borromean Islands – daily connections by boat; Ascona (21 km), Locarno (25 km) and other resorts of Lake Maggiore.

Lungo Lago 3-2, Cannero Riviera 28051 Novara
Tel (0323) 788046 **Fax** 788048
Location in resort, overlooking lake, with garden and 2 car parks
Food & drink breakfast, lunch, dinner
Prices rooms L65,000-L130,000; DB&B L85,000
Rooms 30 double, 6 single, all with bath or shower; all rooms have central heating, phone
Facilities sitting-room, piano bar, dining-room, lakeside terrace; tennis, pool, solarium, boat, windsurfing, 2 bicycles
Credit cards AE, DC, MC, V
Children welcome; separate dining-room for children, baby-sitter on request
Disabled 8 rooms accessible; lift/elevator
Pets accepted if well behaved, but not in main sitting-room
Closed Nov to mid-Mar
Proprietors Sga Gallinotto and sons

The north-west

Seaside villa, Finale Ligure

Punta Est

The Italian Riviera west of Genoa is for the most part disappointing: most of its resorts are dreary, and most of its hotels mediocre. Happily, both the Punta Est and Finale Ligure are exceptions. The hotel is converted from a splendid 18thC villa which stands high and proudly pink above the buzz of the main coastal road, overlooking the sea. Signor Podesta, who used to be a sculptor, has acted as resident architect since the hotel was first created in the late 1960s, and with great success. By preserving the original features of the house and adding to it in a sympathetic style, he has managed to preserve the atmosphere of a private villa. The interior is cool and elegant – all dark-wood antiques, fine stone arches, fireplaces and tiled floors. But with such an impressive setting, for most months of the year the focus is on the outdoor terraces, pool and gardens, with their pines, potted plants and lovely views.

Breakfast is taken (off Staffordshire china) in a sort of canopied greenhouse – a lovely sunny spot, surrounded by greenery. Other meals are served in a dining-room in the annexe, where stone arches and beams create a vaguely medieval setting. You can choose between international and Ligurian dishes, including bass cooked with strong aromatic local herbs. The beach is only a couple of minutes' walk down the hillside.

Nearby Finale Borgo (3 km), Alassio (26 km).

Via Aurelia l, Finale Ligure 17024 Savona
Tel (019) 600612 **Fax** 600611
Location E of the historic town, in private gardens; private car parking
Food & drink breakfast, lunch, dinner
Prices rooms L150,000-L280,000; meals L40,000-L60,000
Rooms 30 double, 4 single, 5 suites; all with bath and shower; all rooms have central heating, phone; minibar, TV in 25 rooms
Facilities sitting-room, bar, TV room, conference room, piano bar; swimming-pool, half tennis court, solarium
Credit cards AE, V
Children accepted, provided they are under control
Disabled access difficult
Pets not accepted
Closed Oct to Easter
Proprietors Podesta family

The north-west

Lakeside guest-house, Isola dei Pescatori

Verbano

The Isola dei Pescatori may not have the *palazzo* or gardens of neighbouring Isola Bella (unlike the other islands, it has never belonged to the wealthy Borromeo family), but it is just as charming in its own way. The cafés and the slightly shabby, painted fishermens' houses along the front are, perhaps, reminiscent of a Greek island – though not an undiscovered one.

The Verbano is a large russet-coloured villa occupying one end of the island, its garden and terraces looking across the lake to Isola Bella. It does not pretend to be a hotel of great luxury, but it can offer lots of character and local colour, and the Zacchera family are friendly hosts. There are beautiful views from the bedrooms, and 11 of the 12 have balconies. Each room is named after a flower; most are prettily and appropriately furnished in old-fashioned style, with painted furniture; those which were a little tired-looking have apparently been refurbished.

But the emphasis is really on the restaurant, with home-made pastas a speciality. If weather prevents eating on the terrace you can still enjoy the views through the big windows of the dining-room. 'Excellent food, friendly staff,' says a recent visitor.

Nearby Isola Bella (5 minutes by boat); Stresa, Pallanza, Baveno

Via Ugo Ara 2, Isola dei Pescatori, Stresa 28049 Novara **Tel** (0323) 30408 **Fax** 33129 **Location** on tiny island with waterside terraces; regular boats from Stresa, where there is ample car parking space **Food & drink** breakfast, lunch, dinner **Prices** rooms L140,000 with breakfast; DB&B L110,000; FB L140,000 **Rooms** 12 double, 8 with bath, 4 with shower; all rooms have central heating **Facilities** dining-room, sitting-room, bar, terrace **Credit cards** AE, DC, MC, V **Children** accepted **Disabled** no special facilities **Pets** accepted **Closed** never **Proprietors** Zacchera family

The north-west

Converted monastery, Ivrea

Castello San Giuseppe

This *castello* was originally a monastery for Carmelite monks before Napoleon took it over as a fort, and although it is high on an isolated hill commanding views over the surrounding lakes, inside the walled grounds the atmosphere remains far more reflective than military. There is lots to explore. The hotel is centred around a peaceful inner garden, with ornamental pond, ancient cedars, monkey trees, magnolias, Sicilian figs and olive trees. The open reception has a sitting-area with comfortable chairs. Upstairs, the bedrooms are rustically stylish, in the best Italian tradition – wrought-iron beds, red-tiled floors, flowing curtains wafting in the breeze from the hills beyond. The best rooms have frescoed ceilings. The dining-room, with its frescoed, vaulted ceiling, high-backed chairs and candles, leaves the single diner crying out for a hand to hold. Fortunately the cuisine is more than sufficiently diverting, incorporating some interesting regional dishes, and there is a limited but good choice of wines. Breakfast is served in a more informal room upstairs.

A recent visitor enjoyed the cuisine but found the hotel and garden rather neglected. More reports please.

Nearby Lake Sirio (2 km); Ivrea (3 km); local castles.

Chiaverano d'Ivrea 10010
Torino
Tel (0125) 424370 **Fax** 641278
Location 3 km NE of Ivrea,
near Chiaverano; in grounds,
with ample car parking
Food & drink breakfast,
dinner
Prices rooms L115,000-
L165,000 with breakfast; meals
L45,000-L65,000
Rooms 9 double, 4 with bath,
5 with shower; 7 single, 2 with
bath, 5 with shower; all rooms
have central heating, phone,
TV
Facilities dining-room,
breakfast-room, bar, TV room,
banqueting hall
Credit cards AE, DC, MC, V
Children welcome
Disabled no special facilities
Pets allowed if small and quiet
Closed never
Proprietor Pasquale and
Renata Naghiero

The north-west

Ca' Peo

This rambling farmhouse in the hills east of Portofino has been in the Solari family for four generations. Franco and Melly Solari opened their attractive, bay-windowed dining-room, with its magnificent views over the bay and hills, to guests in 1973. Melly produces the generous seasonal menus, while Franco provides the wine chosen from the 350 different vintages in his cellar. Both now enjoy a high reputation, and booking for the restaurant is essential.

In addition to its home-like atmosphere, the house has many delightful features, including black slate fixtures of varying antiquity (a local speciality – slate is mined in the hills around here). Accommodation is in apartments with a kitchen and dining area, all modern, in an annexe set into olive terraces below the main building; they are comfortable and airy, with new pine furniture and bright sofas.

This makes a quiet, attractive base for exploring the Gulf de Tigullio, between Portofino and Sestri Levante – provided you don't mind negotiating the winding access road.

Nearby walks in chestnut woods; Portofino (30 km); Cinque Terre within reach.

Via dei Caduti 80, Leivi 16040 Genova
Tel (0185) 319696 **Fax** 319671
Location 6 km N of Chiavari, in hills; with garden and car parking
Food & drink breakfast, lunch, dinner
Prices rooms L160,000 with breakfast
Rooms 5 apartments; all have phone, TV, kitchen facilities
Facilities dining-room, sitting-room, bar, wine cellar

Credit cards V
Children accepted
Disabled access difficult
Pets in bedrooms only
Closed November; restaurant, Mon, Tue lunch
Proprietors Franco and Melly Solari

The north-west

Eden

Such is the popularity of Portofino – a chic and enchanting little port – that even out of season you are likely to have to wait to get into the town, and in season the wait for a parking space can last for hours. Naturally, the charms of the place are affected by the crowds. But stay the night and you can see a different Portofino; you can dine on the waterfront in relative peace, and watch the fishermen coming and going before the crowds arrive.

Hotel rooms are at a premium. There is the grand (and expensive) Hotel Splendid, and a few much smaller, more modest hotels. The Eden is one of these – a tiny place down a narrow street a couple of minutes from the waterfront. The garden, shaded by a large palm and a mass of greenery, is a quiet enclave in the middle of the resort. Meals are taken here on the terrace when weather permits, or in the trattoria-style dining-room which overlooks the garden. The only other public area is the lobby-cum-bar, with the reception desk tucked under the stairs. Bedrooms are light and fresh, with neat, spotless bathrooms.

It has been a while since we had any feedback on the Eden from readers; reports would be very welcome.

Nearby lighthouse; San Fruttuoso (by boat or 2 hr walk).

Portofino 16034 Genoa
Tel (0185) 269091
Fax 269047
Location in middle of resort, with private garden in front; public car park only (L27,000 per day)
Food & drink breakfast, lunch, dinner
Prices rooms L150,000-L200,000 with breakfast; meals L40,000-L60,000
Rooms 12 double, all with bath; all have central heating, phone, TV; some have air-conditioning
Facilities dining-room with outdoor terrace, bar
Credit cards AE, DC, MC, V
Children welcome if well behaved
Disabled no special facilities
Pets accepted, but not in restaurant
Closed never
Proprietor Osta Ferruccio

The north-west

Helvetia

The Helvetia's claim that it has 'the quietest and most enchanting position of Sestri Levante' is no exaggeration; it stands at one end of the appropriately named Baia del Silenzio. The hotel is distinguished by its spotless white façade, and the yellow and white canopies that shade its balconies and terrace.

Lorenzo Pernigotti devotes himself wholeheartedly to his guests and provides the sort of extras – including 15 gleaming yellow bikes – that you might expect to find in a four-star hotel; but the Helvetia remains small and personal; one satisfied guest says he 'felt just like part of the family'.

The sitting-room/bar has the air of a private home – antiques, coffee-table books, newspapers, potted plants – and the breakfast room is lovely and light, with views of the bay. Bedrooms are light and airy, overlooking either the bay – there are six with their own balconies – or the gardens. The day starts on the delightful terrace, with an unusually liberal help-yourself breakfast. Behind the terrace luxuriant gardens climb up the hillside, with tables in the shade of palm trees. Serious sunbathers can take to sunbeds. And there is a tiny pebble beach just across the road.

Nearby Beauty spots of the eastern Riviera; eg Portofino (28 km).

Via Cappuccini 43, Sestri Levante 16039 Genova
Tel (0185) 41175 **Fax** 47216
Location overlooking small beach, with private garage and limited free car parking
Food & drink breakfast
Prices rooms L120,000-L140,000 with breakfast; 30% reduction for children under 6 sharing parents' room
Rooms 28 double, 14 with bath, 14 with shower; all rooms have central heating, phone, hairdrier, radio, colour TV, video, minibar
Facilities sitting-room, TV/video room, dining-room, bar, terrace; solarium, ping-pong, free bicycles
Credit cards MC, V
Children welcome; small beds provided
Disabled no special facilities
Pets dogs accepted but not in dining-room
Closed Nov to Feb
Proprietor Lorenzo Pernigotti

Lakeside hotel, Arona

Hotel Giardino

We get mixed reports on this comfortable lakeside hotel, though no one disputes the attractions of its position, with a large terrace looking across the road to Lake Maggiore, or the friendliness of the staff. The dining-room is undistinguished, but the bedrooms have some individuality.

■ Via Repubblica 1, 28041 Arona (Novara) **Tel** (0322) 45994 **Fax** (0322) 249401 **Meals** breakfast, lunch, dinner **Prices** rooms L122,000 with breakfast; FB L125,000 **Rooms** 56, all with bath or shower, central heating, TV, minibar, phone **Credit cards** AE, DC, V **Closed** never

Seaside villa, Bordighera

Villa Elisa

An attractive old house set among sub-tropical gardens in the quiet area at the back of this popular family resort. Public rooms are peaceful and civilized, bedrooms spacious and pleasantly old-fashioned. Reasonable prices by local standards.

■ Via Romana 70, 18012 Bordighera (Imperia) **Tel** (0184) 261313 **Fax** (0184) 261942 **Meals** breakfast, lunch, dinner **Prices** L95,000-L150,000 **Rooms** 35, all with bath or shower, phone, TV, minibar **Credit cards** AE, MC, V **Closed** Nov to mid-Dec

Restaurant-with-rooms, Cannobio

Pironi

We are pleased to welcome the Pironi back to these pages after a year-long closure. It is an arcaded medieval building at the heart of the unspoilt lakeside village of Cannobio, and when we last saw it the hotel too seemed perfectly preserved. Reports on the new regime very welcome.

■ Via Marconi 35, 28052 Cannobio (Novara) **Tel** (0323) 70624 **Fax** (0323) 72398 **Meals** breakfast, lunch, dinner **Prices** rooms L110,000 with breakfast **Rooms** 12, all with bath, central heating, phone, minibar **Credit cards** AE, DC, MC, V **Closed** Nov to Feb

Mountain chalet, Champoluc

Villa Anna Maria

A chalet-style 1920s villa in a quiet, wooded hillside setting close to the village of Champoluc – main community of a steep-sided valley beneath the Monte Rosa. Wood panelling, simple but cosy furnishings and country decorations. Most rooms have bathrooms.

■ Via Croues 5, 11020 Champoluc (Aosta) **Tel** (0125) 307128 **Fax** (0125) 307984 **Meals** breakfast, lunch, dinner **Prices** rooms L70,000-L105,000; meals L35,000-L40,000 **Rooms** 20, all with central heating, phone, TV **Credit cards** V **Closed** restaurant only, Oct to Nov and May to late Jun depending on weather

The north-west

Converted monastery, Cioccaro di Penango

Locanda del Sant'Uffizio

The addition of bedrooms in the late 1980s made this well-established restaurant a very attractive small hotel. Original features have been preserved, and furnishings are a mix of antique and chic modern. Readers approve of the fine food and warm welcome. Attractive swimming-pool.

■ 14030 Cioccaro di Penango (Asti) **Tel** (0141) 917271 **Fax** (0141) 916068 **Meals** breakfast, lunch, dinner **Prices** DB&B L220,000; FB L280,000 **Rooms** 31, all with bath or shower, central heating, minibar, TV **Credit cards** DC, MC, V **Closed** 3 weeks in both Jan and Aug

---

Mountain chalet, Cogne

Bellevue

A substantial hotel, in the same family since its construction in the 1920s, in a glorious setting on the flat grassy floor of a valley from which the Gran Paradiso and other Alps rise. Traditional family hotel standards are well kept up, and some rooms are more than averagely elegant.

■ Rue Grand Paradis, 11012 Cogne (Aosta) **Tel** (0165) 74825 **Fax** (0165) 749192 **Meals** breakfast, lunch, dinner **Prices** DB&B L93,000-L180,000 **Rooms** 44, all with bath or shower, central heating, phone, hairdrier, radio **Credit cards** MC, V **Closed** Oct to mid-Dec

---

Mountain chalet, Courmayeur

La Grange

This 13thC chalet-style farmhouse, with stone walls, stone roof and wooden trimmings, has made a handsome little hotel. The rustic style is carried through into the welcoming interior, with country antiques dotted around. Bedrooms are plain but comfortable and well equipped.

■ Entreves, 11013 Courmayeur (Aosta) **Tel** (0165) 89274 **Fax** (0165) 89316 **Meals** breakfast, snacks **Prices** rooms L70,000-L100,000 **Rooms** 23, all with bath or shower, central heating, TV, minibar, phone **Credit cards** AE, DC, MC, V **Closed** Mar to Jun, Oct to Nov

---

Country hotel, Garlenda

La Meridiana

A little oasis of peace, a short drive inland from the Riviera, among woods and vines. The Meridiana has a special appeal to golfers, with 18 holes next door, but non-golfers should not be put off: it is in any case a luxurious retreat, with excellent food and a large pool.

■ 17033 Garlenda (Savona) **Tel** (0182) 580271 **Fax** (0182) 580150 **Meals** breakfast, dinner **Prices** rooms L190,000-L300,000; suites L280,000-L360,000 **Rooms** 30, all with bath, phone, TV (satellite), minibar **Credit cards** AE, DC, MC, V **Closed** beginning Dec to end Feb

The north-west

Seaside hotel, Laigueglia

Splendid

The well in the dining-room and the various vaulted ceilings testify to the monastic origins of this neat hotel in the middle of Laigueglia. Furnishings mix antique and modern happily. A key feature is the small back garden, with its inviting pool, where drinks are served.

■ Piazza Badaro 3, 17020 Laigueglia (Savona) **Tel** (0182) 690325 **Fax** (0182) 690894 **Meals** breakfast, lunch, dinner **Prices** rooms L55,000-L150,000 with breakfast; DB&B L75,000-L105,000; 20% reduction for children under 7 **Rooms** 50, all with bath or shower, central heating, phone **Credit cards** AE, DC, MC, V **Closed** Oct to Mar

Country hotel, Mele

Hotel Fado 78

Gianni Canepa and his English wife Christine have made their modest country hotel a welcoming port of call. The 19thC shuttered house has been modernized inside and the plain, comfortable bedrooms are in a modern extension. Lovely little garden, good views, excellent food.

■ Via Fado 82, 16010 Mele (Genova) **Tel** (010) 631802 **Meals** breakfast, lunch, dinner, snacks **Prices** rooms L45,000-L75,000; breakfast L9,000, meals L35,000 **Rooms** 8, all with bath or shower, central heating, phone, TV **Credit cards** not accepted **Closed** never

Country hotel, Orta San Giulio

La Bussola

This modern building enjoys splendid views over Lake Orta and its island of San Guilio, and has been built (in traditional villa style) to make the best of them. The dining-room is simple, light and spacious, and there is a small terrace. The large garden includes a fair-sized secluded pool.

■ 28016 Orta San Giulio (Novara) **Tel** (0322) 90198 **Fax** (0322) 90198 **Meals** breakfast, lunch, dinner **Prices** rooms L100,000-L121,000; DB&B L105,000 (obligatory Jun-Sep) **Rooms** 16, all with bath or shower, phone, central heating; 7 rooms have minibar **Credit cards** AE, MC, V **Closed** Nov

Lakeside hotel, Orta San Giulio

Leon d'Oro

'Great location, nice restaurant, and a charming little town on a charming little lake; a prize for the price.' A fair summary (from a reader) of this otherwise unremarkable hotel. The lakeside terrace looks on to the island of San Giulio, and next to the hotel is the beautiful and animated Piazza Motta.

■ 28016 Orta San Giulio (Novara) **Tel** (0322) 90254 **Fax** (0322) 90303 **Meals** breakfast, lunch, dinner **Prices** rooms L65,000-L85,000; meals L30,000-L50,000 **Rooms** 32, all with bath or shower, central heating; phone in 12 rooms **Credit cards** AE, MC, V **Closed** Jan

The north-west

Lakeside hotel, Orta San Giulio

Orta

The endearingly shabby façade of the Orta forms one side of the main piazza of Orta San Giulio, and its café tables spill out on to the square. Around the corner, the restaurant terrace overhanging Lake Orta gives glorious views. The hotel is pleasantly spacious and old-fashioned.

■ 28016 Orta San Giulio (Novara) **Tel** (0322) 90253 **Fax** (0322) 905646 **Meals** breakfast, lunch, dinner **Prices** rooms L70,000-L130,000 with breakfast **Rooms** 35, all with bath or shower, central heating, phone, view of lake; TV on request **Credit cards** AE, DC, MC, V **Closed** Nov to Feb

---

Seaside hotel, Ospedaletti

Delle Rose

Ospedaletti is famed for its flowers, and the garden is perhaps the main attraction of the Hotel Delle Rose, containing thousands of blooming cacti. The setting is relatively quiet, the bedrooms (most with bath) bland but neat, the dining-room more elegant, with silver on the tables.

■ Via de Medici 17, 18014 Ospedaletti (Imperia) **Tel** (0184) 689016 **Meals** breakfast, lunch, dinner **Prices** rooms L80,000-L95,000; DB&B L90,000 **Rooms** 14, all with bath, central heating, phone **Credit cards** not accepted **Closed** never

---

Town guest-house, Portovenere

Albergo Genio

A tiny, simple, family-run hotel partly occupying a medieval tower at the entrance to the popular tourist spot of Portovenere. The bedrooms are basic, though they all have bathrooms; but they are the cheapest in town, and the tower and its terraces do not lack character.

■ Piazza Bastrieri 8, 19025 Portovenere (La Spezia) **Tel** (0187) 900611 **Meals** no meals available **Prices** rooms L68,000-L88,000 **Rooms** 7, all with shower, central heating **Credit cards** MC, V **Closed** Jan and half of Feb

---

Restaurant-with-rooms, San Giorgio Monferrato

Castello di San Giorgio

A quite grand little pink-painted mansion, mainly dating from the 16thC, set in extensive parkland. The elegant restaurant, with vaulted ceiling and murals, is the focus, and you must eat here – expensively, if Maurizio Grossi has his way – to stay here. Rooms are relatively plain.

■ Via Cavalli d'Olivola 3, 15020 San Giorgio Monferrato (Alessandria) **Tel** (0142) 806203 **Fax** (0142) 806203 **Meals** breakfast, lunch, dinner **Prices** rooms L110,000-L160,000; breakfast L15,000, meals L60,000-L90,000 **Rooms** 11, all with bath, central heating, phone, colour TV, minibar **Credit cards** AE, DC, V **Closed** restaurant only, Mon

Mountain chalet, Sauze d'Oulx

Il Capricorno

To the British, Sauze is a downmarket ski resort, but it attracts quite a smart Italian clientele, winter and summer. The Capricorno is a cosily traditional chalet – rough beams, hand-made furniture – in an isolated position on the wooded slopes above the village.

■ Case Sparse 21, Le Clotes, 10050 Sauze d'Oulx (Torino) **Tel** (0122) 850273 **Meals** breakfast, lunch, dinner **Prices** rooms L150,000-L180,000; meals L50,000-L65,000 **Rooms** 8, all with shower, central heating, phone, TV **Credit cards** DC, V **Closed** May to mid-June, mid-Sep to Nov

Converted castle, Sestri Levante

Grand Hotel dei Castelli

This hotel was included in early editions of the guide on the strength of its splendid location, high up on Sestri Levante's wooded peninsula, and despite its decorative state. In 1992 it reopened after a year-long process of renovation; we haven't been able to inspect the results yet – reports welcome.

■ Via Penisola 26, 16039 Sestri Levante (Genova) **Tel** (0185) 487220 **Fax** (0185) 44767 **Meals** breakfast, lunch, dinner **Prices** rooms L255,000-L280,000; DB&B L215,000-L240,000 **Rooms** 45, all with bath, central heating, air-conditioning, phone, TV, minibar, hairdrier **Credit cards** AE, DC, MC, V **Closed** winter

Seaside hotel, Sestri Levante

Miramare

One of several pink, shuttered 19thC houses that line the Baia del Silenzio – but inside cool and contemporary. Huge arched windows make the best of the sea views, and the terrace is an idyllic spot for breakfast. Friendly staff but unremarkable food, say reporters.

■ Via Cappellini 9, 16039 Sestri Levante (Genoa) **Tel** (0185) 480855 **Fax** (0185) 41055 **Meals** breakfast, lunch, dinner **Prices** rooms L190,000-L210,000; reduction for children **Rooms** 43, all with bath or shower, phone, colour TV, minibar; apartments have sitting-room and kitchenette **Credit cards** AE, MC, V **Closed** never

Restaurant-with-rooms, Soriso

Al Sorriso

One of Italy's few Michelin two-star restaurants, set in an unremarkable village some way from Lake Orta. The dining-room is the picture of elegance, the service professional. Bedrooms are more ordinary (and more affordable) than you might expect.

■ 28018 Soriso (Novara) **Tel** (0322) 983228 **Fax** (0322) 983328 **Meals** breakfast, lunch, dinner **Prices** rooms L130,000-L190,000 with breakfast; meals about L100,000-L140,000 **Rooms** 7, all with bath or shower, phone, TV, minibar **Credit cards** MC, V **Closed** 2 weeks Jan, 3 weeks Aug; restaurant only, Mon and Tue lunch

The north-west

Conte Biancamano

'Faded grandeur' may be a cliché, but it is difficult to avoid in the case of this city-centre hotel (close to Turin's railway station). It is now modestly run, but the sitting-room is palatial in dimensions and style; bedrooms are more ordinary but still comfortable.

■ Corso Vittorio Emanuelle II 73, 10128 Turin **Tel** (011) 562 3281 **Fax** (011) 562 3789 **Meals** breakfast, snacks **Prices** rooms L115,000-L180,000 with breakfast **Rooms** 27, all with bath or shower, central heating, phone, TV, radio, minibar, hairdrier **Credit cards** AE, DC, MC, V **Closed** Aug

Villa Sassi-El Toulà

A noble 17thC villa, unrivalled in Turin. Many original features have been retained: marble floors, ornate doors and 17thC candelabra. But Villa Sassi is not cheap, and reporters have questioned its value for money, finding the welcome indifferent and the food variable.

■ Traforo del Pino 47, 10132 Turin **Tel** (011) 890556 **Fax** (011) 890095 **Meals** breakfast, lunch, dinner **Prices** rooms L200,000-L380,000 **Rooms** 17, all with phone, TV, minibar **Credit cards** AE, DC, V **Closed** Aug; restaurant only, Sun

Lombardia

Hotels in Lombardia

Lombardy is an enormous region, stretching from the high Alps bordering Switzerland almost as far as the Adriatic and Ligurian seas. It contains Lake Como, with Lakes Maggiore and Garda forming its boundary in the west and east respectively, and has at its heart the economic and industrial centre of Italy: Milan.

Of all big, glossy Italian cities, none is glossier than Milan and only Rome is bigger. Despite its considerable heritage – notably a marvellous cathedral, important art collections and the world's most famous opera house – its role as Italy's economic capital dominates the visitor's view, and most steer clear. The result is that Milan's hotels are business-oriented – and as big and glossy as the city itself.

Surprisingly though, we have been able to find two excellent small hotels in Milan (see page 47) and the Gran Duca di York (Tel (02) 874863, fax 869 0344, 33 rooms, no restaurant) is another which deserves a mention; despite its grand entrance, it is relatively plain, even basic, but it has more warmth and character than most and is quietly situated about a quarter of a mile from the cathedral. Also centrally placed, but too large for full recommendations, are the Manzoni (Tel (02) 760 05700, fax 784212), a calm, comfortable and reasonably priced hotel, and (if you can stand the extravagance) the Grand Hotel Duomo (Tel (02) 8833, fax 86462027) set in a historic building close to the *duomo* itself and to the famous central shopping arcades.

Our main lakeside recommendations concentrate on Lake Como and Lake Garda. Bellagio is the main resort on Lake Como with Menaggio a close second – try the Bellavista (Tel (0344) 32136, fax 31793) in Menaggio itself, or the Loveno (Tel (0344) 32110) in the village of Loveno 2 km away – a 13-room hotel with a shady garden and views of the lakes and mountains.

On Lake Garda, the main resort for the southern end is Sirmione, beautifully situated on the lake, and with the massive Castle of the Scaligers, Roman remains and lovely gardens to visit, but also very conveniently placed for the main Milan-Venice motorway and therefore very busy during the day with trippers trying to 'see' Lake Garda, Verona and Venice in a day. The Golf et Suisse (Tel (030) 916176, fax 916304), is a peaceful, modern, 30-room hotel, a mile out of town but still on the lake and with its own beach and jetty.

This page acts as an introduction to the features and hotels of Lombardy, and gives brief recommendations of reasonable hotels that for one reason or another have not made a full entry. The long entries for this region – covering the hotels we are most enthusiastic about – start on the next page. But do not neglect the shorter entries starting on page 44: these are all hotels that we would happily stay at.

Lombardia

Lakeside hotel, Bellagio

Florence

Bellagio is the pearl of Lake Como. It stands on a promontory at the point where the lake divides into two branches, and the views from its houses, villas and gardens are superb. The Florence is a handsome 18thC building occupying a prime position at one end of the main piazza, overlooking the lake. A terrace under arcades, where drinks and snacks are served, provides a welcoming entry to the hotel and the interior is no less appealing. Whitewashed walls, high vaulted ceilings and beams create a cool, attractive foyer; to one side, elegant and slightly faded seats cluster round an old stone fireplace. The atmosphere of rustic old-world charm is carried through to the vaulted dining-room.

Bedrooms have the same old-fashioned charm as the public rooms, furnished with cherry-wood antiques and attractive fabrics; the most sought after, naturally, are those with balconies and views over the lake. Meals (including breakfast) can be taken on a delightful lakeside terrace under shady trees across the street from the hotel, watching the various craft ply across the lake.

In the evening there is jazz in the elegant cocktail bar – one of Lake Como's smarter nightspots. The hotel has been in the same family for 150 years, and is now in the hands of brother and sister, Ronald and Roberta Ketzlar, who both speak good English and made a recent visitor 'very welcome'.
Nearby Villa Serbelloni; the Madonna del Ghisallo (37 km).

Piazza Mazzini, Bellagio 22021 Como
Tel (031) 950342 **Fax** 951722
Location on main piazza overlooking lake, with waterside terrace and garage
Food & drink breakfast, lunch, dinner
Prices rooms L110,000-L125,000; DB&B L97,000; FB L105,000
Rooms 32 double, 23 with bath, 8 with shower; 6 single; all rooms have central heating

Facilities dining-room, bar, reading and TV room, terrace
Credit cards AE, DC, MC, V
Children accepted
Disabled no special facilities
Pets well behaved ones accepted, but not in restaurant
Closed 20 Oct to 15 Apr
Proprietor Ronald Ketzlar

Lombardia

Restaurant with rooms, Capriate San Gervasio

Vigneto

Capriate San Gervasio is a few minutes' drive from the main autostrada from Milan to Venice, convenient for an overnight stop. The Vigneto is a comfortable villa, perched on a river bank, surrounded by a beautifully kept small garden and terrace. The bedrooms are reasonably sized, with modern furniture, decorated in rather sombre beige and tans; those at the front look out over the tree-lined banks of the river. The dining-room is formal, with many pictures on the walls, and looks out over the covered terrace where you can eat in the summer months. The restaurant is popular with the locals.

Nearby Bergamo (17 km); Milan (35 km).

Capriate San Gervasio 24042
Bergamo
Tel (02) 909 9351 **Fax** 0179
Location 12 km SW of
Bergamo, 2 km N of A4, on
banks of river Adda; with
private car parking
Food & drink breakfast,
lunch, dinner
Prices rooms L120,000-
L180,000 with breakfast; meals
L60,000-L80,000
Rooms 12 rooms, all with
shower, phone, TV

Facilities 2 sitting-rooms,
dining-room, conference
facilities
Credit card AE, V
Children accepted
Disabled no special facilities
Pets not accepted
Closed Mon; Aug; restaurant
only, Tue
Proprietor Casina Rosella

Lombardia

Lakeside hotel, Gargnano

Baia d'Oro

The Baia d'Oro is a distinctive old yellow-and-green building, right on the shore, its little pier jutting out into the dark blue waters of Garda and its terrace commanding superb views of the mountains beyond. This outside terrace provides the focal point of the hotel: in the summer months you breakfast, lunch and dine outside. If you are lucky enough to arrive by boat you can moor at the pier and step straight into the hotel.

It is a small, friendly establishment run by the Terzi family. Gianbattista is an artist – you can see some of his water-colours of the lakes in the rooms of the hotel. It was his wife who transformed the building from a private home to a to a delightful hotel which has retained its former intimacy; their eldest son, Gabriele, has recently taken over the day-to-day management.

The main public room is the restaurant – a light and inviting area with baskets brimming with fruit, bowls of freshly cut flowers, pretty arches and glass doors opening on to the terrace. The great majority of the main dishes here are fish – either from the sea or straight from the lake. Bedrooms are bright and lovingly cared for, several with lakeside balconies.

Nearby Gardone Riviera, Desenzano, Sirmione, Garda, Malcesine

Via Gamberera 13, Gargnano 25084 Brescia
Tel (0365) 71171 **Fax** 72568
Location in resort, with private car parking
Food & drink breakfast, lunch, dinner
Prices rooms L62,000-L105,000; meals L50,000-L90,000
Rooms 11 double, all with bath and shower; 2 single with shower; all have central heating, phone, minibar

Facilities dining-room, bar, TV room, sitting-room
Credit cards AE, MC, V
Children accepted
Disabled access difficult
Pets dogs accepted
Closed end Oct to Easter
Proprietors Terzi family

Lombardia

Lakeside hotel, Gargnano

Giulia

From a *pensione* with no private bathrooms, the Giulia has gradually been upgraded over the years to a three-star hotel. But happily it retains the atmosphere of a family-run guest-house – albeit a large one. It is a beautiful, spacious villa, built over a hundred years ago in Victorian style with Gothic touches. Signora Bombardelli, the proud owner, has been here for over 40 years, and thanks to all her hard work (for which she has received various awards) the Giulia is one of the most delightful places to stay on the entire lake.

For a start, it has a wonderful location, with gardens and terraces running practically on the water's edge. Inside, light and airy rooms lead off handsome corridors – a beautiful dining-room with Murano chandeliers, gold walls and elegant seats; a civilized sitting-room with Victorian armchairs; and bedrooms which range from light and modern to large rooms with timbered ceilings, antiques and balconies overlooking the garden and lake. At garden level a second, simpler dining-room opens out on to a terrace with ample space and gorgeous views. At any time of day, it is a lovely spot to linger among the palm trees and watch the boats plying the blue waters of Garda.

Nearby ferry services to villages and towns around Lake Garda.

Gargnano, Lago di Garda
25084 Brescia
Tel (0365) 71022 **Fax** 72774
Location 150 m from middle
of resort, with garden and
terrace down to lake; private
car park
Food & drink breakfast,
lunch, dinner
Prices DB&B L60,000; FB
L130,000
Rooms 14 double, 3 single; all
with bath or shower; all rooms
have central heating, phone,

TV, minibar
Facilities dining-room,
veranda taverna, sitting- room,
TV room, terrace; beach,
swimming-pool, sauna
Credit cards AE, DC, MC, V
Children accepted
Disabled access difficult
Pets accepted
Closed mid-Oct to mid-Mar
Proprietor Rina Bombardelli

Lombardia

San Giorgio

This large white 1920s villa on the shores of Lake Como stands out against a backdrop of wooded hills and immaculate gardens running right down to the shore. A path lined with potted plants leads down through neatly tended lawns to the lakeside terrace and the low-lying stone wall which is all that divides the gardens from the pebble beach and the lake. There are palm trees, arbours and stone urns where geraniums flourish. For a trip on the lake the ferry landing-stage lies close by.

The interior is no disappointment. The public rooms are large and spacious, leading off handsome halls. There are antiques wherever you go, and attractive touches such as pretty ceramic pots and copper pots brimming with flowers. The restaurant is a lovely light room with breathtaking views and the salon is equally inviting, with its ornate mirrors, fireplace and slightly faded antiques. Even the ping-pong room has a number of interesting antique pieces. Bedrooms are large and pleasantly old-fashioned. Antiques and beautiful views are the main features, but there is nothing grand or luxurious about them – hence the reasonable prices. One of our reporters rates this his favourite hotel – 'sensational view, friendly reception, firm bed, great towels'.

Nearby Tremezzo, Cadenabbia, Villa Carlotta (2-4 km); Bellagio (10 min boat crossing from Cadenabbia).

Via Regina 81, Lenno, Tremezzo 22019 Como
Tel (0344) 40415
Location on lakefront in private park, with parking for 30 cars, garage for 6
Food & drink breakfast, lunch, dinner
Prices rooms L95,000-L170,000 with breakfast; DB&B L86,000-L118,000; meals L35,000
Rooms 26 double, 20 with bath, 6 with shower; 3 single, one with bath; all rooms have central heating
Facilities dining-room, hall, reading-room, ping-pong room, terrace; tennis
Credit cards MC, V
Children accepted
Disabled access difficult
Pets not accepted
Closed Oct to Apr
Proprietor Margherita Cappelletti

Lombardia

Restaurant with rooms, Maleo

Sole

Franco Colombani fulfilled a lifelong ambition when, in the mid-1980s, he completed restoration of this 15thC coaching inn. Today it is reckoned among the finest restaurants in Italy. Franco has brought his own distinctive personality to the traditional regional cuisine that is his quiet obsession. Dark, tasty stews, roast meats and fish are accompanied by vegetables from the kitchen garden and fine wines from Franco's unfathomable cellars.

The building itself displays the same robust restraint as the cooking. The exterior is marked solely by a gilt wrought iron sun. Inside, the walls are white-washed, the ceilings timbered and the arched chambers carefully scattered with antique furniture, copper pots and ceramics. There are three dining-areas: the old kitchen, with its long table, open fire and old gas hobs where on occasion dishes are finished in front of the guests; a smaller dining-room, with individual tables; and the stone-arched portico which looks out on to the idyllic garden. The bedrooms all have individual high points, and good bathrooms. Those above the dining-room are traditional, while those overlooking the garden have a less impressive mix of old and new furnishings.

Nearby Piacenza; Cremona (22 km).

Via Trabattoni 22, 20076
Maleo
Tel (0377) 58142 **Fax** 458058
Location behind church, off
main piazza of village, 20 km
NE of Piacenza; car parking
available
Food & drink breakfast,
lunch, dinner
Prices rooms L180,000-
L290,000; meals L80,000
Rooms 8 double, all with bath;
all rooms have central
heating, phone, TV, minibar

Facilities 2 dining-rooms,
sitting-room; garden
Credit cards AE, MC, V
Children welcome
Disabled no special facilities
Pets welcome
Closed hotel Jan and Aug;
restaurant Sun eve, Mon
Proprietor Franco Colombani

Lombardia

Restaurant with rooms, Pomponesco

Il Leone

Pomponesco was once a flourishing town under the Gonzaga family. Now it is a shadow of its former self, surrounded by unsightly modern suburbs. But the old part still has a certain faded charm, and just off the main piazza lies the Leone – an old peeling building which once belonged to a 16thC nobleman.

This is primarily a place to eat (it calls itself a trattoria). There are only eight bedrooms, and by far the most attractive features are the dining-areas. The *pièce de résistance* is the coffered 16thC ceiling and frieze in the main restaurant. Elsewhere the decoration is suitably elegant: 'old master' paintings, gilt wall lamps, a terrazzo floor and tables immaculately laid. Food here is among the best in the region, and local specialities include the traditional dish of braised beef with polenta, which was one of the popular dishes of the Gonzagas.

Beyond the restaurant a flower-filled inner courtyard leads to the bedrooms. These are built around an inviting pool and garden area where a country house atmosphere prevails. In contrast with the elegance of the restaurant, the bedrooms have a stark modernity, but they are comfortable and well maintained.
Nearby Mantua, Modena, Parma all within reach.

Piazza IV Martiri 2,
Pomponesco 46030 Mantova
Tel (0375) 86077 **Fax** 86145
Location on small piazza, next to river Po, with garden and car parking
Food & drink breakfast, lunch, dinner
Prices rooms L53,000-L76,000; DB&B L80,000
Rooms 6 double, 3 single; all with shower; all rooms have central heating, phone, minibar

Facilities dining-room, bar, TV room; swimming-pool
Credit cards AE, DC, MC, V
Children accepted
Disabled access difficult
Pets accepted
Closed Jan; restaurant only, Sun pm and Mon
Proprietor Antonio Mori

Lombardia

Country villa, Alzate Brianza

Villa Odescalchi

A rather formal and plush 17thC villa, popular with business visitors, with lush gardens and grand park behind. Bedrooms are tall and spacious; the dining-room is in a modern conservatory extension.

■ Via Anzani 12, 22040 Alzate Brianza (Como) **Tel** (031) 630822 **Fax** (031) 632079 **Meals** breakfast, lunch, dinner **Prices** rooms L115,000-L180,000 with breakfast; DB&B L140,000-L150,000; FB L160,000-L170,000 **Rooms** 63, all with bath or shower, phone, minibar, colour TV **Credit cards** AE, MC, V **Closed** never, restaurant Tue

---

Lakeside villa, Argegno

Albergo Belvedere

'Inexpensive but wonderful little hotel, marvellously located on shores of Como. Excellent although small rooms, beautiful food – lunch by the lakeside dreamy. Very friendly and co-operative people'. So says a recent reporter, confirming our recommendation. The lady of the house is Scots – hence the tartan bar.

■ Via Milano 8, 22010 Argegno (Como) **Tel** (031) 821116 **Meals** breakfast, lunch, dinner **Prices** rooms L50,000-L90,000 with breakfast; meals L35,000 **Rooms** 17 **Credit cards** DC, MC, V **Closed** Nov to Mar

---

Lakeside hotel, Bellagio

Hotel du Lac

One of Bellagio's most popular hotels, with a welcoming atmosphere, a delightful setting on the piazza (and an inviting arcaded terrace), and high standards throughout. Signora Leoni's British origins show in such things as the towels and breakfasts (real marmalade, real orange juice).

■ Piazza Mazzini 32, 22021 Bellagio (Como) **Tel** (031) 950320 **Fax** (031) 951624 **Meals** breakfast, lunch, dinner **Prices** rooms L90,000-L132,000; lock-up garage L12,000 **Rooms** 48, all with bath or shower, central heating, phone, air-conditioning, TV (satellite), minibar, hairdrier **Credit cards** MC, V **Closed** end-Oct to Easter

---

Lakeside hotel, Bellagio

La Pergola

Unlike most of Bellagio's hotels, this one faces the eastern shore of Como – it is tucked away in the tiny village of Pescallo, just to the south. The view is splendid, the house ancient and rustic, the furnishings simple and old-fashioned, the whole operation a family affair.

■ Pescallo, 22021 Bellagio (Como) **Tel** (031) 950263 **Meals** breakfast, lunch, dinner **Prices** rooms L32,000-L62,000 **Rooms** 11 **Credit cards** AE, DC, MC, V **Closed** Nov to Mar; restaurant only, Tue

Lombardia

Agnello d'Oro

This picturesque, tall and incredibly narrow building lies at the heart of old Bergamo, on a tiny square with a fountain. The restaurant is cosy and characterful, with red-checked cloths on the tables, and ceramics and copper pans covering the walls and ceilings. Bright bedrooms, verging on the basic.

■ Via Gombito 22, 24100 Bergamo **Tel** (035) 249883 **Fax** (035) 235612 **Meals** breakfast, lunch, dinner **Prices** rooms L52,000-L85,000; breakfast L10,000, dinner L50,000 **Rooms** 20, all with bath or shower, central heating, phone, TV **Credit cards** AE, DC, V, MC **Closed** never

---

Gourmet

For the very best food in this gastronomic city you have to head downtown, but in the charming old *città alta* you can still eat well – at the Gourmet, for example. There is a shady terrace for summer dining. Spacious, light, smartly furnished bedrooms with luxury bathrooms.

■ Via San Vigilio 1, 24100 Bergamo **Tel** (035) 256110 **Meals** breakfast, lunch, dinner **Prices** rooms L72,000-L110,000; meals about L70,000 **Rooms** 10, all with bath or shower, phone, TV, minibar **Credit cards** AE, DC, MC, V **Closed** restaurant only, Tue

---

Il Sole

On the corner of the lovely Piazza Vecchia, the Sole catches a lot of Bergamo's tourist trade. The restaurant does not have quite the cosy charm of the Agnello d'Oro, but does not disappoint – and there is an attractive courtyard for summer meals. Plain bedrooms, but modest prices.

■ Via Bartolomeo Colleoni 1, Piazza Vecchia, Citta Alta, 24100 Bergamo **Tel** (035) 218238 **Fax** (035) 240011 **Meals** breakfast, lunch, dinner **Prices** rooms 83,000 with breakfast **Rooms** 11, all with bath or shower, TV, phone and minibar **Credit cards** AE, DC, MC, V **Closed** restaurant only, Thu

---

Montefiori

The three villas that make up the Montefiori are all modern, but you wouldn't know it – the style is distinctly old-world, with arched windows and elegant antique-style furnishing. The hotel is up the hillside from Lake Garda, secluded amid exotic gardens; many of the rooms have balconies with views.

■ Lago di Garda, 25083 Gardone Riviera (Brescia) **Tel** (0365) 290235 **Fax** (0365) 21488 **Meals** breakfast, lunch, dinner **Prices** rooms L80,000-L140,000 with breakfast; FB L110,000-L125,000 **Rooms** 35, all with bath or shower, central heating, TV, phone, radio **Credit cards** AE, DC, V **Closed** never

Lombardia

Lakeside villa, Gardone Riviera

Villa Fiordaliso

This tall but small villa on the shores of Lake Garda is one of the most exclusive hotels in northern Italy. The emphasis is on the restaurant, which occupies several elegant rooms – and spills on to the waterside terrace. The few bedrooms are richly decorated and beautifully furnished.

■ Corso Zanardelli 132, 25083 Gardone Riviera (Brescia) **Tel** (0365) 20158 **Fax** (0365) 290011 **Meals** breakfast, lunch, dinner **Prices** DB&B L170,000-L290,000 **Rooms** 7, all with bath, central heating, minibar, TV, radio, phone **Credit cards** AE, V **Closed** Jan and Feb

---

Lakeside villa, Gardone Riviera

Villa del Sogno

The 'Dream Villa' earns its name by its position, overlooking Lake Garda and secluded in its own luxuriant park with a swimming-pool and vast terrace. The interior is a mix of traditional and modern, much of it renovated in the past few years.

■ Via Zanardelli 107, Fasano di Gardone Riviera, 25083 Gardone Riviera (Brescia) **Tel** (0365) 290181 **Fax** (0365) 290230 **Meals** breakfast, lunch, dinner **Prices** rooms L170,000-L340,000 with breakfast; DB&B L160,000-L200,000 **Rooms** 34, all with bath or shower, central heating, phone, TV **Credit cards** AE, DC, MC, V **Closed** mid-Oct to Mar

---

Town hotel, Mantua

Hotel Broletto

Sandwiched between the arcaded Piazza delle Erbe and the huge Piazza Sordello, the little Broletto has an unbeatable location. It is a new building in an old shell, with the emphasis on clean simplicity. Bedrooms are compact, staff friendly.

■ Via Accademia 1, 46100 Mantua **Tel** (0376) 326784 **Fax** (0376) 221297 **Meals** breakfast **Prices** rooms L92,000-L127,000 with breakfast **Rooms** 17, all with bath or shower, central heating, air-conditioning, minibar, phone, radio **Credit cards** AE, DC, MC, V **Closed** Christmas and New Year

---

Town hotel, Mantua

San Lorenzo

There are fine views of historic Mantua from the terrace of this centrally situated hotel, close to the famous Piazza delle Erbe. Within, the modern hotel (opened in 1967) has an old-fashioned ambience, with ornate furnishings. Bedrooms are tastefully furnished with handsome antiques.

■ Piazza Concordia 14, 46100 Mantua (Mantova) **Tel** (0376) 220500 **Fax** (0376) 327194 **Meals** breakfast **Prices** rooms L127,000-L190,000 **Rooms** 41, all with bath or shower, central heating, air-conditioning, phone, TV, minibar **Credit cards** AE, DC, MC, V **Closed** never

Lombardia

Town inn, Milan

Antica Locanda Solferino

A surprise in glossy Milan: a simple and modestly priced inn with a rather rustic character. Compact, prettily decorated bedrooms with traditional-style bathrooms. The inn incorporates a separately managed, cosily traditional Paris-style bistro.

■ Via Castelfidardo 2, 20121 Milan **Tel** (02) 659 2706 **Fax** (02) 657 1361 **Meals** breakfast, brunch **Prices** rooms L110,000-L130,000 **Rooms** 11, all with bath, central heating, phone **Credit cards** AE, MC, V **Closed** 15 days in Aug

---

Town hotel, Milan

Pierre Milano

A welcome addition to Milan scene – the old hotel Torino, reborn in 1987 as a hotel of great style and luxury, with a calm atmosphere and personal service. It is set in a relatively quiet area, about 1 km SW of the duomo. Rooms mix occasional antiques into modern decorative schemes.

■ Via de Amicis 32, 20123 Milan **Tel** (02) 7200 0581 **Fax** (02) 805 2157 **Meals** breakfast, lunch, dinner, snacks **Prices** rooms L230,000-L570,000 with breakfast; suite L590,000-L780,000 **Rooms** 47, all with bath or shower, central heating, air-conditioning, phone, hairdrier, TV, radio, minibar **Credit cards** AE, DC, MC **Closed** Aug

---

Restaurant-with-rooms, Ranco

Sole

The fifth generation of Brovellis is now in charge here (Carlo), assisted by the sixth (Davide). Carlo's renowned fish specialities are served in friendly but formal style on the lake-view terrace or the refined restaurant. Accommodation is in newly built, swish suites, with terraces and views.

■ Piazza Venezia 5, Lago Maggiore, 21020 Ranco (Varese) **Tel** (0331) 976507 **Fax** (0331) 976620 **Meals** breakfast, lunch, dinner **Prices** rooms L255,000; meals about L110,000 **Rooms** 8, all with bath, central heating, minibar, lake-view terrace, air-conditioning, safe, TV **Credit cards** AE, DC, MC, V **Closed** Jan

---

Country hotel, Riva di Solto

Miranda 'da Oreste'

This modest, modern hotel may be thin on charm, but it is well run and enjoys a splendid position, high up above Lake Iseo, with views shared by the rooms, restaurant, terrace, garden and fair-sized swimming-pool. And you will find few respectable hotels in Italy offering lower prices.

■ Zorzino, 24060 Riva di Solto (Bergamo) **Tel** (035) 986021 **Fax** (035) 986021 **Meals** breakfast, lunch, dinner **Prices** rooms L37,000-L53,000; DB&B L48,000 **Rooms** 22, all with bath or shower, central heating, phone **Credit cards** AE, MC, V **Closed** Jan

Lombardia

Town hotel, Sabbioneta

Al Duca

Family-run, no-frills but spick-and-span hotel behind a Renaissance façade, close to the central square of a neglected but historic town. The emphasis is on the restaurant – a modest but well-run trattoria. Rooms are modern and bright.

■ Via della Stamperia 18, 46018 Sabbioneta (Mantova) **Tel** (0375) 52474 **Meals** breakfast, lunch, dinner **Prices** rooms L45,000-L70,000; lunch and dinner L25,000-L30,000 **Rooms** 10, all with bath or shower, central heating, intercom **Credit cards** AE, MC, V **Closed** Jan

---

Country villa, San Fedele d'Intelvi

Villa Simplicitas

A saffron-coloured 19thC country villa perched high above the lakes. Each room has its own particular interest – a rocking-chair here, a grand old mirror there – and there are breathtaking views to the lakes or mountains. Staff very welcoming and relaxed.

■ Tremezzo, 22010 San Fedele d'Intelvi (Como) **Tel** (031) 831132 **Meals** breakfast, lunch, dinner **Prices** DB&B L121,000; FB L132,000 **Rooms** 14, all with bath, central heating **Credit cards** not accepted **Closed** Oct to April

---

Lakeside villa, Torno

Villa Flora

The greatest asset of this unpretentious pinkish-orange villa is its superb lakeside situation. Bedrooms vary from spacious to cramped but all are clean, simple and functional. The sitting-room, with its brocade and ornate ceiling, has more character.

■ Via Torrazza 10, Lago di Como, 22020 Torno (Como) **Tel** (031) 419222 **Fax** (031) 418318 **Meals** breakfast, lunch, dinner **Prices** rooms L50,000-L90,000; meals L24,000-L50,000; reductions for children **Rooms** 20, all with shower, phone **Credit cards** MC, V **Closed** Jan, Feb; restaurant only, Tue

---

Lakeside hotel, Valsolda

Stella d'Italia

The shaded, gravelled terrace of this much-extended lakeside villa juts right out into the waters of Lake Lugano, offering marvellous views. The house is spacious, prettily refurbished and pleasantly 'lived-in', with pictures, comfortable furniture and lots of books. The food impresses reporters.

■ Piazza Roma 1, San Mamete, 22010 Valsolda (Como) **Tel** (0344) 68139 **Fax** (0344) 68729 **Meals** breakfast, lunch, dinner **Prices** rooms L77,000-L124,000 with breakfast; reductions for children under 10 **Rooms** 35, all with bath or shower, central heating, balcony, phone **Credit cards** AE, MC, V **Closed** mid-Oct to Apr; restaurant only, Wed

Lombardia

Lakeside hotel, Varenna

Hotel du Lac

The name could not be more appropriate: this small hotel, down an alley off the central piazza, overhangs the waters of Como – and the position is its main attraction. Dinner on the terrace (excellent food and service) is memorable. Inside, neat modern furnishings dominate.

■ Via del Prestino 4, 22050 Varenna (Como) **Tel** (0341) 830238 **Fax** (0341) 831081 **Meals** breakfast, lunch, dinner **Prices** rooms L148,000-L243,000 with breakfast; DB&B L130,000-L180,000; suite L180,000-L255,000; parking L15,000 **Rooms** 18, all with bath or shower, central heating, phone, TV **Credit cards** AE, DC, MC, V **Closed** mid-Dec to Feb; restaurant mid-Oct to mid-Mar

Converted castle, Voghera

Castello di San Gaudenzio

A convenient stopover for travellers on the A7 and A21 motorways, and an impressive hotel in any case. The 14thC brick-built castle has been immaculately restored and sensitively furnished in mainly modern styles. Immensely spacious, and good value.

■ Cervesina, 27050 Voghera (Pavia) **Tel** (0383) 3331 **Fax** (0383) 333409 **Meals** breakfast, lunch, dinner **Prices** rooms L150,000-L180,000; suite L300,000 **Rooms** 48, all with bath or shower, central heating, air-conditioning, TV, minibar, phone, radio **Credit cards** AE, DC, MC, V **Closed** never

The north-east

Hotels in the north-east

The remarkable city of Venice, set on islands in a salt-water lagoon, is the focal point of the area and a 'must' to visit for its beautiful buildings, art treasures and the sheer originality of the place. But whether you stay in the city or travel in from a base outside depends on whether you can stand the high prices and the noise and bustle, even late into the night.

A feast of small hotels in Venice are described on the following pages. Some alternatives, too big for a full recommendation in this guide, are: La Fenice et Des Artistes (Tel (041) 523 2333, fax 520 3721, 65 rooms) next to the opera house; the Monaco and Grand Canal (Tel (041) 520 0211, fax 520 0501, 70 rooms) set in an excellent position right on the Grand Canal as its name suggest; and the Gritti Palace (Tel (041) 794611, fax 520 0942, 97 rooms), an extraordinarily luxurious hotel set in a beautiful position, also on the Grand Canal. And we must mention the legendary and extravagant Cipriani (Tel (041) 520 7744, fax 520 3930, 95 rooms) outside the city of Venice itself and reached by the hotel's private launch.

Staying at the fashionable holiday resort of Venice Lido enables you to combine sightseeing with a beach holiday. The Quattro Fontane (Tel (041) 526 0227, fax 526 0726, 70 rooms) would make an acceptable alternative to the Villa Mabapa (page 77) or Villa Parco (page 88).

The Alto Adige, in the extreme north of Italy, is more like Austria than the rest of Italy and is often known as the South Tirol. It is largely a German-speaking area so place names – and hotel tariffs and brochures – are often given in Italian and German. Merano is the biggest resort and a central base for the area as a whole – we give several hotel recommendations on pages 57–61 and 69. The other major towns are Bolzano – see the Castel Guncina on p78 – and Trento – see the Accademia on p69. A near-miss for a full entry in this area is the Villa Madruzzo (Tel (0461) 986220), an imposing and formal red-and-yellow building set in beautiful gardens on the hillside above Trento.

Cortina d'Ampezzo is the main resort in the Dolomites – a smart ski resort in winter, with a lot of other winter sports on offer as well, but also suitable for a summer visit. The Menardi on page 79 is our recommendation here, but the 45-room Parc Hotel Victoria (Tel (0436) 3246, fax 4734) is also attractively rustic. Equally well known to skiers is Selva, the main resort of Val Gardena; our favourite here is the secluded Sporthotel Granvara (Tel (0471) 795250, fax 794336). In Corvara, not far from the Cappella (page 79) is the equally polished and only slightly larger 50-room Perla (Tel (0471) 836132, fax 836568).

This page acts as an introduction to the features and hotels of North-east Italy, and gives brief recommendations of reasonable hotels that for one reason or another have not made a full entry. The long entries for this region – covering the hotels we are most enthusiastic about – start on the next page. But do not neglect the shorter entries starting on page 78: these are all hotels that we would happily stay at.

The north-east

Country villa, Asolo

Villa Cipriani

Asolo is a beautiful medieval hilltop village commanding panoramic views. The Villa Cipriani is a mellow ochre-washed house on the fringes of the village, the entrance leading directly from the street into a tiled hall with Oriental-style rugs and a grandfather clock, brass wall lights and an efficient welcome from reception. It belongs to the Cigahotels group, but there is no chain-hotel atmosphere – staff are friendly and attentive.

A tall covered terrace furnished in rustic style, and with an unusual pierced minstrel's gallery, leads out through glass doors into the prettiest of gardens, well stocked with flowers and partly laid to grass – a mass of roses, azaleas and mature trees. The restaurant areas dog-leg around the outside of the villa, over-hanging the valley below, with views out through plate-glass windows. For cooler evenings, there is a cosy bar. The bedrooms all have lovely views, and are decorated in old-fashioned style, with prints, fresh flowers and antiques adding interest and colour. Pretty tiles have been used for the bathrooms. The views, the comfort and the peaceful garden combine to make this a most relaxing country hotel. Food is reported to be excellent.

Nearby Treviso (35 km); Padua, Vicenza, Venice within reach.

Via Canova 298, Asolo 31011 Treviso
Tel (0423) 952166 **Fax** 952095
Location on NW side of village; with small garden and private car parking
Food & drink breakfast, lunch, dinner
Prices rooms L280,000-L410,000; meals about L90,000
Rooms 31 double; all rooms have colour TV, phone, air-conditioning
Facilities dining-room, bar, conference room
Credit cards AE, DC, MC, V
Children accepted
Disabled lift/elevator
Pets accepted
Closed never
Manager Giuseppe Kamenar

The north-east

Elefante

Bressanone is a pretty little town at the foot of the Brenner Pass, more Austrian than Italian in character. The same is true of the charming old Elefante, which owes its name to a beast which was led over the Alps for the amusement of Emperor Ferdinand of Austria. The only stable which could house the exhausted creature was that next to the inn, so the innkeeper painted an elephant on the side of his inn and changed its name.

There is an air of solid, old-fashioned comfort throughout. Green-aproned staff lead you through corridors packed with heavily carved and beautifully inlaid pieces of antique furniture. The colours are sumptuous: scarlets, greens, copper, gold; turn a corner, and you may encounter an enormous display of purple iris and tulips in a simple iron pot. The bedrooms are generous and handsomely furnished with graceful antiques and solid old pieces. The breakfast room is panelled entirely in intricately carved wood and the main restaurant is wood-floored, with a moulded ceiling and windows looking out on to a little garden area. Much of the produce served here comes from the large walled garden, and from the adjacent farm belonging to the hotel. The formal sitting-room has been decorated in an elegant 18thC style, with mirrors, chandeliers and plush armchairs.

Nearby cathedral; Novacella monastery (3 km); the Dolomites.

Via Rio Bianco 4, Bressanone
39042 Bolzano
Tel (0472) 32750 **Fax** 36579
Location at N end of town, in gardens with car parking and garages
Food & drink breakfast, lunch, dinner
Prices rooms L115,000 -L230,000 with breakfast
Rooms 28 double, all with bath and shower; 16 single, 15 with bath, one with shower; all have central heating, colour TV, phone
Facilities 2 dining-rooms, sitting-room, bar; outdoor swimming-pool
Credit cards V
Children welcome
Disabled not suitable
Pets accepted by arrangement
Closed Jan to Feb **Manager** Karl-Heinz Falk

The north-east

Leuchtenburg

This solid stone-built 16thC hostel once housed the peasant servants of Leuchtenburg castle, an arduous hour's trek up the steep wooded mountain behind.

Today, guests in the *pensione* are cosseted, while the castle lies in ruins. The young Sparer family do the cosseting, providing good, solid breakfasts and 3-course dinners of regional cuisine in an unpretentious, home-like atmosphere. The white-painted, low-arched dining-chambers occupy the ground floor; above is the reception, with a large table littered with magazines and surrounded by armchairs.

There is a further sitting-area on the second floor, leading to the bedrooms. These have pretty painted furniture, tiled floors and attractive duvet covers; the rooms on the third floor are plainer. All the rooms are of a reasonable size, and some share the wide views enjoyed from the terrace, across vineyards to the Lago di Caldaro, perhaps better known (at least to wine buffs) as Kalterer See.

Nearby Swimming and fishing in lake.

Campi al Lago 100, Caldaro 39052
Tel & fax (0471) 960093
Location 5 km SE of Caldaro (Kaltern), 15 km SE of Bolzano; in courtyard surrounded by vineyards, with adequate car parking
Food & drink breakfast, dinner
Prices rooms L100,000-L120,000 with breakfast; meals L12,000-L18,000
Rooms 13 double, 2 with bath, 11 with shower; 3 single with shower; 2 family rooms, one with bath, one with shower; one suite for 2 to 4; all rooms have central heating
Facilities dining-area, sitting-area, bar; private beach
Credit cards none
Children accepted
Disabled no special facilities
Pets accepted
Closed Nov-Easter
Proprietor Paul and Markus Sparer

The north-east

Country villa, Cavasagra

Villa Corner della Regina

Driving through the flat agricultural land west of Treviso, it is something of a surprise to come upon this stately Palladian mansion, set in its vast estate and formal grounds at the end of a gravel drive. Lemon trees in huge terracotta pots and an ancient wisteria decorate your path to the entrance on the ground floor, to the side of a vast, sweeping set of stone steps. Once inside, you are greeted with a magnificent floral display, and it is clear that much of the original grandeur of the villa has been preserved, despite the provision of modern comforts.

The grandiose central reception room runs the full width of the villa; intricately carved French windows survey the drive, with floor-to-ceiling drapes trimmed in pink contrasting with the dark panelling and matching the deeply cushioned chairs and sofas. The bedrooms are huge, light and airy. They are all decorated differently and named rather than numbered: 'the Butterfly Room' or 'the Rose Room', for example. They offer a combination of both character and luxury, with period antiques, decorative painted plaster walls, abundant flowers and prints, and thick pile carpets. The grounds are beautifully kept and the pool beside the villa has plenty of space for relaxation.

Nearby Palladian villas; Venice (40 km).

Cavasagra, Treviso 31050 Treviso
Tel (0423) 481481 **Fax** 451100
Location 15 km W of Treviso, 3 km S of road to Vicenza; in formal gardens and parkland, with ample car parking
Food & drink breakfast, lunch, dinner
Prices rooms L125,000-L400,000 with breakfast
Rooms 4 double, 7 suites in villa and 12 apartments in annexe, all with bath; all have TV, telephone, minibar
Facilities dining-rooms, breakfast room (in old orangery), sitting-room; heated outdoor swimming-pool, sauna, tennis
Credit cards AE, DC, MC, V
Children accepted
Disabled not suitable
Pets dogs accepted in annexe
Closed never
Proprietor Conte Nicolo and Contessa Dona Dalle Rose

The north-east

Villa Ducale

Driving along the N11 highway from Padua to Venice, you follow an old canal whose banks are scattered with beautiful 18thC villas, where wealthy Venetians used to escape from the city in summer. Villa Ducale is one of them – surrounded by formal gardens, with statues, a fountain, ancient trees and arbours.

The entrance to the hotel is rather grand. The marble- floored reception area leads into a vast chandeliered dining-hall, with a more modest breakfast room to one side. A grand staircase leads to the bedrooms. Upstairs, the floors are the original decorative wooden parquet, overlaid with patterned rugs. In the bedrooms, much of the furniture is antique and in some the original softly painted walls and ceilings remain. The larger rooms have balconies and all are of a generous size. Bathrooms have decorative tiles and gilt fittings, which in lesser surroundings might seem pretentious. The smaller rooms at the rear overlook horse chestnut trees. The welcome and service are not a strong point. When we last visited, no dinner was available because the chef had driven off the road. We have no complaint about that, but no attempt was made to make alternative dinner arrangements.

Nearby Venice (20 km); Padua (21 km); Treviso (33 km)

Riviera Martiri della Liberta 75, Dolo 30031 Venezia
Tel (041) 420094
Location 2 km E of Dolo
Food & drink breakfast, dinner; lunch on request
Prices rooms L70,000-L105,000; DB&B L75,000 (minimum 3 days)
Rooms 14 double, 4 with bath, 10 with shower; one single; all rooms have phone, terrace
Facilities sitting-room, bar, TV room, dining-room, games room
Credit cards AE, V
Children accepted
Disabled not suitable
Pets not accepted
Closed never
Proprietors Bressan family

The north-east

Mas del Saügo

Secluded hostelries don't come much more remote than this. A good 2 km up a winding forest track that leads to nowhere but the Lagorai mountains, the Mas del Saügo is surrounded by nothing but open meadow, forest, and fresh air.

Donatella Zampoli, a local cook, and Lorenzo Bernardini, a painter and designer, embarked on their great adventure in 1985. The state of the derelict barn adjacent to this immaculately restored 17thC farmhouse gives some idea of their achievement. Inside, Lorenzo combined original features with his own distinctive Tyrolean-Cubist styles. The smaller dining-room is all wood, with the original decorated plaster ceiling and traditional ceramic boiler, while the larger dining-room is more formal. A wooden staircase leads down to the enchanting bar in the converted cattle stalls below. Everywhere there are gorgeous smells of wood or herbs – or food. The four bedrooms are individually decorated: some with stone walls and exposed beams, others wood-panelled, all offering peace and tranquillity. Lorenzo and Donatella have sold the Mas to the Vinante family, who look set to continue their high standards of hospitality – though it will be hard to match Donatella's six-course gourmet menus and Lorenzo's range of accompanying wines. Prior booking is obligatory.
Nearby Mountain walks, winter skiing at Cavalese (4 km).

Masi 38033 Cavalese
Tel (0462) 30788
Location up mountain track, 4 km SW of Cavalese, 40 km SE of Bolzano; in fields, with ample car parking
Food & drink breakfast, lunch, dinner
Prices rooms L120,000-L200,000; lunch and dinner L120,000-L150,000
Rooms 3 double, one single, all with shower; all rooms have central heating, hairdrier

Facilities dining-room, bar
Credit cards V
Children not accepted under 8 years
Disabled no special facilities
Pets not accepted
Closed hotel never; restaurant only, Thu
Proprietors Vinante family

The north-east

Castel Labers

On the hillside to the east of Merano, Castel (or Schloss) Labers is surrounded by its own vineyards, orchards and mountain walks through alpine pastures. The hotel has been in the Neubert family since 1885, but the building itself dates back to the 11th century.

An impressive stone staircase with wrought-iron balustrades leads from the white-walled entrance hall and up to the bedrooms. These all have charming wooden double doors, with sealed wooden floors, simple old furniture, and goose feather duvets in crisp white cotton covers.

The castle gardens are packed with trees and flowering shrubs, which can be admired from the conservatory restaurant, whose windows are draped in country cottons. Leading off this is another restaurant area, with a church-like vaulted wooden ceiling and old panelling round the walls. Fresh local produce is well presented and deliciously cooked.

'Absolutely fantastic, tremendous food, friendly proprietors', enthuses one recent guest.

Nearby promenades along the Passirio river in Merano; Tirolo Castle (5 km); Passirio valley, the Dolomites.

Via Labers 25, Merano 39012 Bolzano
Tel (0473) 234484 **Fax** 34146
Location 2.5 km E of Merano, with private grounds, garage and parking (locked at night)
Food & drink breakfast, lunch, dinner
Prices rooms L90,000-L100,000; DB&B L90,000-L120,000
Rooms 22 double, 20 with bath, 2 with shower; 9 single, 2 with bath, 7 with shower; 10 family rooms, all with bath; all have central heating, phone
Facilities dining-room, dining/conservatory, bar, music/reading room, conference room; outdoor heated swimming-pool, tennis
Credit cards AE, DC, MC, V
Children welcome
Disabled not suitable
Pets dogs accepted, but not in dining-room **Closed** Nov to Mar **Proprietors** Stapf-Neubert family

The north-east

Converted castle, Merano

Castel Freiberg

The Freiberg is every inch the grand medieval castle. It commands an exposed hilltop position high above Merano, but its ramparts enclose a beautiful sheltered garden with sweet-scented shrubs, and its walls conceal a hotel which is at once luxurious, welcoming and full of character.

The entrance is very grand, with suits of armour and ancient weapons along the whitewashed walls, and vaulted ceilings. Throughout the castle there are small sitting-areas, usually by a window with superb eagle's-eye views down over the valley. The small, intimate bar with an old painted wooden bench adjoins a tiny chapel, but by far the most stunning rooms are the dining-rooms, completely panelled in honey-coloured pine with enormous wood-burning stoves clad in turquoise ceramic tiles.

The house-boys, in black-and-green striped jackets, lead you to the spacious bedrooms – all comfortably fitted out in an opulent, antique style.

Nearby Promenades along Passirio River in Merano; Passirio valley, the Dolomites.

Via Labers, Merano 39012 Bolzano
Tel (0473) 244196 **Fax** 244488
Location 8 km NE of Merano, with walled garden and park; car parking close to hotel, and garaging available
Food & drink breakfast, lunch, dinner
Prices rooms L170,000-L330,000
Rooms 28 doubie, 7 single, one suite, all with bath and shower; all rooms have phone, radio, sitting-area; TV on request
Facilities 3 dining-rooms, basement taverna, TV room, 2 sitting-rooms, bar, chapel, veranda; indoor (heated) and outdoor swimming-pools, fitness room, solarium, tennis
Credit cards AE, DC, MC, V
Children not suitable
Disabled not suitable
Pets not accepted
Closed Nov to mid-Apr
Proprietors Bortolotti family

The north-east

Converted castle, Merano

Fragsburg

A lovely drive along a narrow country lane, through mixed woodland and past Alpine pastures where goats and cattle graze, brings you to the wooded outcrop, high up to the east of Merano, where sits the Hotel Fragsburg (or Castel Verruca) – 300 years old, and a hotel for over 100 years..

Externally, Fragsburg still looks very much the hunting lodge, with carved wooden shutters and balconies decked with flowering plants. It enjoys splendid views (notably of the Texel massif), shared by many of the bedrooms; these have been decorated recently in sparkling white, with abundant wood panelling, some old and some new. Downstairs, hearty meals can be enjoyed either in the low-ceilinged dining-areas which have recently been elegantly refurbished, or on one of the terraces. Below are what appear to be dolls' houses; actually they house the bees which provide honey for the wholesome buffet breakfast. In the extensive wooded garden there are areas for lazing in the sun – including a wooden shelter reserved for all-over tanning. 'Superb meals; one of our all-time favourites', enthuses a recent visitor.

Nearby Promenades along the Passirio river in Merano; Passirio valley, the Dolomites.

Via Fragsburg 3, PO Box 210, 39012 Merano, Bolzano
Tel (0473) 244071 **Fax** 244493
Location 6 km NE of Merano, with gardens; ample car parking space, and garages available
Food & drink breakfast, lunch, dinner
Prices DB&B L85,000-L115,000; FB L105,000-L135,000
Rooms 14 double, 10 with bath, 4 with shower; 3 single, all with shower; 2 family rooms; all rooms have central heating, phone, balcony, TV, safe
Facilities dining-rooms, sitting-room, terrace; table-tennis, heated outdoor swimming-pool **Credit cards** not accepted **Children** welcome **Disabled** not suitable **Pets** dogs accepted by arrangement
Closed Nov to Easter
Proprietors Ortner family

The north-east

Medieval manor, Merano

Castel Rundegg

Despite its smart facilities, this ancient white-painted house retains a lot of charm. The pretty sitting-room, with plush seats and antiques, overlooks the garden through delicate wrought iron gates. The restaurant has a cellar-like atmosphere, with its stone-vaulted ceiling and alcove rooms. The bedrooms are luxurious, and many of them have special features – the turret room, reached up spiral steps, commands a 360-degree view.

Nearby promenades along Passirio river; Passirio valley, the Dolomites.

Via Scena 2, Merano 39012 Bolzano
Tel (0473) 34100 **Fax** 37200
Location on E side of town; in gardens, with car parking and garages
Food & drink breakfast, lunch, dinner
Prices DB&B L132,000-L294,000; reductions for children under 12
Rooms 22 double, 20 with bath, 2 with shower; 5 single, all with shower; 2 family rooms, both with bath; all rooms have central heating, colour TV, radio, minibar, phone
Facilities 3 dining-rooms, bar, sitting-room; heated indoor swimming-pool, health and beauty farm
Credit cards AE, DC, MC, V
Children welcome
Disabled lift/elevator available
Pets small dogs accepted on request **Closed** last 3 weeks Jan
Proprietors Sinn family

The north-east

Villa Mozart

Here is a truly extraordinary hotel. Set in a peaceful residential area of Merano, it has been entirely decorated in the Jugend style of art nouveau, with not a single detail overlooked.

The villa was built in 1907 and was renovated to the existing design in the late 1970s. Black and white are dominant throughout the hotel, with splashes of colour sparingly applied. In the airy conservatory, where breakfast is served, gauze curtains throw a soft light on posies of vivid fresh flowers; in the dining-room, a single yellow tulip next to a black candle picks up the soft yellow of the walls. The bedrooms are done out in black, gold and soft yellows, with the honey-coloured parquet floors, giving warmth and contrast to the beautiful black-and-white patterned rugs. Every last knife, teacup and finger plate in the Villa Mozart is part of a 'homogeneous whole', the design principle laid down by Josef Hoffmann in 1901. But this is no museum piece – the seats are for relaxing on, the rugs for walking over and the elegant staff make a good job of cosseting their guests. Dinner is no longer confined to the weeks when the cookery courses are running but it must be reserved in advance.
Nearby promenades along Passirio river in Merano.

Via San Marco 26, Merano
39012 Bolzano
Tel (0473) 30630 **Fax** 211355
Location in peaceful residential area; with garden and covered car parking
Food & drink breakfast, dinner
Prices rooms L150,000 with breakfast; DB&B L210,000
Rooms 7 double, all with bath; 2 single, both with shower; all rooms have colour TV, phone, radio, minibar, health-beds

Facilities bar, restaurant, breakfast conservatory; heated indoor swimming- pool, sauna, solarium
Credit cards AE, MC, V
Children accepted
Disabled lift/elevator
Pets not accepted
Closed Nov to Easter
Proprietors Andreas and Emmy Hellrigl

The north-east

Villa Margherita

Yet another country villa in the Venetian hinterland, offering peace, seclusion and a lot of real estate for your money, while being well placed for excursions into Venice itself – and you don't even need to worry about parking when you get there, because there is a regular half-hourly bus service from a stop almost in front of the villa.

Villa Margherita was built in the 17thC as Villa Contarini, one of a series of grand country residences lining the Brenta river – the weekend retreats, as it were, of Venetian nobles. It has been open as a hotel only since late 1987. It is less imposing than some of its rival villa-hotels from the outside, but charmingly furnished and decorated within, particularly in the public areas. The breakfast room is gloriously light, with French windows on to the garden, while the sitting-room has *trompe l'oeil* frescos and an open fireplace. Bedrooms are plainer, perhaps lacking character, but thoroughly comfortable (and some are notably spacious).

The highly regarded restaurant is a short walk from the main building. Service is exactly what you would expect: attentive, and rather formal.

Nearby Venice (10 km), Padua (20 km).

Via Nazionale 416, Mira Porte
30030 Venezia
Tel (041) 426 5800 **Fax** 5838
Location on banks of Brenta river at Mira, 10 km W of Venice; ample car parking
Food & drink breakfast, lunch, dinner
Prices rooms L100,000-L180,000; meals from L38,000
Rooms 18 double, 3 with bath, 15 with shower; 1 single with shower; all have central heating, phone, air-conditioning, TV, minibar
Facilities breakfast room, sitting-room, bar, restaurant (200 m walk); jogging track
Credit cards AE, DC, MC, V
Children accepted
Disabled some rooms on ground floor
Pets by arrangement
Closed never
Manager Stefano Maggiolini

The north-east

Country villa, Oderzo

Villa Revedin

Amid open countryside just outside the little town of Gorgo al Monticano, the Villa Revedin is sheltered within its own mature, tree-screened park. Formal gardens at the front and an old fountain lead on to the park through cool tree-lined paths.

The villa dates from the 15th century, and the antique atmosphere is well preserved in the huge main salon, which has an imposing grand piano. The restaurant (which attracts local customers, particularly for its fish specialities) is more relaxed, in the familiar Italian sophisticated-rustic style, with wooden ceiling, terracotta tiled floor and cream decorations. The hotel's sitting areas have large leather sofas and chairs, and there is a pretty open fireplace for cooler evenings.

Most of the bedrooms are of generous size; all have pretty views out over the park and gardens. Although most of the furniture is modern, the tall ceilings, shuttered windows, open fireplaces and tasteful decoration lend charm.

This is a luxury hotel, but it is charming and welcoming in a way that most such hotels are not. 'Excellent value, considering the location and meals,' says a recent visitor.

Nearby Treviso (32 km); Venice within reach; Venetian villas.

Via Palazzi 4, Gorgo al Monticano, Oderzo 31040 Treviso
Tel (0422) 740669
Location 4 km E of Oderzo, signposted just N of Gorgo al Monticano; in private grounds with ample car parking
Food & drink breakfast, lunch, dinner
Prices rooms L80,000-L160,000
Rooms 14 double, 14 single, 4 family rooms; all with bath and shower; all rooms have TV, radio, phone
Facilities breakfast room, dining-room, function room, bar, sitting-room, conference room (30 people)
Credit cards AE, DC, MC, V
Children very welcome
Disabled not suitable
Pets not accepted
Closed restaurant only, Jan
Management Programma Revedin s.r.l

The north-east

Villa Quaranta

Ospedaletto earned its name as a stopping-off point on the way to and from the Brenner pass; the Chapel of Santa Maria di Mezza Campagna was where travellers stayed. The original 13thC chapel, with its Ligozzi frescos, now forms one side of the Villa Quaranta's pretty inner courtyard; the remainder of the buildings are 17thC. The main house is rather imposing, but the hotel's reception, dotted with antiques, is in the less intimidating parts behind, with the bedrooms set around the courtyard. The bedrooms are scrupulously clean, with plain carpets, polished stained-wood furniture, and bright shower rooms of pine and white ceramics. Downstairs, there is a snug little converted cellar where the splendid buffet breakfast is served. The staff are generally eager to please, and Pierantonio Zarotti keeps an eye on things from his garden office.

The formal dining-halls in the main house form the restaurant: awe-inspiring frescoed walls, stone-arched doors and tiled floors, appropriately furnished with red leather straight- back chairs. The food here is an excellent mix of regional and international cuisine. There is no longer a shortage of garden chairs from which to enjoy the wonderful grounds.

Nearby Verona (minibus service to opera); Lake Garda (12 km).

Via Brennero, Ospedaletto di Pescantina 37026 Verona
Tel (045) 715 6211 **Fax** 6306
Location on SS12, 15 km NW of Verona
Food & drink breakfast, lunch, dinner
Prices rooms L185,000-L370,000 with breakfast
Rooms 28 double, 4 single, 11 family rooms, all with bath; all rooms have central heating, air-conditioning, phone, TV, radio, minibar

Facilities 4 dining-rooms, bar, TV room; swimming-pool, 2 tennis courts
Credit cards AE, DC, MC, V
Children no special facilities
Disabled lift/elevator
Pets not accepted
Closed hotel never; restaurant Mon
Manager Pierantonio Zarotti

The north-east

Country hotel, Rasun di Sopra

Ansitz Heufler

This converted 16thC castle is a bit too close to the road up the Anterselva valley to rate as truly idyllic. But it is undoubtedly one of the most beautiful buildings in the area, inside and out. Fir trees shelter the chairs and tables scattered on the lawn in front; once inside, traffic is soon forgotten: a large pine table serves as reception where guests are met by young and cheerful staff.

All the public rooms are pine-panelled, with rugs and skins, rustic wooden tables, benches and amply cushioned sofas and armchairs. The main sitting-room on the first floor is the real gem: here the panelling is intricately inlaid, and there is a vast traditional ceramic stove reminiscent of a castle tower. Breakfast is taken in the snug bar, while other meals are served by smart, lace-aproned waitresses in the equally cosy dining-rooms. The *carte* offers good solid Tyrolean fare, with liberal use of alcohol. Chocolate truffles in Grand Marnier can be just what the doctor ordered when it's snowing outside. The bedrooms, set around a large open hall and gallery, are all of ample size, though you have to mind your head on low door lintels at times. In the majority, the pine fixtures are original.

Nearby Walking, cycling, and winter skiing at Brunico.

39030 Rasun di Sopra
Tel (0474) 46288 **Fax** 48199
Location in wooded Anterselva valley, 10 km E of Brunico; with garden and car parking
Food & drink breakfast, lunch, dinner
Prices rooms L100,000-L170,000 with breakfast; meals L35,000-L56,000
Rooms 9 double, 3 with bath, 6 with shower; all rooms have central heating, telephone

Facilities dining-room, sitting-room, breakfast room, bar
Credit cards AE,DC, MC, V
Children accepted
Disabled no special facilities
Pets accepted
Closed November; 15 May to 15 Jun
Manager Valentin Pallhuber

Converted castle, San Paolo

Schloss Korb

Rising up above the fertile vineyards and orchards that surround the outskirts of Bolzano is the 11thC medieval tower which forms the centrepiece of Schloss Korb.

The entrance to the hotel is a riot of colour – flowering shrubs and plants set against walls of golden stone and whitewash. Inside, furnishings and decorations are in traditional style, and antiques and fresh flowers abound. Reception is a cool, dark, tiled hall, set about with brass ornaments and armoury – the oldest part of the hotel. Surrounding the main restaurant areas is a terrace, hanging out over the valley and awash with plants, where breakfast and drinks can be enjoyed.

The bedrooms in the castle are generous in size, with separate sitting-areas and lovely views out over the vineyards. Duvet covers give a warm, friendly feel. The detached annexe behind the main building has a heated indoor pool and lift/elevator – the latter being the attraction for some of the guests.

The daughter of the family (shadowed everywhere by her enormous Great Dane) speaks fluent English.

Nearby sights of Bolzano; Merano within reach; the Dolomites.

Missiano, San Paolo 39050
Bolzano
Tel (0471)636000 **Fax** 636033
Location 8 km W of Bolzano,
in gardens on estate with
vineyards and large car park
Food & drink breakfast,
lunch, dinner
Prices rooms L90,000-
L180,000 with breakfast;
DB&B L115,000; reductions
for children in family room
Rooms 54 double, 2 single, all
with bath or shower; all rooms
have central heating, phone,
TV
Facilities dining-room,
conference rooms, bar,
sitting-rooms (one with TV);
sauna, beauty salon, outdoor
and heated indoor swimming-
pools, tennis **Credit cards** not
accepted **Children** welcome
Disabled lift to annexe
bedrooms, but access awkward
for wheel- chairs **Pets** accepted
Closed Nov to Mar
Proprietors Dellago family

The north-east

Lakeside inn, San Vigilio

Locanda San Vigilio

In general the east side of Lake Garda is more downmarket than the west. A conspicuous exception is the Punta de San Vigilio; this verdant peninsula, dotted with olive trees and grazing ponies, is entirely owned by Count Agostino Guarienti, who lives in the impressive 16thC villa that dominates the headland. To the left of the big house, down a cobbled lane, nestling between the hillside and a miniature harbour, is this secluded inn of more modest proportions, which a recent visitor recommends for its complete peacefulness. Inside, blue carpets lend sophistication to the rustic furniture, white walls and wooden doors. Bedrooms are decorated in suitable antique style.

It is in the evening that the Locanda really comes into its own. With the day-trippers departed, guests are free to wander the peninsula, take a drink at one of the tables on the harbour wall, or join the Count for the evening meal in the Locanda (he eats here practically every night). The restaurant is candle-lit, and there is a walled garden dining-terrace with giant canvas parasols; both overlook the lake. The menu is recited to guests by the smart, cheerful staff. Lake Garda carp is an inevitable house speciality, but there can be no better setting for it.

Nearby Garda (2 km).

San Vigilio 37016 Garda
Tel (045) 725 6688 **Fax** 6551
Location 2 km W of Garda, on promontory; parking available 150 metres away
Food & drink breakfast, lunch, dinner
Prices rooms L300,000-L420,000 with breakfast
Rooms 7 double, 4 suites, all with bath and shower; all rooms have central heating, air-conditioning, phone, TV
Facilities restaurant, dining-terrace, sitting-room, bar; walled garden
Credit cards AE, DC, V
Children accepted if well behaved
Disabled no special facilities
Pets accepted if well behaved
Closed Dec to Mar
Proprietor Count Agostino Guarienti

The north-east

Gardesana

Torri del Benaco is one of the showpiece villages of Lake Garda – a picturesque fishing port of immaculately restored medieval houses, a 14thC castle and an attractive waterfront with beautiful lake views. The Gardesana has a plum position on the main piazza, facing the busy little harbour.

The building has a long history, as its exterior would suggest, with its stone arcades and mellow stucco walls; but the entire interior was smartly modernized in the late 1970s to produce an essentially modern and rather smart hotel. Bedrooms have recently been further refurbished and are almost all identical – wooden furnishings, soft green fabrics, and plenty of little extras – and most have views of the lake, sufficiently beautiful to have elicited a poem from Stephen Spender when he stayed here in the 1950s.

The historic Hall of the Ancient Council makes a suitably elegant dining-room, and there are a few tables for à la carte meals on the balcony which overlooks the lake. There is a much more extensive ground-floor terrace for drinks. Breakfast is sumptuous, with ham, cheese, pâté, yoghurt.

Nearby Bardolino (11 km), Malcesine (21 km).

Piazza Calderini 20, 37010 Torri del Benaco, Lago di Garda (Verona)
Tel (045) 722 5411 **Fax** 5771
Location in middle of resort, on waterfront; private car parking 150 m away
Food & drink breakfast, dinner
Prices rooms L65,000-L160,000, DB&B L90,000-L150,000; reduction for children sharing parents' room

Rooms 30 double, 4 with bath, 26 with shower; 3 single, all with shower; all rooms have central heating, air-conditioning, phone, TV
Facilities dining-room, bar, TV room, lakeside terrace
Credit cards AE, DC, MC, V
Children welcome
Disabled no special facilities
Pets not accepted
Closed Nov and Dec
Proprietor Giuseppe Lorenzini

The north-east

Accademia

The old centre of Trento is much quieter now that traffic restrictions are in force, and this recently converted medieval house lies on a tiny street right in the heart of it. Quaint wooden shutters and geranium-filled window boxes break up the four storeys of the elegant cream-stucco façade. Inside, all is in the best contemporary taste: white vaulted chambers, parquet floors, classic modern furniture, and strategically placed antique pieces and old maps. There are plenty of comfortable sofas, some on a small wooden gallery above the bar – ideal for a quiet drink. The smart staff have an air of calm efficiency about them. The atmosphere is carried through to the bedrooms which are bright and airy, only the singles being a bit on the small side. You will find all the facilities you could wish for – tastefully presented, of course – right down to the electric shoe polishing machine on the landing. Breakfast is a particular pleasure when taken on the walled terrace, shaded by a giant horse-chestnut tree. The restaurant – another white vaulted room, with crisp white tablecloths and simple wooden and wicker chairs – is a Trento favourite. The *gnochetti di ricotta* are not to be missed.

Nearby Church of Santa Maria, Piazza del Duomo.

Vicolo Colico 4/6, 38100 Trento
Tel (0461) 233600 **Fax** 230174
Location in historic middle of town, between *duomo* and Piazza Dante
Food & drink breakfast, lunch, dinner
Prices rooms L170,000-L250,000; meals from L40,000
Rooms 32 double, 16 with bath, 16 with shower; 9 single with shower; 2 family rooms with bath; all rooms have central heating, telephone, TV, minibar, hairdrier
Facilities dining-room, sitting-room, bar, breakfast room, terrace
Credit cards AE, DC, V
Children accepted
Disabled lift/elevator
Pets accepted
Closed hotel never; restaurant Mon
Proprietor Sig. Fambri

The north-east

Town guest-house, Venice

Accademia

Though it is not quite the bargain it used to be, the Accademia is still a place of immense charm and character with prices that most people can afford and a very convenient but tranquil location. But what really distinguishes the *pensione* is its gardens – the spacious patio facing the canal, where tables are scattered among potted plants and classical urns, and the grassy garden at the back where wisteria, roses and fruit trees flourish.

It was originally built as a private mansion, and earlier this century housed the Russian consulate. There are still touches of grandeur, and the furnishings for the most part are classically Venetian. But there is no trace whatever of formality.

Reception is a spacious hallway-cum-salon, with ample seating, stretching between two gardens. The airy breakfast room has chandeliers and a beamed ceiling supported by columns; but, weather permitting, guests will inevitably opt to start their day in the garden, and end it there with evening drinks. Most of the bedrooms are rather old-fashioned, with a haphazard collection of antiques, and some are surprisingly spartan, but the new owners have embarked on a major renovation.

Nearby Accademia gallery, Grand Canal.

Fondamenta Maravegie, Dorsoduro 1058, Venice 30123
Tel (041) 523 7846 **Fax** 9152
Location on side canal just S of Grand Canal, with gardens front and back
Food & drink breakfast
Prices rooms L88,000-L186,000; extra bed L42,000
Rooms 20 double, 8 with bath, 8 with shower; 6 single, 5 with bath; all rooms have central heating, phone
Facilities breakfast room, bar,
sitting-room
Credit cards AE, DC, MC, V
Children welcome
Disabled no special facilities
Pets small animals accepted
Closed never
Manager Giovanna Salmaso and Massimo Dinato

The north-east

Alboretti

Enthusiastic students of Venetian painting will find this little hotel the most convenient in Venice. It lies right alongside the gallery of the Accademia, the world's finest collection of Venetian art. It is also well placed for exploration further afield: water-bus landing-stages on the Grand Canal lie just a few steps from the entrance to the hotel. Like many small hotels in Venice, the Alboretti occupies a building which is several centuries old, but what distinguishes it from many others is the warm welcome and the genuine family atmosphere – something of a rarity in Venice. Reception is a cosy wood-panelled room with a model of a 17thC galleon in its window; the sitting-room is but the upper TV room is a comfortable retreat (the TV is rarely used). The restaurant offers traditional and creative cooking, and Signora Linguerri is proud of her range of Italian wines.

The style of the bedrooms is predominantly simple and modern, though a few rooms have an antique or two. Like the rest of the hotel, they are well cared for and spotlessly clean; but the bathrooms are tiny. The most peaceful are those overlooking the pretty leafy courtyard at the back of the hotel.

Nearby Accademia gallery, Zattere, Gesuati church.

Accademia 882, Venice 30123
Tel (041) 523 0058 **Fax** 521 0158
Location between the Grand Canal and Giudecca Canal; nearest landing-stage
Food & drink breakfast, dinner
Prices rooms L100,000-L165,000 with breakfast
Rooms 13 double, 3 with bath, 10 with shower; 6 single, all with showers; one family room with bath; all rooms have central heating, phone

Facilities sitting-room, dining-room, TV room, bar
Credit cards AE, MC, V
Children welcome – cots on request
Disabled no special facilities
Pets small dogs only accepted
Closed never
Proprietor Anna Linguerri

The north-east

Town hotel, Venice

Flora

Such is the popularity of this small hotel, tucked away in a cul-de-sac close to St Mark's, that to get a room here you have to book weeks or even months in advance. You only need to glimpse the garden to understand why it is so sought after. Creepers, fountains and flowering shrubs cascading from stone urns create an enchanting setting for morning coffee and croissants, or evening drinks in summer. It is undoubtedly one of the prettiest and quietest gardens in Venice – somehow far removed from the hubbub of St Mark's.

The lobby is small and inviting, enhanced by the views of the garden through a glass arch. The atmosphere is one of friendly efficiency, reception acting as a mini tourist information bureau for the many English-speaking guests. There are some charming double bedrooms with painted carved antiques and other typically Venetian furnishings, but beware of other comparatively spartan rooms, some of which are barely big enough for one, let alone two. Prices are quite steep – but a recent guest endorses our view that the setting and the intimate atmosphere make it well worth the cost.

Nearby Piazza San Marco

Calle Larga 22 Marzo 2283/a, San Marco, Venice 30124
Tel (041) 520 5844 **Fax** 522 8217
Location 300 m from Piazza San Marco in cul-de-sac
Food & drink breakfast
Prices rooms L112,000-L215,000 with breakfast
Rooms 32 double, 6 single, 6 family rooms; all with bath and/or shower; all rooms have air-conditioning, phone
Facilities breakfast room, bar, sitting-room
Credit cards AE, DC, MC, V
Children accepted
Disabled no special facilities
Pets accepted
Closed Jan
Proprietor Roger Romanelli

The north-east

Pausania

The San Barnaba area, traditionally the home of impecunious Venetian nobility, is quiet and picturesque, and now highly desirable as the better-known San Marco area becomes increasingly tourist-ridden and overpriced. The Pausania is a small hotel lying close to the last surviving floating vegetable shop in Venice – a colourful barge on the San Barnaba canal.

The building is quintessentially Venetian, a weathered Gothic *palazzo* with distinctive ogee windows. Inside, timbered ceilings, Corinthian columns, an old well-head and a battered stone staircase are features of the original building. Bedrooms are smartly furnished in tastefully restrained and restful blues and creams. Occupants of rooms with a view (overlooking the canal) may be gently awakened by bells from a nearby campanile, but not indecently early. Breakfast is served in a light, modern extension overlooking a secluded garden. Unusually for a small city hotel, there are several comfortable spaces to sit, including a sunny canal-side landing and a lounge of beams and classical supporting pillars. Reasonable prices, and exceptionally friendly and helpful staff – rare virtues in Venice.

Nearby Scuola dei Carmini, Accademia gallery.

Dorsoduro 2824, Venice 30124
Tel (041) 522 2083
Location short walk W of Grand Canal; with terrace
Food & drink breakfast
Prices rooms L90,000-L200,000 with breakfast
Rooms 23 double, 5 with bath, 18 with shower; 3 single, all with shower; 5 family rooms, one with bath, 4 with shower; all rooms have central heating, TV, air-conditioning, phone

Facilities breakfast room, bar, reading-room
Credit cards AE, MC, V
Children welcome
Disabled not suitable
Pets only small ones accepted
Closed never
Proprietor Guido Gatto

The north-east

Town hotel, Venice

La Residenza

This grand Gothic *palazzo* dominates the quiet, neglected square of Campo Bandiera e Moro. Just to enter is an experience: press the button on the lion's mouth on the left of the huge entrance doors and they swing open to reveal an ancient covered courtyard. A wrought-iron gate moves to one side to admit you up the ancient stone steps to the reception and sitting-room – a vast hall with mullioned windows, furnished with soft couches and antiques. The soft pastel shades of the walls add to the feeling of faded grandeur and immersion in Venice's history. Our inspector was not allowed to see any bedrooms; look before you leap.
Nearby Scuola di San Giorgio degli Schiavoni.

Campo Bandiera e Moro
3608, Castello, Venice 30122
Tel (041) 528 5315
Fax (041) 523 8859
Location on a small square,
100m back from the main
waterfront; nearest
landing-stage Arsenale
Food & drink breakfast
Prices rooms L90,000-
L145,000 with breakfast
Rooms 14 double, 5 with bath,
9 with shower; 2 single, both
with shower; all rooms have
air-conditioning, phone, TV,
minibar **Facilities** large sitting-
room **Credit cards** AE, DC,
MC, V **Children** not accepted
Disabled not suitable **Pets** not
accepted **Closed** Jan until
carnival; end Nov to mid-Dec.
Proprietor Sg Tagliapietra

The north-east

Santo Stefano

If you follow the popular route from Piazza San Marco to the Accademia gallery you will walk across the Campo Santo Stefano (which, just to confuse you, is also called the Campo Francesco Morosini). It is a large, lively and rambling square whose best-known features are the alarmingly tilted *campanile* of the church of Santo Stefano and the café / *gelateria* Paolin, whose reputation for making the best ice-creams in town is well deserved.

Close to all the activity lies the Santo Stefano, a welcoming and well-cared-for little hotel whose front rooms have views of the piazza. It is not a spacious place; downstairs there is only a modest reception area, a tiny breakfast room and an even tinier courtyard at the back; and upstairs the bedrooms are barely big enough for two. But lack of size is made up for in other ways. The decoration is exceptionally pretty – many of the bedrooms are decked out with painted furniture and pretty pink fabrics – and it is kept in immaculate condition throughout.

Finally, another bonus – for Venice the prices are low.

Nearby Accademia gallery, Grand Canal.

Campo Santo Stefano, San Marco 2957, Venice 30124
Tel (041) 520 0166
Location on large square about 500 m W of Piazza San Marco; nearest landing-stage San Samuele
Food & drink breakfast
Prices rooms L80,000-L190,000; air-conditioning extra L10,000
Rooms 6 double, 2 single, 3 family rooms, all with shower; all rooms have phone, minibar, air-conditioning, TV
Facilities breakfast room, hall, tiny rear courtyard
Credit cards MC, V
Children accepted
Disabled not suitable
Pets not accepted
Closed never
Proprietor Dr Giorgio Gazzola

The north-east

Seguso

Sitting on the wide sunny promenade of the Zattere gives you the distinct feeling of being by the seaside. The quayside is lapped by the choppy waters of the wide Guidecca canal. This open setting, with a grand panorama across the lagoon, is just one of the charms of the Seguso. A *pensione* in the old tradition, it is family-run, friendly and solidly old-fashioned. And (unlike most hotels in Venice or indeed in any of the main Italian cities) prices are modest; the Seguso is not noted for its food, but half-board here costs no more than bed and breakfast alone in hotels of similar comfort closer to San Marco.

The best bedrooms are the large ones at the front of the house, overlooking the canal – though for the privilege of the views and space you may have to forfeit the luxury of a private bathroom (only half the rooms have their own facilities). The main public rooms are the dining-room, prettily furnished in traditional style, and the modest sitting-room where you can sink into large leather chairs and peruse ancient editions of travel and guide books. Breakfast is taken on a small terrace at the front of the hotel – delightful.

Nearby Accademia gallery, Gesuati church.

Zattere 779, Dorsoduro, Venice 30123
Tel (041) 528 6858
Fax 522 2340
Location 5 minutes S of Accademia, overlooking Guidecca canal; nearest landing-stage Zattere
Food & drink breakfast, lunch, dinner
Prices rooms L95,000-L130,000; DB&B L90,000-L121,000; reductions for children **Rooms** 31 double, 5 single; 9 with bath, 9 with shower; all rooms have phone
Facilities dining-room, sitting-room, terrace
Credit cards AE, MC, V
Children welcome
Disabled no special facilities
Pets accepted
Closed Dec to Feb
Proprietors Seguso family

The north-east

Seaside villa, Venice Lido

Villa Mabapa

Despite the extensions to the original 1930s family house, giving this comfortable hotel more rooms than we normally allow in these pages, Villa Mabapa still manages to give the impression of a private home. What is more, it is good value, particularly in comparison with the large, better-known hotels on the beach at the Lido. The hotel is set in a garden beside the lagoon, with a private landing stage (the public water-bus stop is a few minutes away). The location may be slightly out of the way, being neither on the main Lido thoroughfare nor on the beach, but it does have the bonus of wonderfully peaceful rooms, a garden and a summer dining terrace giving wonderful sunset views.

The hotel consists of two buildings. Villa Mabapa itself contains the high-ceilinged public rooms and some traditional-style bedrooms; the best are on the first floor – as is the sitting-room, with a terrace giving views of the lagoon. Within the garden is the modern annexe of Villa Morea, with more up-to-date bedrooms.

The name? It consists of the first syllables of the words mamma, bambino and pappa. A family home indeed.
Nearby Venice (10/20 minutes by ferry).

Riviera San Nicolo' 16, Venice Lido 30126 Venice
Tel (041) 526 0590 **Fax** 9441
Location on the lagoon side of the Lido, with fine views of city; in pretty garden
Food & drink breakfast, lunch, dinner
Prices rooms L105,000-L290,000; meals about L40,000
Rooms 47 double, 15 single, all with bath or shower; all have TV, phone; 30 rooms have air-conditioning

Facilities dining-room, dining terrace, bar, sitting-room
Credit card AE, DC, MC, V
Children accepted
Disabled some rooms suitable
Pets no dogs allowed in dining-room
Closed mid-Nov to just before Christmas
Proprietor Sg Vianello

The north-east

Country villa, Arcugnano

Villa Michelangelo

This rather severe-looking 18thC villa was a Capuchin college before it became a hotel, and there is a monastic purity about its decorative style even now. Black slate floors and leather chairs contrast with white walls. Extensive grounds, fair-sized pool.

■ Via Sacco 19, 36057 Arcugnano (Vicenza) **Tel** (0444) 550300 **Fax** (0444) 550490 **Meals** breakfast, lunch, dinner **Prices** rooms L165,000-L270,000; meals about L70,000 **Rooms** 34, all with bath or shower, central heating, air-conditioning, phone, TV, radio, minibar **Credit cards** AE, DC, MC, V **Closed** restaurant only, Sun eve, Mon

---

Converted castle, Bolzano

Castel Guncina

Yet another of north-east Italy's handsome hilltop castles with fine views, in this case over the valley and town of Bolzano. Surrounded by trees and vineyards, the hotel also offers an attractive pool and tennis-courts. Comfortable and well-equipped bedrooms, varying in size and outlook.

■ Via Miramonti 9, Guncina, 39100 Bolzano **Tel** (0471) 285742 **Fax** (0471) 46345 **Meals** breakfast, lunch, dinner **Prices** rooms L50,000-L160,000 with breakfast **Rooms** 18, all with bath, central heating, phone, TV, radio, minibar **Credit cards** MC, V **Closed** Feb; restaurant only, Tue

---

Town hotel, Bressanone

Hotel Dominik

A deeply comfortable and well-run modern hotel, close to the river on the green fringes of Bressanone. The spacious and well-equipped bedrooms are rather anonymous, but public areas have more style, and the garden is pretty. Large, indoor swimming-pool.

■ Via Terzo di Sotto 13, 39042 Bressanone (Bolzano) **Tel** (0472) 30144 **Fax** (0472) 36554 **Meals** breakfast, lunch, dinner **Prices** rooms L160,000-L278,000 **Rooms** 29, all with bath, central heating, phone, TV, radio, hairdrier, minibar **Credit cards** AE, MC, V **Closed** early Nov to mid-Mar

---

Restaurant-with-rooms, Cividale del Friuli

Locanda al Castello

Although quite properly described as a restaurant with rooms, this crenellated hilltop building is a welcoming and restful place to stay, with a large terrace accommodating easy chairs. The two dining-rooms are uncomfortably large, but the bedrooms have a pleasantly rustic Alpine feel, and spotless bathrooms.

■ Via del Castello 18, 33043 Cividale del Friuli (Udine) **Tel** (0432) 733242 **Fax** (0432) 700901 **Meals** breakfast, lunch, dinner **Prices** rooms L59,000-L91,000 **Rooms** 10, all with bath or shower, phone **Credit cards** V **Closed** a few days in Nov

The north-east

Mountain chalet, Colfosco

Hotel Cappella

A typical (and small) example of the classical Sud Tirol hotel – modern (late 1960s), but in Alpine chalet style; thoroughly comfortable and welcoming, with richly traditional furnishings; well equipped with sports facilities (pleasant indoor pool); and set in spectacular scenery, with skiing or walking from the door.

■ 39030 Colfosco (Bolzano) **Tel** (0471) 836183 **Fax** (0471) 836561 **Meals** breakfast, lunch, dinner **Prices** rooms L110,000-L180,000; reduction for children **Rooms** 40, all with bath or shower, central heating, phone, radio, TV **Credit cards** DC, MC, V **Closed** mid-Apr to mid-Jun, end Sep to mid-Dec

Country hotel, Cortina d'Ampezzo

Hotel Menardi

This old farmhouse on the northern side of Cortina has evolved over the years from country inn to pensione to polished hotel. Despite the elegant antiques and modern comforts, it retains its traditional warmth. The large garden is a secluded delight.

■ Via Majon 110, 32043 Cortina d'Ampezzo (Belluno) **Tel** (0436) 2400 **Fax** (0436) 862183 **Meals** breakfast, lunch, dinner **Prices** rooms L65,000-L130,000 with breakfast; DB&B L92,000-L160,000; FB L100,000-L175,000 **Rooms** 48, all with bath, central heating, phone **Credit cards** V **Closed** Oct to mid-Dec and mid-Apr to mid-Jun

Country hotel, Fiè Allo Sciliar

Hotel Turm

A polished, warmly welcoming hotel in the best Sudtirol tradition, between Bolzano and the well-known ski resorts of Val Gardena. There are cosy sitting-rooms, a rustic bar, indoor and outdoor pools. And the proprietor has built up an impressive collection of paintings on the walls.

■ Piazza della Chiesa 9, 39050 Fiè Allo Sciliar (Bolzano) **Tel** (0471) 725014 **Fax** (0471) 725474 **Meals** breakfast, lunch, dinner **Prices** rooms L70,000-L200,000 with breakfast; DB&B L80,000-L115,000 **Rooms** 23, all with bath, central heating, TV, radio, phone **Credit cards** MC, V **Closed** mid-Nov to mid-Dec

Country hotel, Merano

Der Pünthof

Part of the Pünthof dates back to the Middle Ages, when it was a farmhouse, and the breakfast rooms retain traces of the original decoration on their panelled walls. Some bedrooms also have an antique atmosphere, but most are in little, detached chalets of recent vintage, with their own kitchen facilities. Good pool.

■ Via Steinach 25, 39022 Merano (Bolzano) **Tel** (0473) 48553 **Fax** (0473) 49919 **Meals** breakfast, dinner **Prices** rooms L90,000-L190,000 with breakfast **Rooms** 18, all with bath or shower, central heating, colour TV, radio, minibar, phone, safe **Credit cards** DC **Closed** mid-Nov to Feb

Country villa, Mogliano Veneto

Villa Condulmer

For about the price of a two-star hotel in Venice you can stay in this lovely 18thC villa only a 20-minute drive away. Public rooms are adorned with rococo frescos, extravagant Murano-glass chandeliers and period furniture. Bedrooms are also grand but less ornate.

■ Via Zermanese, Zerman Mogliano, 30121 Mogliano Veneto (Treviso) **Tel** (041) 457100 **Fax** (041) 457134 **Meals** breakfast, lunch, dinner **Prices** rooms L84,000-L147,000; luxury rooms L210,000; meals L63,000-L84,000 **Rooms** 45, all with phone, minibar; some rooms have air-conditioning **Credit cards** AE, DC, MC, V **Closed** 8 Jan to 15 Feb

Country villa, Paderno di Ponzano

El Toulà

People come from far and wide to experience the restaurant of this lovingly converted old farmhouse, where classic dishes are re-interpreted according to new ideas. Bedrooms vary from extremely comfortable to extremely luxurious. An expensive treat.

■ Via Postumia 63, 31050 Paderno di Ponzano (Treviso) **Tel** (0422) 969023 **Fax** (0422) 969994 **Meals** breakfast, lunch, dinner **Prices** rooms L315,000-L400,000; suites L600,000 **Rooms** 10, all with bath, central heating, phone, colour TV, minibar **Credit cards** AE, DC, V **Closed** never

Town hotel, Padua

Hotel Majestic Toscanelli

This 1960s building looks nothing special, but it occupies an unusually quiet spot in the heart of old Padua, and was renovated a couple of years ago in confident style. Bedrooms are carefully coordinated and very comfortable, with sparkling shower rooms. Tuscan proprietors – hence the name.

■ Piazzeta dell'Arco 2, 35122 Padua **Tel** (049) 663244 **Fax** (049) 876 0025 **Meals** breakfast, lunch, dinner **Prices** rooms L140,000-L175,000; suite L220,000 **Rooms** 32, all with bath or shower, phone, air-conditioning, TV, minibar, radio **Credit cards** AE, DC, MC, V **Closed** never

Town hotel, Padua

Hotel Donatello

This is much the best-placed base in Padua for tourists, taking its name from the creator of the famous equestrian statue that it overlooks. The bright trattoria-style restaurant has a pavement café with a good view of the basilica. Simple, modernized rooms.

■ Via del Santo 102, 35123 Padua **Tel** (049) 875 0634 **Fax** (049) 875 0829 **Meals** breakfast, lunch, dinner **Prices** rooms L120,000-L205,000 **Rooms** 49, all with bath or shower, phone, minibar **Credit cards** AE, DC, MC, V **Closed** mid-Dec to mid-Jan; restaurant only, Wed

The north-east

Town hotel, Padua

Albergo Leon Bianco

'Charming' may not be quite the right word for this smart little hotel, with its plate-glass doors and smooth modern furnishings. But it has a stylish air, and a good position overlooking the famous Caffè Pedrocchi. Breakfast can be taken on a small roof terrace.

■ Piazzetta Pedrocchi 12, 35100 Padua **Tel** (049) 875 0814 **Fax** (049) 875 6184 **Meals** breakfast **Prices** rooms L117,000-L159,000 **Rooms** 22, all with bath or shower, colour TV, phone, minibar, air-conditioning **Credit cards** AE, DC, MC, V **Closed** never

---

Converted castle, Pergine

Castel Pergine

This conspicuous hilltop castle enjoys marvellous views in all directions. Inside, enormous vaulted rooms serve as the restaurant; bedrooms have whitewashed or wood-panelled walls, and old carved beds with bright duvets. There is a peaceful, walled garden. 'Incredible value', says a reporter.

■ 38057 Pergine (Trento) **Tel** (0461) 531158 **Meals** breakfast, lunch, dinner **Prices** rooms L68,000-L80,000; 40% reduction for children under 6 **Rooms** 23, all with phone; most have shower **Credit cards** not accepted **Closed** mid-Oct to Apr

---

Converted castle, San Floriano del Collio

Castello de San Floriano

The beautifully furnished rooms of this tiny hotel, contained in two renovated houses of a fortified village, are named after prestigious wines, emphasising the vinous interest of the Formentini family. Lovely gardens, with golf, tennis and a pool. English breakfasts.

■ Via Oslavia 5, 34070 San Floriano del Collio (Gorizia) **Tel** (0481) 884051 **Fax** (0481) 884214 **Meals** breakfast **Prices** rooms L160,000-L220,000 with breakfast **Rooms** 12, all with bath or shower, central heating, air-conditioning, TV, minibar, phone **Credit cards** DC, MC, V **Closed** Dec to Mar

---

Country villa, Scorze

Villa Conestabile

Not a luxury hotel, but excellent value at half the cost of a similar standard of accommodation in the city. It still has touches of grandeur – elaborate chandeliers, grand staircases and fine pieces of furniture – but the restaurant and bar are comparatively simple.

■ Via Roma 1, 30037 Scorzè (Venezia) **Tel** (041) 445027 **Fax** (041) 584 0088 **Meals** breakfast, lunch, dinner **Prices** rooms L71,000-L101,000; meals L35,000-L60,000 **Rooms** 24, all with central heating, phone, TV;most with bath or shower **Credit cards** AE, MC, V **Closed** restaurant only, first 3 weeks in Aug

The north-east

Restaurant-with-rooms, Solighetto

Locanda da Lino

Restaurant with rooms, and chalk with cheese. You eat pasta and grills in a jolly room hung with copper pans and pictures, or in a courtyard hung with vines; you sleep in a beautifully furnished modern ground-floor room with a distinctive decorative theme – perhaps the super-slick 'Marcello Mastroianni'.

■ Via Brandolini 31, 31050 Solighetto (Treviso) **Tel** (0438) 82150
Fax (0438) 980577 **Meals** breakfast, lunch, dinner **Prices** rooms
L75,000; meals L40,000 **Rooms** 17, all with bath, central heating, phone,
TV, minibar **Credit cards** AE, DC, MC, V **Closed** Mon, Christmas Day,
July

Converted castle, Tesimo

Schloss Fahlburg

An imposing Sudtirol schloss, with spires at its corners giving a slightly fairytale air, and the obligatory panoramic views. Inside, it is cool and uncluttered, the white walls showing off the handsome furniture and splendid ceilings. Breakfast is an impressive buffet.

■ Prissiano 83, 39010 Tesimo (Bolzano) **Tel** (0473) 90930 **Fax** (0473)
90930 **Meals** breakfast **Prices** rooms L53,000-L106,000; suite L129,000
Rooms 8, all with bath, central heating **Credit cards** AE, MC, V
Closed end Nov to Easter

Mountain chalet, Tires

Stefaner

A fairly modern chalet, high up in a beautiful Dolomite valley, that is run more as a home than a hotel. Furnishings are simple and cosy, with plenty of plants and ornaments. Bedrooms are bright and airy, with geranium-decked balconies. Charming and enthusiastic proprietors.

■ San Cipriano, 39050 Tires (Bolzano) **Tel** (0471) 642175 **Fax** (0471)
642005 **Meals** breakfast, dinner **Prices** DB&B L48,000-L62,000
Rooms 15, all with bath or shower, **Credit cards** not accepted
Closed mid-Nov to mid-Dec

Restaurant-with-rooms, Torcello

Locanda Cipriani

The Locanda Cipriani, on the popular excursion island of Torcello, is a fashionable spot for lunch or dinner (40 minutes by water-bus, much less by water-taxi) with a large terrace area. The rustic double rooms overlook the garden whence come the salads and flowers for the tables.

■ Piazza S Fosca 29, 30012 Torcello (Venice) **Tel** (041) 730757
Fax (041) 735433 **Meals** breakfast, lunch, dinner **Prices** DB&B L260,000;
FB L350,000 **Rooms** 6, all with bath, phone; double rooms have
sitting-room **Credit cards** AE, DC, MC, V **Closed** early Nov to mid-Mar

The north-east

Country hotel, Torri del Benaco

Hotel Europa

Regular visitors to the Europa call it 'a happy, welcoming hotel', offering excellent value. It is an old villa up the hillside from Lake Garda, in gardens and olive groves. Inside, most of the character has been ironed out in favour of cleanliness and simplicity. Dinner on the stroke of 7.30.

■ Via Gabriele d'Annunzio 13, 37010 Torri del Benaco (Verona) **Tel** (045) 722 5086 (winter 629 6619) **Fax** (045) 629 6632 **Meals** breakfast, dinner, snacks **Prices** rooms L45,000-L145,000 with breakfast; DB&B L65,000-L97,000; min stay 3 days **Rooms** 18, all with central heating, phone; most rooms have bath or shower **Credit cards** not accepted **Closed** mid-Oct to Easter

---

Restaurant-with-rooms, Treviso

Le Beccherie

Le Beccherie is a long-established, unpretentious but highly regarded restaurant at the heart of charming old Treviso, with a few simple rooms above it. Across the tiny piazza is the same proprietor's Albergo Campeol, containing more comfortable rooms with bathrooms.

■ Piazza G Ancillotto 10, 31100 Treviso **Tel** (0422) 540871 **Fax** (0422) 540871 **Meals** breakfast, lunch, dinner **Prices** rooms L56,000-L91,000 with breakfast **Rooms** 27, all with central heating; 16 rooms have radio and phone **Credit cards** AE, DC, MC, V **Closed** restaurant only: Thu evening, Fri and 3 weeks late July

---

Town inn, Tricesimo

Boschetti

This long-established, family-run inn is as compelling as a restaurant (its modern interpretations of traditional dishes earn a Michelin star) as it is as a hotel. The emphasis in the rooms is on comfort and good housekeeping, rather than on character.

■ Piazza Mazzini 10, 33019 Tricesimo (Udine) **Tel** (0432) 851230 **Fax** (0432) 851216 **Meals** breakfast, lunch, dinner **Prices** rooms L85,000-L120,000 **Rooms** 32, all with bath or shower, phone, TV **Credit cards** AE, DC, V **Closed** 5 to 20 Aug; restaurant only, Mon

---

Town hotel, Venice

Abbazia

A converted abbey standing in a rather shabby area near the station – but inside, the atmosphere could not be more respectable. The former church is the sitting-room (with the pulpit still intact). Bedrooms are somewhat monastic and austere, but perfectly well kept and comfortable. A charming garden lies behind.

■ Cannaregio 66, 30121 Venice **Tel** (041) 717333 **Fax** (041) 717949 **Meals** breakfast **Prices** rooms L150,000-L250,000 with breakfast **Rooms** 40, all with bath or shower, central heating, TV, minibar **Credit cards** AE, DC, MC, V **Closed** never

Town hotel, Venice

American

A shuttered, terraced *palazzo* tucked behind the Accademia, recently restored and converted into a hotel. Bedrooms have Venetian-style painted furniture; public areas are comfortably and tastefully done with plenty of personal touches. The canal-side location is exceptionally pleasant and peaceful.

■ San Vio 628, 30123 Venice **Tel** (041) 520 4733 **Fax** (041) 520 4048 **Meals** breakfast **Prices** rooms L105,000-L262,500 **Rooms** 30, all with bath or shower, air-conditioning, TV, minibar, phone, radio **Credit cards** AE, DC, MC, V **Closed** never

Town hotel, Venice

Ateneo

Another of Venice's *palazzo* hotels, decked out in a civilized, traditional style with Murano glass light fittings and painted furniture. The reception is agreeable and the lack of restaurant no problem in this area by the Fenice theatre.

■ San Marco 1876, 30124 Venice **Tel** (041) 520 0777 **Fax** (041) 522 8550 **Meals** breakfast **Prices** rooms L85,000-L200,000 with breakfast **Rooms** 23, all with air-conditioning, central heating, phone, TV, radio, minibar **Credit cards** AE, MC, V **Closed** never

Town hotel, Venice

Bel Sito

A central but reasonably priced and quiet option, well looked-after inside. A patio of potted plants and parasols makes a pleasant vantage-point for people-watching. The best rooms are at the rear; front rooms are darker and more old-fashioned.

■ Campo Santa Maria del Giglio, San Marco 2517, 30124 Venice **Tel** (041) 522 3365 **Fax** (041) 520 4083 **Meals** breakfast **Prices** rooms L86,800-L183,000 with breakfast **Rooms** 38, all with bath or shower, phone, air-conditioning, minibar **Credit cards** AE, MC, V **Closed** never

Town hotel, Venice

Bucintoro

This modest, cement-rendered block (conveniently close to the vaporetto stop at Arsenale) shares the fine Giudecca waterfront views of many more elaborate hotels. Tables and chairs are set on the quayside, screened by tubs of flowers. Inside it is light and neat – plain, but personal and well looked-after.

■ Riva Schiavoni 2135, 30122 Venice **Tel** (041) 522 3240 **Fax** (041) 523 5224 **Meals** breakfast, dinner **Prices** rooms L55,000-L126,000; DB&B L82,000-L92,000 **Rooms** 28, all with bath or shower, phone **Credit cards** not accepted **Closed** Dec and Jan

The north-east

Town guest-house, Venice

Calcina

Ruskin's plaque reveals the long-established enthusiasm of regular visitors to this little hotel. Today, facing the sunny straits of the Giudecca canal, it is similarly hard to resist. Inside it is simple: flowers and cottagey chairs in the entrance lounge, and many cheerful modern paintings. Friendly and informal.

■ Zattere 780, 30123 Venice **Tel** (041) 520 6466 **Fax** (041) 522 7045 **Meals** breakfast **Prices** rooms L40,000-L143,500 **Rooms** 40, all with central heating, phone; most with bath or shower **Credit cards** AE, DC, MC, V **Closed** Jan

---

Town hotel, Venice

Pensione alla Salute da Cici

This calm, civilized place has a classically elegant lobby of columns and marble floors beneath exposed rafters. It lies in an interesting part of Venice, between the Salute basilica and the Accademia. Furnishings are quietly tasteful. A tiny, sheltered garden offers a few sunny tables for a drink.

■ Fondamenta Ca Balla 222, 30123 Venice **Tel** (041) 523 5404 **Fax** (041) 522 2271 **Meals** breakfast **Prices** rooms L85,000-L120,000 **Rooms** 50, all with central heating, phone; 28 rooms with bath or shower **Credit cards** not accepted **Closed** early Nov to Feb

---

Town hotel, Venice

Kette

Recently refurbished in an ambitiously formal style of *faux* marble and much wood panelling, this hotel is now somewhat institutional. Bedrooms and all public areas are well kept and comfortable with smartly matching uniform furnishings. Displays of Murano glass and a few *objets d'art* add some personality.

■ San Marco 2053, 30124 Venice **Tel** (041) 520 7766 **Fax** (041) 522 8964 **Meals** breakfast **Prices** rooms L120,000-L220,000 with breakfast; suites L220,000-L380,000 **Rooms** 50, all with bath or shower, central heating, air-conditioning, TV, safe, minibar, hairdrier **Credit cards** AE, V **Closed** never

---

Town hotel, Venice

Nuovo Teson

In a tiny square just off the Riva degli Schiavoni (a short walk or *vaporetto* ride to San Marco), this is a modern building, recently renovated. Bedrooms are small, but pretty with Venetian furniture and glass lamps. The only public space is a plainish breakfast room enclosing a small bar-lounge area, but several reasonable restaurants lie nearby, notably Al Covo directly opposite.

■ Riva degli Schiavoni 3980, 30122 Venice **Tel** (041) 522 9929 **Fax** (041) 528 5335 **Meals** breakfast **Prices** rooms L100,000-L150,000 with breakfast; 15% off for mentioning the guide **Rooms** 30, all with shower, central heating, radio, music **Credit cards** AE, MC, V **Closed** Nov to Jan

The north-east

Town hotel, Venice

Paganelli

This modest, friendly place gives itself no airs at all, but shares approximately the same lagoon views as much more august and expensive hotels on the Riva degli Schiavoni. Breakfast is served in a nearby annexe in the adjoining side-street. Largest and smartest bedrooms face the waterfront.

■ Riva degli Schiavoni 4687, 30122 Venice **Tel** (041) 522 4324 **Fax** (041) 523 9267 **Meals** breakfast **Prices** rooms L90,000-L150,000 with breakfast; 30% reduction for young children **Rooms** 23, all with phone, most with bath or shower **Credit cards** AE, MC, V **Closed** restaurant only, mid-Nov to mid-Mar

---

Town hotel, Venice

Do Pozzi

Quietly located in a tiny enclosed square near San Marco, this neat little hotel has fairly standardized furnishings and modern bedrooms. The palm-fringed courtyard set with café tables is a popular spot; so too is the adjoining Raffaele restaurant, festooned with copper utensils and antique weaponry.

■ Via XXII Marzo, 30124 Venice **Tel** (041) 520 7855 **Fax** (041) 522 9413 **Meals** breakfast; bar service **Prices** rooms L100,000-L212,000; meals L30,000 **Rooms** 35, all with bath or shower, central heating, minibar, air-conditioning, phone, TV **Credit cards** AE, DC, MC, V **Closed** never

---

Town hotel, Venice

San Cassiano

A gorgeous Gothic façade faces the Grand Canal and Ca d'Oro; access, via tortuous, narrow alleyways from the nearest *traghetto* point, can be tricky. Inside the *palazzo* is handsomely furnished with Murano chandeliers and antique-look pieces. It retains many original features and timbered ceilings. The light, elegant breakfast room with waterfront views is the main focal point.

■ Santa Croce 2232, 30135 Venice **Tel** (041) 721033 **Meals** breakfast **Prices** L80,000-L105,000 **Rooms** 35, all with bath or shower, air-conditioning, colour TV, radio, phone, minibar, hairdrier **Credit cards** AE, DC **Closed** never

---

Town guest-house, Venice

San Fantin

An intriguing façade, studded with cannonballs and guarded by a whimsical lion, distinguishes this hotel, in a quiet corner near the Fenice theatre. Amicably run by a mother-and-daughter team, the hotel is simple but cared-for, as indicated by a profusion of pictures.

■ Campiello de la Fenice 1930/a, San Marco, 30124 Venice **Tel** (041) 523 1401 **Meals** breakfast **Prices** rooms L70,000-L180,000 **Rooms** 14, all with central heating; most with shower **Credit cards** not accepted **Closed** winter

The north-east

Town hotel, Venice

San Moisé

A delightful canalside location near San Marco is an obvious attraction. Warbling gondoliers glide past within inches. This newly restored place has intrinsic good points too, and is sprucely kitted out in a mix of modern furnishings given period Venetian flavour with rugs and elaborate glass chandeliers.

■ San Marco 2058, 30124 Venice **Tel** (041) 523 6720 **Meals** breakfast **Prices** L78,750-L104,000 **Rooms** 18, all with bath or shower, some rooms have phone, minibar **Credit cards** AE, DC, MC, V **Closed** never

---

Town hotel, Venice

Santa Marina

An attractive, yellow-washed building on a corner-site of a relatively untouristy square near the Rialto, near several pleasant cafés. Inside decorations and furnishings are predictably hotel-like, but the welcome is civil and the ambience relaxing. Bedrooms are light and clean, modern lines softened by occasional Venetian flourishes.

■ Castello, Campo Santa Maria 6068, 30122 Venice **Tel** (041) 523 9202 **Fax** (041) 520 0907 **Meals** breakfast **Prices** rooms L150,000-L230,000 **Rooms** 16, all with bath or shower, central heating, air-conditioning, phone, TV, minibar **Credit cards** AE, DC, MC, V **Closed** never

---

Town hotel, Venice

Scandinavia

The rambling piazza is lively on market-days, but the hotel is formal and almost hushed inside, decorated with much marble, walnut veneer and Murano glassware. Solid antique-style furnishings and many paintings give it an air of superiority. A nearby trattoria is under the same management.

■ Campo Santa Maria Formosa, Castello 5240, 30122 Venice **Tel** (041) 522 3507 **Fax** (041) 523 5232 **Meals** breakfast; lunch and dinner at nearby Trattoria Al Burchiello **Prices** rooms L100,000-L250,000 with breakfast **Rooms** 34, all with central heating, phone, minibar, air-conditioning; TV on request, most with bath **Credit cards** AE, MC, V **Closed** never

---

Town hotel, Venice

Torino

Grander inside than its exterior suggests, this Gothic *palazzo* has kept many interesting architectural features, and the style remains firmly traditional, though a number of new bedrooms have recently been added with modern bathrooms.

■ Calle delle Ostreghe 2356, San Marco, 30124 Venice **Tel** (041) 520 5222 **Fax** (041) 522 8227 **Meals** breakfast **Prices** rooms L100,000-L220,000 with breakfast **Rooms** 20, all with shower, central heating, air-conditioning, phone, radio, TV, minibar **Credit cards** AE, DC, MC, V **Closed** never

Town villa, Venice Lido

Villa Parco

A simple, reasonably priced place a few minutes away from the waterfront in a quiet residential area. The building is in art nouveau style, though furnishings are mainly modern. As well as breakfast, you can get snacks from the bar.

■ Via Rodi 1, 30126 Venice Lido (Venice) **Tel** (041) 526 0015 **Fax** (041) 526 7620 **Meals** breakfast **Prices** rooms L100,000-L180,000 **Rooms** 20, all with bath or shower, central heating, phone, TV, air-conditioning, minibar **Credit cards** AE, DC, MC, V **Closed** Dec to Carnival (Feb)

Town hotel, Verona

Torcolo

A faded ochre building offering solid value in an excellent location close to the Arena and the city centre. Bedrooms are decorated in a variety of styles – Italian 18thC, art nouveau and modern – and most are not as noisy as you might expect. Breakfast can be served outside on a terrace.

■ Vicolo Listone 3, 37121 Verona **Tel** (045) 800 7512 **Meals** breakfast **Prices** rooms L46,000-L78,000 **Rooms** 19, all with bath or shower, central heating, air-conditioning, phone **Credit cards** not accepted **Closed** 2 weeks Jan

Emilia-Romagna

Area introduction

Hotels in Emilia-Romagna

The Via Emilia, the Roman road (now a motorway) stretching along the foothills of the Apennine mountains from Piacenza to Rimini, gives the region its name, and most of the main towns are located along it.

Bologna, the regional capital, is primarily a business centre with business-style hotels to match; but it is also a city of learning (it has the oldest university in Europe) and art (including beautiful Renaissance buildings) so there is much to attract the tourist, and we are able to recommend the three hotels owned by the Orsi family, described on pages 90–92.

Our only recommendation for Modena – too big for a full entry in this guide – is the Canalgrande (Tel (059) 217160, fax 221674, 78 bedrooms), a stylish, peaceful and comfortable villa set in beautiful gardens in the middle of the city.

Finding a satisfactory hotel in Parma is nearly as difficult but we can add the Villa Ducale (Tel (0521) 272727, fax 70756), a 28-room hotel set in shady grounds, as an alternative to the Torino described on page 96. And for Ferrara, the luxurious Duchessa Isabella (Tel (0532) 202121, fax 202638) is worth mentioning as an alternative to the Ripagrande (page 95) although it is equally expensive.

The Adriatic coast of this region is not notable for small hotels, hence the lack of recommendations in this guide. Ravenna is the most important port – try the simple but central Centrale Byron (Tel (0544) 22225, 59 rooms) if you need to stay there – and there are numerous beach resorts up and down the coast offering plenty of sea, sun and sand. The Albergo Caravel (Tel (0533) 330106, fax 330107) is one of the few examples of an alternative to the large, busy seaside hotels. This hotel has only 22 rooms and is set in a shady garden 100 m from the beach at Lido di Spina.

Should you need a room in the backwater town of Sarsina, try the Al Piano (Tel (0547) 94848 fax 95153) – a simply furnished mansion in a splendid hillside position, dropped from the guide this year following reports from disappointed visitors. It has enjoyed enthusiastic support in the past, so more reports would be very welcome.

This page acts as an introduction to the features and hotels of Emilia-Romagna, and gives brief recommendations of reasonable hotels that for one reason or another have not made a full entry. The long entries for this region – covering the hotels we are most enthusiastic about – start on the next page. But do not neglect the shorter entries starting on page 95: these are all hotels that we would happily stay at.

Emilia-Romagna

Corona d'Oro 1890

The Corona d'Oro lies in the historic old city, close to the two famous leaning towers, in a cobbled street which for most of the time is closed to traffic. Enticing food shops (including a wonderful delicatessen) give you some idea of why the city is nicknamed Bologna La Grassa (the Fat) – and you certainly will not find it hard to eat well in this part of town.

The Corona d'Oro became a hotel in 1890, though the original building dates back to 1300. It is here that Italy's first printing press was established and there are still a few features surviving from the original palace. In the early 1980s the hotel was bought by a packaging magnate, who elevated it from a simple hotel to four-star status, successfully combining the old features with the stylish new. The 14thC portico and Renaissance ceilings were preserved, while the plush bedrooms were provided with all modern conveniences. The showpiece was the hallway, with its fine art nouveau frieze supported on columns. Light streaming from above, fresh flowers and the central feature of lush feathery plants combined to create a cheerful, inviting entrance.

Nearby Piazza Maggiore and Piazza del Nettuno.

Via Oberdan 12, Bologna 40126
Tel (051) 236456 **Fax** 262679
Location in middle, close to the two leaning towers in Piazza di Porta Ravegnana; with private car parking
Food & drink breakfast
Prices rooms L183,000-L355,000
Rooms 27 double, one with bath, 27 with shower; 8 single, all with shower; all rooms have central heating, colour TV, minibar, phone, safe, air-conditioning
Facilities bar, conference room, sitting-area, TV room
Credit cards AE, DC, MC, V
Children accepted
Disabled lift/elevator
Pets only small ones accepted
Closed Aug
Proprietor Mauro Orsi

Emilia-Romagna

Town hotel, Bologna

Dei Commercianti

As its name suggests, the Commercianti (in the same group as
the Corona d'Oro, page 90) caters primarily for businessmen,
but in a city with few tourist hotels it is a useful little place to
know about, particularly since it was spruced up two or three
years ago. Bedrooms are neat and modern, apart from the
occasional old beam to remind you that you are in a medieval
building. There is no restaurant – just a café-like breakfast room.
In a corner off reception is a little sitting-area with pretty blue
flowered sofas. The hotel has an air of efficiency rather than
notable character, but it is well run and for a reasonably priced
base serves its purpose well.

Nearby San Petronio, Fontana and Piazza del Nettuno.

Via Pignattari 11, Bologna
40124
Tel (051) 233052 **Fax** 224733
Location in middle of city, off
Piazza Maggiore, with private
car parking
Food & drink breakfast
Prices rooms L95,000-
L163,000 with breakfast
Rooms 23 double, 8 single; all
with shower; all have central
heating, colour TV, minibar,
phone, air-conditioning
Facilities bar/breakfast room,
sitting-area, TV room
Credit cards AE, DC, MC, V
Children accepted; beds and
cots available
Disabled lift/elevator available
Pets small ones only
Closed never
Proprietor Paolo Orsi

Emilia-Romagna

Orologio

The Corona d'Oro (page 90), Commercianti (page 91) and the Orologio are all under the same management; of the three – all close together in central Bologna – this has in the past been the poor relation, but in 1990 the Orologio was completely renovated to bring it up to the standards of the others (or at least the standard of the Commercianti); unfortunately the prices now match, too.

The Orologio can claim the best location of the three – just off the main square in the historic heart of Bologna, flanking a pedestrianized thoroughfare and facing the handsome Palazzo Communale. The hotel's formula is simple: freshly decorated and well-equipped bedrooms, and much better than average breakfasts served in a smart, bright little sitting/breakfast area.

Recent visitors endorse our recommendation, commenting on the 'extremely pleasant and helpful staff', the 'very attractive' and 'well lit' bedrooms and the 'very good breakfast, still including the freshly squeezed orange juice'. But one (who stayed in a front room on an upper floor) also warns of disturbance from the tolling of a bell nearby.

Nearby basilica of San Petronio, Fontana del Nettuno

Via IV Novembre 10, Bologna 40123
Tel (051) 231253
Fax 260552
Location in middle of city, on pedestrian thoroughfare, with private car parking and garage
Food & drink breakfast
Prices rooms L95,000-L165,000 with breakfast
Rooms 21 double, 8 single, all with bath; all rooms have central heating, phone, air-conditioning, minibar, TV,
safe
Facilities breakfast room, bar
Credit cards AE, DC, MC, V
Children accepted
Disabled no special facilities
Pets small ones only
Closed never
Proprietor Mauro Orsi

Emilia-Romagna

Gigiolè

Brisighella is a picturesque small town 13 km south-west of Faenza. The Gigiolè stands across from the main church – a vaguely French-looking shuttered building with a shaded terrace in front.

The French style extends to the food: Tarcisio Raccagni, the chef, has been put on a par with the famous Paul Bocuse. Like Bocuse he places great stress on using seasonal local ingredients of top quality and the results are superb: succulent meats, delicious soups and imaginative use of vegetables and herbs – top quality *nouvelle cuisine* but at prices you can afford and in helpings that don't leave you hungry. The setting is late 18thC, with stone arches, ceramics and copper pots. Table-cloths are white and crisp, and glasses gleam. Service is 'grave but efficient'.

After all this, the bedrooms come as a bit of an anti-climax; but they are adequate, and give little cause for complaint. Some of the newly decorated rooms are quite pretty, with white modern furnishings and fabrics, and good new bathrooms; others are being redecorated. Ask for a room at the back if peace is a priority. 'Very friendly welcome, splendid food, excellent value; I should gladly return', says a reporter.

Nearby Faenza; Florence, Ravenna, Bologna, Rimini within reach.

Piazza Carducci 5, Brisighella
48013 Ravenna
Tel (0546) 81209
Location in middle of town, 13 km SW of Faenza on S302; no private car parking, but space available in the piazza
Food & drink breakfast, lunch, dinner
Prices rooms L55,000-L75,000; meals L45,000
Rooms 7 double, 5 single, 2 family rooms; all with bath; all rooms have central heating, phone
Facilities dining-room, bar, TV room
Credit cards AE, DC, V
Children welcome
Disabled access difficult
Pets welcome if clean and well behaved
Closed one week Feb, one week Mar; restaurant only, Mon
Proprietor Tarcisio Raccagni

Emilia-Romagna

Converted monastery, Portico di Romagna

Al Vecchio Convento

A sleepy medieval village, Portico di Romagna lies on the borders of Tuscany and Emilia-Romagna, in the valley of l'Acquacheta. The Vecchio Convento lies in the middle of the village. It was built in 1840 and converted only in the mid-1980s into a hotel by the Raggi family – and, thanks to them, it still maintains the feel of an old country house.

Tiles, beams and old fireplaces create a delightfully rustic setting and the warmth and hospitality of the family is part of the great charm of the place. The husband is the chef, renowned for his expertise in the kitchen, particularly his home-made pastas served with fresh herbs or *funghi* and white truffles. The ground floor is devoted mainly to the dining area – four rooms, each with the feel of a Tuscan farmhouse, ranging from a tiny vaulted room with a huge stone fireplace to the much larger old granary, with its timber ceiling and arched windows overlooking the verdant valley.

Many of the antiques from the original buildings are still in place, and this applies even to the bedrooms. Handsome and elaborate antique beds are features of rooms that are otherwise quite plain and simple. Even the new attic rooms at the top of the house have a certain rustic charm.

Nearby Faenza (46 km), Ravenna (70 km), Florence (80 km).

Via Roma 7, Portico di Romagna 47010 Forli
Tel (0543) 967752 **Fax** 967877
Location 30 km SE of Forli, in village; with some private parking in a garage
Food & drink breakfast, lunch, dinner
Prices rooms L70,000-L100,000 with breakfast; meals L40,000-L60,000
Rooms 11 double, 9 with shower; 3 single, 2 with shower; all rooms have phone

Facilities bar, dining-room, hall/sitting-room
Credit cards AE, DC, V
Children welcome
Disabled access difficult
Pets not accepted **Closed** never
Proprietors Marisa Raggi and Giovanni Cameli

Emilia-Romagna

Country villa, Barbiano di Cotignola

Villa Bolis

Beautifully restored 17thC country house with many original features, and furnished with period antiques plus some elegant modern additions. Modern *trattoria*-style restaurant, which serves Romagnolo dishes, has a terrace overlooking the main swimming pool.

■ Via Corriera 5, Lugo, 48010 Barbiano di Cotignola (Ravenna) **Tel** (0545) 78347 **Fax** (0545) 78859 **Meals** breakfast, lunch, dinner **Prices** rooms L75,000-L140,000 **Rooms** 11, all with bath or shower, central heating, phone, radio; TV on request **Credit cards** AE, DC, MC, V **Closed** Aug; restaurant only, Mon

Town hotel, Busseto

I Due Foscari

It is hard to believe that this Gothic building is only a few decades old, so convincing are its beamed ceilings, heavy antiques and iron candelabras. The restaurant (with terrace) dominates – food and service excellent – but the equally traditional rooms are satisfactory.

■ Piazza Carlo Rossi 15, 43011 Busseto (Parma) **Tel** (0524) 92337 **Fax** (0524) 91625 **Meals** breakfast, lunch, dinner **Prices** rooms L60,000-L100,000 **Rooms** 20, all with bath or shower, phone, TV **Credit cards** AE, DC, MC, V **Closed** Aug and Jan; restaurant only, Mon

Country hotel, Castelfranco Emilia

Villa Gaidello Club

Paola Giovanna and her architect sister renovated this 250-year-old farmhouse in the 1970s, creating three comfortable apartments in the old family home. The interior is appropriately furnished with country antiques, and the grounds include a lake as well as a small swimming-pool.

■ Via Gaidello 18, 41013 Castelfranco Emilia (Modena) **Tel** (059) 926806 **Fax** (059) 926620 **Meals** breakfast, lunch, dinner **Prices** rooms L110,000-L220,000 **Rooms** 3, all with bath, minibar, TV **Credit cards** DC, MC, V **Closed** Aug; restaurant only, Sun dinner and Mon

Town hotel, Ferrara

Ripagrande

The entrance hall of this Renaissance *palazzo*, converted in 1980, raises expectations high, with its exposed beams, glossy antiques and ancient stone columns. Bedrooms, in contrast, are smartly modern split-level affairs. You eat in a canopied courtyard, or a bistro-style restaurant.

■ Via Ripagrande 21, 44100 Ferrara **Tel** (0532) 765250 **Fax** (0532) 764377 **Meals** breakfast, lunch, dinner **Prices** rooms L190,000-L320,000 with breakfast; meals L40,000-L60,000 **Rooms** 42, all with bath or shower, central heating, air-conditioning, minibar, colour TV, phone **Credit cards** AE, DC, MC, V **Closed** never

Emilia-Romagna

Town hotel, Parma

Torino

In the heart of the city, just a stone's throw from the main sights (with the bonus of a private garage) – yet very reasonably priced. Bedrooms are spartan but clean, well cared-for and recently refurbished. Breakfast includes cakes and local specialities.

■ Via A Mazza 7, 43100 Parma **Tel** (0521) 281047 **Meals** breakfast
Prices rooms L95,000-L145,000 **Rooms** 33, all with bath or shower,
central heating, piped music, TV, phone **Credit cards** AE, DC, MC, V
Closed first 3 weeks Aug, and Christmas

Country guest-house, Sasso Marconi

Locanda dei Sogni

A peaceful alternative to central Bologna, 8 km to the south: a neat, yellow-washed modern villa in hilly surroundings, where you are treated as a guest in Manuela Belvederi's home. The Locanda is stylishly furnished, with a tasteful mix of the modern and the antique.

■ Via Pieve del Pino 54, 40037 Sasso Marconi (Bologna) **Tel** (051)
847028 **Meals** breakfast, lunch, dinner **Prices** L150,000 with breakfast;
meals L50,000 **Rooms** 5, all with bath or shower, central heating, phone
Credit cards AE, DC, MC, V **Closed** Jan and Feb

Town inn, Soragna

Locanda del Lupo

Rather large for our purposes, but an exceptionally comfortable place to stay in an area where we cannot offer many alternatives. The 18thC coaching inn, in a small town near Cremona, is quite a grand building, with spacious rooms harmoniously furnished with antiques.

■ Via Garibaldi 64, 43019 Soragna (Parma) **Tel** (0524) 690444
Fax (0524) 69350 **Meals** breakfast, lunch, dinner **Prices** rooms
L110,000-L180,000; suite L250,000; DB&B L135,000-L155,000
Rooms 46, all with bath or shower, central heating, air-conditioning,
phone, TV, radio **Credit cards** AE, DC, V **Closed** late Jul to late Aug

Tuscany

Area introduction

Hotels in Tuscany

No other region of Italy is as rich in good small hotels as Tuscany. The greatest concentrations of hotels are naturally around the tourist highlights of Florence, Siena and San Gimignano. But on recent visits we have been struck by the momentum that tourism is gaining in the countryside between Florence and Siena – the Chianti wine region. There have been fine hotels in this area for many years; but alongside the old favourites there are some new discoveries to which, with the new format of the guide, we are now able to give fuller descriptions on the following pages.

Finding notably welcoming places to stay along the Tuscan coast is not so easy – although many of the better hotels in resorts such as Forte dei Marmi and Marina di Pietrasanta have attractive shady gardens, few have any other distinguishing features. At Livorno is the Villa Godilonda (Tel (0586) 752032, fax 753286), a spotless, modest seaside hotel near two sandy beaches.

Further south and just off the coast (but within easy reach of the long sandy beach at Marina de Castagneto) is an old stone villa, La Torre at Castagneto Carducci (Tel (0565) 775268), which, as its name suggests, stands next to a ruined tower. It has been converted into a simple hotel with 11 rooms, offering B&B and basic evening meals.

The Tuscan island of Elba is big enough to absorb the many summer visitors it attracts without being swamped in the way that some of the smaller and more southerly islands have been. We have one clear recommendation on the island (page 140), but in general its small hotels are, to be honest, less attractive than many of the bigger ones which cannot properly be given entries here. There is a handful of charming and comfortable (but not cheap) hotels with 60 to 100 rooms within a few miles of the port of arrival, Portoferraio. High in the hills to the south, with wonderful views from its terraces and pool, is the Picchiaie (Tel (0565) 933072, fax 933186). Across the bay from Portoferraio, in leafy grounds close to the sea, is the polished Villa Ottone (Tel (0565) 933042, fax 933257). Nearby at Magazzini is the smart and expensive Fabricia (Tel (0565) 933181, fax 933185) with its own beach facilities. On the south side of the island is the Bahia at Cavoli (Tel (0565) 987055, 60 rooms in houses, gardens of olives and cacti).

We have entries for two hotels on the island of Giglio (page 144). Also worth considering is the Arenella – a quiet and comfortable hotel, with great views of the coast (Tel and fax (0564) 809340).

This page acts as an introduction to the features and hotels of Tuscany, and gives brief recommendations of reasonable hotels that for one reason or another have not made a full entry. The long entries for this region – covering the hotels we are most enthusiastic about – start on the next page. But do not neglect the shorter entries starting on page 139: these are all hotels that we would happily stay at.

Tuscany

Country hotel, Artimino

Paggeria Medicea

Artimino is a village of some distinction, drawing visitors to see its museum and nearby Etruscan tombs. It also has a number of imposing buildings, one being a grand villa built by Ferdinand I of Medici, who was struck by the beauty of the surroundings in the 16thC. Now the outbuildings and servants' quarters of this villa have been converted into an elegant and peaceful hotel.

As befits its aristocratic pedigree, the atmosphere is classy, but unshowy. Furnishings are a stylish, unpretentious mix of new and old, and original features such as sloping rafters, chimneys and ceilings have, where possible, been retained both in bedrooms and in public areas.

A short walk across manicured lawns brings you to the restaurant Biagio Pignatta (named after a celebrated Medici chef). Its specialities are Tuscan dishes 'with a Renaissance flavour' (*pappardelle sul coniglio*, for instance – broad noodles with rabbit sauce) on a terrace overlooking hillsides of vines and olives. The estate produces its own wine, which is decanted at your table with religious reverence.

Nearby Etruscan museum; medieval village; Prato (15 km), Florence (18 km).

Viale Papa Giovanni XXIII, Artimino 50040 Firenze
Tel (055) 871 8081
Fax (055) 871 8080
Location 18 km NW of Florence, close to village, with ample car parking
Food & drink breakfast, lunch, dinner
Prices rooms L145,000-L240,000; DB&B L145,000-L205,000
Rooms 34 double, some with bath, most with shower; 3 single with shower; 14 apartments; all have central heating, air-conditioning, minibar, TV, phone, radio
Facilities dining-room, reading-room, TV room; 2 tennis-courts, jogging, swimming-pool
Credit cards AE, DC, MC, V
Children accepted
Disabled no special facilities
Pets accepted, but not in dining-room **Closed** never
Manager Alessandro Gualtieri

Tuscany

Country villa, Candeli

Grand Hotel Villa la Massa

Standing on the banks of the Arno, surrounded by parkland and gentle hills, Villa la Massa (dating from the 17thC) used to be the country residence of one of the most powerful Florentine families. It is now one of the city's most elegant (and expensive) hotels. And with its country setting, expansive lawns, gardens overflowing with flowers, seductive little pool and tennis-courts, it makes a sharp contrast to the city-centre hotels that serious sightseers head for. (Not that staying here rules out sightseeing: there is a free shuttle bus into Florence.)

The main house sets the tone – a rather severe, four-square building with a grand, lofty central lobby and pillared galleries leading to the bedrooms. These are individually furnished and the height of luxury, combining antique-style furniture with modern high-quality fabrics; lots of pampering extras.

The riverside restaurant (Il Verrocchio) is in a rather less grand but still very impressive building; weather permitting, you can dine outside at elegantly laid tables on a terrace lit by romantic lanterns hanging from the trees. With almost as many waiters as diners, service is immaculate.

Nearby Florence (7 km).

Via La Massa 6, Candeli, Florence 50010
Tel (055) 630051
Fax (055) 632579
Location 7 km E of Florence, on Arno in extensive grounds with ample car parking
Food & drink breakfast, lunch, dinner
Prices rooms L262,000-L474,000 (suites L610,000); DB&B L290,000-L342,000 (suites L730,000)
Rooms 32 double, 3 single, 5 suites, all with bath; all have central heating, phone, air-conditioning, TV, minibar
Facilities dining-room, bar, piano bar, sitting-room; tennis, swimming-pool
Credit cards AE, DC, MC, V
Children accepted
Disabled no special facilities
Pets not accepted in dining-room
Closed never
Manager Arturo Secchi

Tuscany

Salivolpi

For no immediately obvious reason, the unremarkable Chianti village of Castellina contains a cluster of Tuscany's most appealing hotels. This welcome addition to the catalogue, open since 1983, offers a much cheaper alternative to its two illustrious neighbours – Tenuta de Ricavo (page 101) and Villa Casalecchi (page 102). It occupies two well-restored farm buildings and one new bungalow in a peaceful open position on the edge of the village – supposedly the location of the ancient Etruscan Castellina – affording broad views across the countryside.

There is a Spanish feel to the older of the houses – iron fittings, exposed beams, white walls, ochre tiles – and the spacious rooms are both neat and stylish, with some splendid old beds and other antiques. The whole place is well cared-for, and has a calm, relaxed atmosphere.

The garden is well tended, with plenty of space, some furniture and a fair-sized swimming-pool. Breakfast ('*molto abbondante*', claims the boss) is served in a crisp little room in the smaller of the houses.

Nearby Siena (18 km); Florence, San Gimignano and other attractions within reach.

Via Fiorentina, Castellina in Chianti 53011 Siena
Tel (0577) 740484
Fax 740998
Location 500 m from middle of village, on the road to San Donato; with gardens and ample open-air car parking
Food & drink breakfast
Prices rooms L95,000 with breakfast
Rooms 19 double with bath; all rooms have central heating, phone

Facilities hall, breakfast room, bar; swimming-pool
Credit cards MC, V
Children accepted
Disabled some rooms with special facilities
Pets not accepted
Closed never
Manager Angela Orlandi

Tuscany

Country hotel, Castellina in Chianti

Tenuta di Ricavo

If away from it all is where you want to get – while retaining the possibility of doing some serious sightseeing – Ricavo is hard to beat. The hotel occupies an entire hamlet, deserted in the 1950s when people left the land for the cities in search of work.

The grouping of houses along a wooded ridge in the depth of the countryside might have been conceived as a film-set replica of a medieval hamlet. The main house, facing a little square of other mellow stone cottages, houses some of the bedrooms, the no-smoking dining-room – smart and restrained, with plain white walls, brick arches and tiled floor – and the several sitting-rooms, which are comfortably furnished with a pleasant jumble of antique chairs and sofas (one of them with a small library of English, Italian, French and German books).

Breakfast can be had in several spots outdoors – perhaps in the shade of linden trees. At the right time of the year the gardens are bright with flowers – one of the highlights is a grand old wisteria – and there are plenty of secluded corners, with the result that the place seems calm and quiet even when the hotel is full. The small garden pool is ideal for quiet cooling off, the larger one out of the way so that lively children are no problem.

A visitor pronounces the hotel 'expensive, but professional and worth it', and the food 'very satisfactory'.

Nearby Siena (22 km); San Gimignano, Florence within reach.

Localita Ricavo, Castellina in Chianti 53011 Siena
Tel (0577) 740221 **Fax** 741014
Location isolated in countryside, about 3 km N of Castellina; in gardens, with ample car parking
Food & drink breakfast, lunch, dinner
Prices rooms L210,000-L310,000; DB&B L150,000-L210,000
Rooms 13 double, 2 single, 10 family rooms; all with bath; all have central heating, phone
Facilities 3 sitting-rooms, bar, dining-room; 2 swimming-pools, table tennis, 2 *boccia* courts **Credit cards** not accepted **Children** welcome
Disabled some ground-floor rooms **Pets** not accepted
Closed Nov to Easter; restaurant only, Tue lunch and Mon
Proprietors Dr Scotoni and Alessandro Lobrano

Tuscany

Country villa, Castellina in Chianti

Villa Casalecchi

It is not difficult to find fault with this unassuming villa immersed in woods and vineyards in the heart of Chianti. It does not set particularly high standards of decoration, house-keeping or cuisine, and not all of those involved in its running are notably welcoming. But Casalecchi is one of those places it is always comfortable to be going back to; perhaps the fact that it does not feel the need to try too hard is part of its charm.

The house sits high on a steepish slope. There is no clearly defined front and back, but you approach from above, and below is the fair-sized pool. Bedrooms fall into two categories: the old ones in the main house, which are lofty, fairly spacious and full of lovely antique furniture; and the ones added on to the downhill side of the house overlooking the pool, which are rather cramped but which have the undeniable attraction of a terrace immediately outside where you can take breakfast with nothing but trees and vines in view – a great advance on the dreary breakfast room. The sitting-areas – one a sort of lobby and the other a more rustic affair looking out over the vineyards – are no more than adequately comfortable. The dining-room, in welcome contrast, boasts splendid old wood-panelled walls.

Nearby Florence, Siena, San Gimignano, Volterra and Perugia.

Castellina in Chianti 53011
Siena
Tel (0577) 740240 **Fax** 741111
Location one km S of
Castellina, in countryside,
with adequate car parking
Food & drink breakfast,
lunch, dinner
Prices rooms L249,000-
L286,000 with breakfast;
DB&B L212,000-L243,000;
20% reduction for children
under 6
Rooms 19 double, 16 with

bath, 3 with shower; all rooms
have central heating, phone
Facilities dining-room,
breakfast room; bar, 2
sitting-rooms; open-air
swimming-pool
Credit cards AE, DC, MC, V
Children accepted
Disabled access difficult
Pets accepted, but not in
public rooms
Closed Oct to Mar
Proprietor Elvira Lecchini-
Giovannoni

Tuscany

Country guest-house, Fiesole

Bencista

'Don't send us too many tourists,' the smooth Simone Simoni begged our inspector – and he genuinely meant it. It is easy to see why the Bencista is so popular. The *pensione* stands on a hillside overlooking Florence and the Tuscan hills; views from the terrace and many of the bedrooms are unforgettable. Added to this are the charms of the building, once a monastery: a handsome hallway, three salons almost entirely furnished with antiques (including a little reading-room with shelves of books and a cosy fire), plus plenty of fascinating nooks and crannies.

No two bedrooms are alike, and each one has some captivating feature – perhaps a beautiful view, a fine piece of furniture, a huge bathroom or, in some, a private terrace. They are nearly all old-fashioned, with plain whitewashed walls and solid antiques, and the accent is more on character than luxury. The dining-room is simple, light and spacious, overlooking gardens where olives, roses and magnolia flourish. Breakfast is taken *al fresco* on the terrace – a glorious spot to start (and end) the day. Meals offer no choice (except soup as an alternative to pasta) but are well cooked, and the house wine is excellent.

Nearby Roman theatre, cathedral and monastery, all at Fiesole.

Via B da Maiano 4, Fiesole 50014
Tel (055) 59163
Location 2.5 km S of Fiesole on Florence road, set in private park overlooking city; garage and ample open-air car parking
Food & drink breakfast, lunch, dinner
Prices DB&B L85,000-L105,000; FB L100,000-L120,000
Rooms 29 double, 28 with bath, 13 with shower; 13 single, 7 with bath; all rooms have central heating
Facilities 3 sitting-rooms, dining-room **Credit cards** not accepted **Children** accepted
Disabled no special facilities
Pets no dogs in restaurant
Closed never
Proprietor Simone Simoni

Tuscany

Country villa, Fiesole

Villa San Michele

According to its brochure the Villa San Michele was designed by Michelangelo – which perhaps accounts in part for the high prices. Rooms are among the most expensive in Italy – only a fraction less than at the hotel's more swanky sister, the Cipriani in Venice – and beyond the reach of most readers; but the guide would be incomplete without this little gem on the peaceful hillside of Fiesole – originally a monastery, built in the early part of the 15th century and enlarged towards the end of it.

What you get for your money is not extravagant decoration or ostentatious luxury but restrained good taste and an expertly preserved aura of the past. The furniture is mostly solid antiques including 17thC masterpieces (religiously maintained every winter, we are told); many of the bedrooms have tiled floors which are themselves of notable antiquity. The bathrooms, on the other hand, are impressively contemporary. The views from the villa are exceptional. One of the great delights of the place is to lunch or dine *al fresco* in the loggia, gazing down slopes of olives and cypresses to the city below. The pool terraces share this glorious view. Breakfast is an American buffet feast; the DB&B prices we quote include an *à la carte* meal, lunch.

Nearby Roman theatre, cathedral and monastery of San Francesco at Fiesole.

Via Doccia 4, Fiesole 50014
Tel (055) 59451 **Fax** 598734
Location on Florence- Fiesole road, in private grounds with car parking available
Food & drink breakfast, lunch, dinner
Prices DB&B L475,000- L820,000; suites L1.3M-L1.8M
Rooms 24 double, 2 single, and 2 suites; all with bath and shower; all rooms have central heating, air- conditioning, music, phone; TV and
minibar on request
Facilities reading- room/bar, piano bar, dining-room with loggia/terrace; heated swimming-pool (open Jun to Sep)
Credit cards AE, DC, MC, V
Children accepted
Disabled access difficult
Pets small dogs accepted, but not in dining-room or in pool area
Closed mid-Nov to mid-Mar
Manager Maurizio Saccani

Tuscany

Town hotel, Florence

Hermitage

The location, just north of the Ponte Vecchio with views to match, is highly central, and highly favoured: few hotels this close to Florence's main drag could be described as peaceful, but this Lilliputian-scale retreat is not inappropriately named. There is an air of tranquillity about it – helped by a judicious amount of double-glazing on the busier riverside aspect.

Everything about the Hermitage is small, like a doll's house – only upside down, with the old-fashioned bedrooms on the lower floors while the reception desk and public rooms are on the fifth floor, overlooking the Arno. It's worth the climb: both bar-lounge and breakfast room are delightfully domestic, in cool lemony yellows made intimate and welcoming with flowers and pictures.

The Hermitage was once no more than one of the typical, older-style pensions that are becoming as rare as hen's teeth in Florence. But it has had a marked face-lift in the past two or three years and is now more tasteful and well-kept than average. A flower-filled roof terrace offers views across the pantiles of old Florence to the Duomo – an appealing place for breakfast.
Nearby Uffizi gallery, Ponte Vecchio.

Vicolo Marzio 1, Piazza del
Pesce, Florence 50122
Tel (055) 287216
Fax (055) 212208
Location in heart of city,
facing the river; car parking
difficult
Food & drink breakfast, snacks
Prices rooms L110,000-
L200,000 with breakfast
Rooms 20 double, 15 with
bath, 3 with shower; 2 single
with shower; all rooms have
central heating, phone,
air-conditioning
Facilities breakfast room,
sitting-room with bar, roof
terrace
Credit cards V
Children welcome
Disabled access difficult
Pets small dogs only
Closed never
Proprietor Vincenzo Scarcelli

Tuscany

Town hotel, north of the *Duomo*

Loggiato dei Serviti

One of Florence's newest charming hotels is in one of its loveliest Renaissance buildings, designed (around 1527) by Sangallo the Elder to match Brunelleschi's famous Hospital of the Innocenti, opposite. Until a few years ago the building housed a modest *pensione* and the beautiful square was a giant car park. But the Loggiato is now elegantly restored and, thanks to the city council's change of heart, exceptionally tranquil.

The decoration is a skilful blend of old and new, all designed to complement the original vaulting and other features with a minimum of frill and fuss. Floors are terracotta tiled, walls rag painted in pastel colours. Furniture and paintings are mostly, but not exclusively, old. There is a small, bright breakfast room in which to start the day (with fruit juice, cheese and ham, brioches, fruit and coffee) and a little bar where you can recover from it, browsing glossy magazines and sipping a Campari.

Visitors have praised the cleanliness of the rooms and the helpful staff; another satisfied customer comments on the 'truly beautiful' bedroom, with 'every article carefully chosen and thought out'.

Nearby church of Santissima Annunziata, Foundlings' Hospital

Piazza SS Annunziata 3,
Florence 50122
Tel (055) 289592 **Fax** 289595
Location a few minutes' walk
N of the *Duomo*, on W side of
Piazza SS Annunziata; garage
service on request
Food & drink breakfast
Prices rooms L140,000-
L210,000; suites
L280,000-L500,000
Rooms 19 double, 6 single, all
with bath or shower; 4 suites,
all with bath or shower; all
rooms have air-conditioning,
TV, phone, minibar, hairdrier,
piped music
Facilities breakfast room, bar
Credit cards AE, DC, MC, V
Children welcome
Disabled not suitable
Pets accepted
Closed never
Proprietor Rodolfo Budini-
Gattai

Tuscany

Town villa, east of the *Duomo*

Monna Lisa

Despite other challengers, the Monna Lisa remains Florence's most charming small hotel – an unusual combination of comfort without pretension. Five minutes' walk from the *Duomo*, the Monna Lisa is an elegant Renaissance *palazzo* around a small courtyard set back from the unprepossessing street façade.The main rooms, on the ground floor, have polished brick floors with Oriental carpets and beamed or vaulted ceilings, plus a very individual collection of antique furniture, paintings and sculpture. In the cosy little salon is the first model for Giambologna's famous Rape of the Sabines, and there is also a collection of drawings and statues by Giovanni Dupre, the neo-classical sculptor, from whom the owner's family is descended. The best bedrooms are huge and high-ceilinged, with old furniture; some overlook the lovely garden, a rare bonus in Florence. But a recent guest thought his bedroom small and the bathroom very cramped, and was critical of housekeeping standards; not surprisingly, this visitor judged the prices too high.

Nearby *Duomo* (about five minutes' walk), Santa Croce, Bargello, Uffizi all within easy walking distance.

Borgo Pinti 27, Florence 50121
Tel (055) 247 9751 **Fax** 9755
Location about 5 minutes'
walk E of the *Duomo*; with
garden and private car parking
Food & drink breakfast
Prices rooms L190,000-
L280,000 with breakfast
Rooms 15 double, 5 single; all
with bath or shower; all rooms
have central heating,
air-conditioning, phone,
minibar, colour TV
Facilities sitting-rooms, bar

Credit cards AE, DC, V
Children accepted
Disabled no special facilities
Pets accepted
Closed never
Manager Riccardo Sardei

Tuscany

City hotel, Florence

Morandi alla Crocetta

This lovely old house, formerly a convent, is the family home of Mrs Kathleen Doyle, an Englishwoman who has lived here since the 1920s. Now widowed, Mrs Doyle and her son share their house with visitors, and have made a great success of it.

The house is decorated throughout with taste and care, and is obviously a home, not just a hotel. Antique Tuscan furnishings, patterned rugs, interesting pictures and fresh flowers abound. You may spot corbels carved with coats of arms in the reception hall, ancient painted tiles or fragments of fresco in the bedrooms, or a portrait of Mrs Doyle as a Renaissance-style beauty at the age of 18.

Current constructional upheavals will soon result in a new breakfast area and bar, but the house's multitude of quaint features and contents of personal interest will remain intact.

The house is convenient for exploring the historic centre of the city, close by the Academy of Fine Arts and the Archaeological Museum. The Doyles take a personal interest in their guests – 'we know them by name, not by room number' – and readers find the atmosphere friendly.

Nearby Cathedral, archaeological museum, Academy of Fine Art.

Via Laura 50, Florence 50121
Tel (055) 234 4747
Fax (055) 248 0954
Location in quiet street, NW of Piazza del Duomo; car parking on street problematic
Food & drink breakfast
Prices rooms L87,000-L137,000 (familiy rooms more); breakfast L16,000
Rooms 4 double, 2 single, 3 family rooms, all with shower; all have central heating, air-conditioning, phone, TV, hairdrier, radio, minibar
Facilities breakfast room, sitting-room
Credit cards AE, DC, MC, V
Children welcome
Disabled no special facilities
Pets small well-behaved dogs accepted
Closed never
Proprietor Kathleen Doyle

Tuscany

Town hotel, Florence

Hotel J and J

A converted monastery provides the setting for this cool, chic hotel some distance east of the Duomo, on the way to the Sant'Ambroggio market and Florence's curiously remote main tourist office. The street is comparatively quiet, and inside the hotel feels a haven from heat and dust, so effective is its air-conditioning and tranquil ambience.

Many original features of the building are still intact – columns, vaulted ceilings, frescos and wooden beams – and furnishings, though stylishly modern in places, are sympathetic to the spirit of the antique setting, and certainly not lacking personality. A small, pretty patio garden at the rear of the hotel, with elegant white parasols and plants in tubs, tempts breakfast-eaters to venture out through the plate-glass doors, though the interior option is equally charming in shades of yellow and green with wicker seating.

Bedrooms vary – all are of high standard and some exceptionally spacious, with split-level floors and seating areas, and high ceilings with exposed beams.

We found the reception knowledgeable and efficient.
Nearby Duomo, church of Santa Croce.

Via di Mezzo 20, 50121
Florence
Tel (055) 240951
Fax (055) 240282
Location east of the duomo,
north of Santa Croce
Food & drink breakfast
Prices rooms L160,000-
L400,000
Rooms 18 double, 2 family
rooms, all with bath; all rooms
have central heating,
air-conditioning, phone,
hairdrier, TV, minibar

Facilities sitting-room, bar
Credit cards AE, DC, MC, V
Children welcome
Disabled no special facilities
Pets not accepted
Closed never
Proprietor James Cavagnari

Tuscany

Hilltop villa, Florence

Torre di Bellosguardo

Giovanni Franchetti and his French wife Michele began renovating his beautiful 16thC family home, on the hilly outskirts south of the Arno, in 1980. Their aim to create 'a peaceful oasis where travellers can feel as comfortable as in their own homes' has certainly succeeded, though few visitors can be lucky enough to live in such delightful surroundings (Bellosguardo – 'beautiful view' – is an apt name.

There are sixteen luxurious guest rooms in the house which, although grand, is not at all gaunt or dreary. Each room is a separate world, as much a sitting-room as a bedroom, carefully and individually furnished with fascinating antiques; some are split-level, others have splendid inlaid panelling. The gardens of well kept lawns and lily ponds, ancient cypress trees and shady terraces (not forgetting a secluded swimming-pool), exert as much pulling power as the interior. The unassuming geniality of the owners is a refreshing contrast to many a haughty hireling in Florence's central hotels.

Energetic guests could easily walk into the city – though the gradients on the return journey may suggest a taxi-ride.

Nearby Ponte Vecchio, Pitti Palace, Passeggiata ai Colli.

Via Roti Michelozzi 2, Florence 50124
Tel (055) 229 8145
Fax (055) 229008
Location on hill overlooking city, just S of Porta Romana; with garden and car parking
Food & drink breakfast, lunch (by swimming-pool)
Prices rooms L230,000-L300,000; suites L400,000-L530,000
Rooms 8 double, 2 single, 6 suites, all with bath; all rooms have central heating, phone; 5 rooms have air-conditioning
Facilities dining-room, sitting-rooms, bar; swimming-pool
Credit cards AE, DC, MC, V
Children accepted
Disabled lift/elevator
Pets accepted
Closed never
Proprietor Giovanni Franchetti

Tuscany

Town guest-house, in shopping district

Tornabuoni Beacci

Via Tornabuoni is one of the most desirable streets of Florence, and the Tornabuoni Beacci is one of the most desirable hotels in the area. The hotel used to be a *deluxe pensione* and it still has the feel of a family home rather than a hotel – largely due to the warm personality of Signora Beacci, who has run the place since 1954. In fact there has been a Beacci here since 1900, when her mother first established the hotel at a nearby location. The present hotel occupies the upper floors of a fine old *palazzo*.

The rather gloomy ground-floor entrance gives no hint of the charming interior of the hotel, where prints and paintings, patterned carpets on wood block floors and classical antiques all create an elegant, yet welcoming atmosphere. The sitting-room is exceptionally comfortable and well furnished. The bedrooms are comfortable and classically furnished. And there is a delightful roof-top terrace, cluttered with potted plants, flowers and creepers, with several tables for breakfast or evening drinks.

The volumes of visitors' books, which date back to the 1920s, are full of glowing praise from famous travellers who have been captivated by this little 'home from home' hotel. Sga Beacci has not updated the information below; prices are estimates.

Nearby Palazzo Strozzi, Palazzo Rucellai, church of Santa Trinità.

Via Tornabuoni 3, Florence 50123
Tel (055) 268377
Location at N end of busy central street, with car parking in paying garage
Food & drink breakfast, lunch, dinner
Prices DB&B L130,000-L275,000
Rooms 20 double, 18 with bath or shower; 10 single, 7 with bath or shower; all have central heating, minibar, air-conditioning, phone; colour TV in some rooms
Facilities sitting-room, bar, restaurant, roof terrace
Credit cards AE, DC, V
Children accepted
Disabled lift/elevator
Pets accepted
Closed never
Proprietor Sga Beacci

Tuscany

Country villa, Florence

Villa Belvedere

This family-run hotel lies in a pleasant hilly residential district on the southern outskirts of the city, commanding excellent views through classically Tuscan cypress trees when Florentine smog permits. The building itself is no great beauty, being practical and modern, but its well kept gardens and small swimming-pool are a great boon in hot weather, and its peaceful surroundings, away from any passing traffic, a relief from the city centre at any time of the year.

The Ceschi-Perrotto family manage their business with welcoming enthusiasm, and have embarked on an ambitious programme of refurbishment. Bedrooms and bathrooms are steadily being upgraded in a smart matching scheme of spriggy motifs, racing greens and high-quality solid wood furnishings. Bathrooms gleam, with white tiles offset by restrained geometric friezes. Public areas are light, spacious and comfortable – and the breakfast room makes the best of the garden.

A limited evening snack menu is available – useful after a tiring day's sightseeing, since there are few restaurants within easy walking distance.

Nearby Pitti Palace, Boboli gardens.

Via Benedetto Castelli 3, Florence 50124
Tel (055) 222501
Fax (055) 223163
Location 3 km S of city, in gardens with some private car parking
Food & drink breakfast, snacks
Prices rooms L180,000-L280,000 with breakfast
Rooms 24 double, 22 with bath, 2 with shower; 3 single, 2 with bath, one with shower; all rooms have central heating, air-conditioning, phone, colour TV, safe
Facilities breakfast room, 2 sitting-rooms, bar, TV room, veranda; swimming- pool, tennis
Credit cards AE, DC, MC, V
Children welcome
Disabled no special facilities
Pets not accepted
Closed Dec to Feb
Proprietors Ceschi-Perotto family

Tuscany

Converted castle, Gaiole in Chianti

Castello di Spaltenna

Gaiole is a quiet little town deep in the Chianti countryside, and the Castello sits romantically at the top of a hill above it, a group of ancient rustic buildings in grassy surroundings, with splendid views of the wooded hills around.

A tiny doorway beside the church leads into the central grassy courtyard (complete with well) of the 'castle' – originally a monastery, in fact. Beyond that, another doorway takes you first into the sitting-rooms and then into the high-ceilinged dining-room – impressively medieval, with huge beams, and gallery leading to the bedrooms. Candles and a log fire at one end contribute further to the atmosphere.

The bedrooms are spacious, with exposed beams, tiled floors and simple antique furniture. The British proprietor, Seamus de Pentheny O'Kelly, took over in 1988. He has refurbished the whole place (it is now centrally heated, springtime visitors will be pleased to note); he has also introduced ambitious food, combining 'creative international cooking' with more traditional Tuscan-based cuisine. Recent visitors judged the prices not justified by the standards of service; more reports, please.

Nearby Siena (28 km), Arezzo (56 km), Florence (69 km).

Gaiole in Chianti 53013 Siena
Tel (0577) 749483
Fax 749269
Location on hilltop close to middle of Gaiole, 28 km NE of Siena
Food & drink breakfast, lunch, dinner
Prices rooms L170,000-L275,000 with breakfast; meals L55,000-L70,000
Rooms 17 double with bath and shower; all rooms have phone, central heating, TV, minibar; some have air-conditioning
Facilities dining-room, 2 sitting-rooms, wine bar, terrace bar; swimming-pool
Credit cards AE, DC, MC, V
Children welcome
Disabled no special facilities
Pets accepted, with small charge
Closed mid-Jan to Feb; main restaurant, Wed dinner
Proprietor Seamus de Pentheny O'Kelly

Tuscany

Country villa, Lucca

Villa la Principessa

La Principessa was built on the ruins of the 14thC country house of a famous Lucchese soldier of fortune. Although some traces of the Gothic mansion were found when it was restored in 1970, most of the villa dates from the 18th and early 19thC when Lucca came under Bourbon rule, and La Principessa was occupied by the last Dukes of Bourbon-Parma.

The villa still has a somewhat French feel in the furnishings and the formal park. The bedrooms have bold colour schemes and modern comforts; the public rooms have a rather more traditional character – notably the grand central sitting-room, with its painted beams, and rugs on a marble floor. The restaurant is elegant but relatively informal, the food excellent.

The hotel has recently been expanded by the restoration of the Principessa Elisa, an adjacent 18thC building, not quite so grand, in which 10 luxury suites have been created.

The pool area, behind the house, is a pleasant place to relax, and on our visits we have always found the staff helpful. La Principessa makes a comfortable (though not cheap) base for those travelling via Pisa airport.
Nearby Pisa (18 km).

SS del Brennero 1600, Massa Pisana, Lucca 55050
Tel (0583) 370037 **Fax** 379019
Location 4 km S of Lucca on SS12r towards Pisa
Food & drink breakfast, lunch, dinner
Prices rooms L200,000-L310,000; suites L370,000; meals from L45,000
Rooms 32 double, 5 single, 15 suites; all with bath or shower; all rooms have phone, air-conditioning, TV

Facilities sitting-room, bar, TV room, breakfast room, dining-room, banquet and congress room; outdoor swimming-pool
Credit cards AE, DC, MC, V
Children accepted
Disabled special facilities in annexe
Pets small dogs accepted, but not allowed in restaurant
Closed early Jan to mid- Feb; Villa restaurant, Wed; Elisa restaurant, Sun
Proprietor Sg G Mugnani

Tuscany

Country estate, Mercatale Val di Pesa

Salvadonica

This delightful assembly of rustic buildings amid olive groves and vineyards will gladden the heart of any lover of Tuscan scenery. With judicious assistance from an EC grant, two entrepreneurial young sisters have energetically converted a family home, on what was until recently a feudal estate, into a thriving bed-and-breakfast and 'agriturismo' business.

Now the two main buildings of the farm – one rich red stucco, the other mellow stone and brick – offer five well-equipped, comfortable guest rooms and ten apartments to let. They have clay-tiled floors and wood-beamed ceilings, and range from the merely harmonious and comfortable to the positively splendid – a brick-vaulted cowshed.

From the paved terraces surrounding the buildings, you look over an olive grove to the neat swimming-pool area. Tennis-courts and riding stables add alternative attractions.

Breakfast is served in a pleasant stone-walled dining room or on a sunny terrace overlooking unspoilt sweeps of countryside, where the local 'Gallo Nero' Chianti wine and excellent olive oil are still produced.

Nearby Florence (20 km).

Via Grevigiana 82, 50024 Mercatale Val di Pesa (Firenze)
Tel (055) 821 8039
Fax (055) 821 8043
Location 18km S of Florence, E of road to Siena
Food & drink breakfast, lunch
Prices rooms L110,00-L122,000 with breakfast
Rooms 5 double, 10 apartments, all with bath or shower; all rooms have central heating, phone, TV on request; apartments have fridge
Facilities swimming-pool, tennis-courts, football
Credit cards AE, MC, V
Children accepted
Disabled no special facilities
Pets not accepted
Closed Dec to Feb, except Christmas/New Year
Proprietors Baccetti family

Tuscany

Converted castle, Monte San Savino

Castello di Gargonza

Gargonza is not so much a castle as a whole village, perfectly preserved in a typically Tuscan landscape, surrounded by cypresses. The various houses, each with its own character and name (the farmer's house, the guard's house, Lucia's house) are let individually, some on a long-term basis, but usually by the week.

Mostly dating from the 13th century, they have been restored and comfortably furnished; but a visitor, initially impressed by the value of a four-person apartment, points out that they are run on a self-catering basis and linen is not changed and beds are not made.

All have kitchens but there is also a restaurant just outside the walls (highly rated – specialities include spinach and ricotta roulade, and wild boar); you can take breakfast in the old oil-pressing house ('il fantoio'). The English-speaking Count is an efficient administrator and charming host.

In the main guest-house ('la forestiera') you can stay for a few nights on B&B terms. Visitors find that a stay here lives up to expectations, but note that some of the furniture is 'tacky'.
Nearby Arezzo (25 km); Chianti; Val di Chiana.

Gargonza, Monte San Savino
52048 Arezzo
Tel (0575) 847021 **Fax** 847054
Location 35 km E of Siena on
SS73, 7 km W of Monte San
Savino; walled village of 18
houses with garden; ample car
parking outside village walls
Food & drink breakfast,
lunch, dinner
Prices rooms L121,000-
L176,000 with breakfast, in
main guest-house; meals
L28,000-L35,000

Rooms 7 double in main
guest-house; 30 double in 18
self-catering houses; all rooms
have phone, central heating;
main guest-house rooms have
minibar **Facilities** 4 sitting-
rooms (2 available for
meetings), TV room; ping-
pong, bowls **Credit cards** AE,
DC, MC, V **Children** accepted
Disabled not suitable **Pets**
small dogs only accepted
Closed Jan **Proprietor** Conte
Roberto Guicciardini

Tuscany

Country estate, Montefiridolfi

Fattoria la Loggia

Montefiridolfi is set in classic Chianti countryside scattered with ancient estates producing wine and olive oil. Many of the mellow, stone farm buildings hereabouts are being turned into tourist accommodation of one sort and another, and Fattoria la Loggia is one of the most successful of its type: a range of spacious and attractive apartments agreeably housed in a hamlet-like collection of rural dwellings, in a hilltop setting with views over gloriously peaceful surroundings. The apartments are let for a minimum of three days in low season, a week in high season. But this is not simply a self-catering complex – breakfast is served, and dinner is available to order in the fine cellar restaurant.

Each unit is carefully furnished with country-style pieces and many personal touches; kitchens and bathrooms, however, are efficiently modern, and are finished to a very high standard.

Visitors can swim, ride, or walk on the estate, which produces its own wine and olive oil. The genial owner, Sr Baruffaldi, is planning to open a museum of modern art, the core of which will be his own impressive collection.

Nearby Florence (15 km), San Gimignano (40 km), Siena (45 km), Volterra (55 km).

Via Collina 40, 50020
Montefiridolfi, Firenze
Tel (055) 824 4288
Fax (055) 824 4283
Location 15km S of Florence,
E of road to Sienna
Food & drink breakfast
(dinner occasionally)
Prices apartments L150,000-
L750,000; min stay 3 days low
season, 7 days high season
Rooms 11 apartments,
sleeping 2 to 8; all have
central heating, fridge and

radio; most have phone
Facilities restaurant;
swimming-pool, table-tennis,
volleyball, bikes, horses,
barbeque, solarium
Credit cards not accepted
Children accepted
Disabled no special facilities
Pets by prior arrangement
Closed never
Proprietor Giulio Baruffaldi

Tuscany

Restaurant-with-rooms, Montignoso

Il Bottaccio

Il Bottaccio, a couple of miles inland from the beaches of Forte dei Marmi, amid pale-coloured hill towns and grey-green olive groves, is in a league of its own: one of the most captivating – and expensive – places you will find in this book.

It is primarily a restaurant (Michelin-starred), serving 10-course meals of 'creative dishes inspired by Mediterranean tradition', which have earned high praise from the gourmet guides (and from our inspector). But it is a fantastic place to stay, too: overlooked by a ruined castle, it was originally an olive oil mill and the D'Anna family have successfully blended old and new in their conversion. Each suite is individual, vast and luxurious, combining fascinating features with great style. For example, the Appartamento delle Macine contains the original wooden workings of the mill, a 17thC fireplace, Eastern rugs and a mosaic-tiled sunken bath. Elsewhere, bathrooms combine local marble with hand-painted tiles to great effect.

The dining-room is at once plain and extraordinary: bentwood chairs stand on a tiled floor beneath a beamed ceiling; but it contains a large pool in which exotic fish waft about.

Nearby Beaches of Forte dei Marmi; Pisa (30 km).

Via Bottaccio 1, 54038
Montignoso
Tel (0585) 340031
Fax 340103
Location 5 km SE of Massa;
with gardens and car parking
Food & drink breakfast,
lunch, dinner
Prices suites L480,000-
L750,000; meals L100,000-
L120,000
Rooms 8 suites, all with bath;
all rooms have phone, TV,
radio

Facilities dining-room, terrace
Credit cards AE, DC, MC, V
Children accepted
Disabled no special facilities
Pets accepted
Closed never
Proprietors Stefano and
Elizabeth D'Anna

Tuscany

Country villa, Panzano in Chianti

Villa le Barone

Le Barone, the attractive 16thC country house of the della Robbia family (of ceramics fame), became a hotel in 1976, but still feels very much like a private home.

The small scale of the rooms helps, but there are several other factors. The antique furniture is obviously a personal collection; reception amounts to little more than a visitors' book in the hall; there are plenty of books around – including English ones – and there are always fresh flower arrangements in the elegant little sitting-rooms; and you help yourself to drinks, recording your consumption as you do so. In the past a minimum stay of three nights has further contributed to the low-key house-party atmosphere; but the rule has now been dropped.

Guests who are not out on sightseeing excursions have plenty of space to themselves in the peaceful woody garden or by the lovely pool, which gives a glorious panorama of the surrounding hills of Tuscany.

The restaurant and some of the rooms are in converted outbuildings. Our most recent report speaks of 'fabulous Tuscan food' and attentive service.

Nearby Siena (31 km), Florence (31 km).

Via San Leolino 19, 50020 Panzano in Chianti (Siena)
Tel (055) 852261 **Fax** 852277
Location 31 km S of Florence off SS222; covered car parking
Food & drink breakfast, lunch, dinner
Prices DB&B L140,000-L160,000 (min 3 nights); reductions for children
Rooms 25 double, 20 with bath, 5 with shower; one single, with shower; 10 rooms have phone, 5 have air-conditioning, and 5 have tea-makers
Facilities self-service bar, TV room, 3 sitting- rooms, dining-room, breakfast room; ping-pong, swimming-pool
Credit cards AE, MC, V
Children welcome
Disabled not suitable
Pets not accepted
Closed Nov to Mar
Proprietor Marchesa Franca Viviani della Robbia

Tuscany

Country villa, Panzano in Chianti

Villa Sangiovese

The Bleulers used to manage the long-established Tenuta di Ricavo at Castellina (see page 101), but have recently established this hotel of their own in Panzano, a few miles to the north and equidistant between Florence and Siena. They opened their doors fully in 1988 after completely renovating the building, and are already winning high praise from readers.

The main villa is a neat stone-and-stucco house fronting directly on to a quiet back-street; potted plants and a brass plate beside the doorway are the only signs of a hotel. Attached to this house is an old, rambling, stone building beside a flowery, gravelled courtyard-terrace offering splendid views.

Inside, all is mellow, welcoming and stylish, with carefully chosen antique furnishings against plain, pale walls. Bedrooms, some with wood-beamed ceilings, are spacious, comfortable, and tastefully restrained in decoration. The dining-room is equally simple and stylish, with subdued wall lighting and bentwood chairs on a tiled floor.

A limited but interesting à la carte menu is offered, which changes each night. A reporter praises the food and the wine.

Nearby Greve (5 km); Siena (30 km); Florence (30 km).

Piazza Bucciarelli 5, 50020 Panzano in Chianti, Firenze
Tel (055) 852461
Fax (055) 852463
Location on edge of town, 5 km S of Greve; with large garden and car parking
Food & drink breakfast, lunch, dinner
Prices rooms L110,000-L170,000; suites L170,000-L210,000; meals about L35,000
Rooms 15 double, one single,

3 suites, all with bath or shower; all rooms have phone
Facilities dining-room, bar, 2 sitting-rooms, library, terrace; swimming-pool
Credit cards MC, V
Children accepted
Disabled no special facilities
Pets not accepted
Closed Jan, Feb; restaurant only, Wed
Proprietors Ulderico and Anna Maria Bleuler

Tuscany

Country inn, Pieve Santo Stéfano

Locanda Sari

Locanda Sari has long been run by Carmen Pierangeli's family as a local inn and convenient port of call on the road over to Ravenna; but the traffic which once passed within feet of the front door now whizzes up a neo-motorway on the other side of the narrow valley, and Carmen has seized the opportunity to turn the Locanda into a place worth travelling to find. The house has been restored with real panache in classy country style. In the bedrooms, rustic antiques and painted reproduction wardrobes sit on glistening tiled floors, with creamy rugs and bedspreads woven to a special pattern; old iron bedheads are fixed to the walls, but the beds themselves are new (and splendidly firm); the shower rooms are compact but smart. The dining-room shows the same simple good taste, but the real attraction here is Carmen's exquisite country cooking, of the kind that tourists rarely taste; most guests agree that the daily batch of ravioli, made with local ricotta, for example, is superb, though it was not to the taste of one reporter.

One visitor found Carmen and husband Pio 'charming and hospitable' and the proximity of the motorway 'a bore but surprisingly unobjectionable'. 'Remarkably good,' says another.
Nearby Sansepolcro (16 km); La Verna (20 km).

Via Tiberina km 177, Pieve Santo Stéfano, Arezzo
Tel (0575) 799129
Location in countryside 3 km N of village, on minor road; car parking across the road
Food & drink breakfast, lunch, dinner
Prices rooms L55,000-L80,000; meals L32,000-L36,000
Rooms 8 double, one with bath, 7 with shower; all rooms have central heating

Facilities dining-room, lobby, bar; small terrace
Credit cards AE, DC
Children welcome
Disabled access difficult
Pets not accepted
Closed never
Proprietor Carmen Pierangeli

Tuscany

Converted monastery, Pistoia

Il Convento

A converted monastery in the verdant hills of Pistoia (between Lucca and Florence), white-painted with a tiled roof, sounds like quite a find – and so it is. Its great attraction is the setting, which is both peaceful and panoramic: you get grand views from the hotel and the terraces of its lush gardens below, which are carefully maintained and include an impressive swimming-pool with a generous tiled surround.

Inside, Il Convento is not all that you might expect – bed-rooms are uncompromisingly modern, with the emphasis firmly on efficient facilities and cleanliness rather than on antiquity or individual character. But the public rooms are more in sympathy with their surroundings – particularly the restaurant, where the original cells have been converted into tiny, intimate dining-rooms. The sitting-room has plenty of space and comfortable chairs and sofas.

We have always been impressed by both the staff and the food. But our most recent reporter judges the restaurant staff 'not particularly helpful' and the food 'good but expensive'. Keep us posted, please.

Nearby sights of Pistoia; Prato, Florence within reach.

Via San Quirico 33,
Pontenuovo, Pistoia 51100
Tel (0573) 452652
Fax 453758
Location 4 km E of Pistoia in Pontenuovo area, on hillside overlooking city; with car parking space
Food & drink breakfast, lunch, dinner
Prices rooms L85,000-L120,000 with breakfast
Rooms 20 double, 4 single; all with bath; all rooms have

central heating, phone, TV
Facilities dining-room, sitting-area, bar, games room; swimming-pool
Credit cards MC, V
Children accepted
Disabled access difficult
Pets not accepted
Closed restaurant only, Mon
Proprietor Paozo Petrini

Tuscany

Country villa, Pistoia

Villa Vannini

Here is a real gem, lying in an area which has surprisingly few small, charming places to stay – in a remote and delightfully quiet setting, high on a hill about 2 km above the small village of Piteccio and not far from the lively little city of Pistoia. To get there, you wind your way up a narrow, roughly surfaced road through unspoiled countryside. The congenial Signora Vannini offers a particularly warm welcome, and looks after her house with loving care. There are various little sitting areas with large vases of flowers, chintz or chunky modern seats, prints and water-colours, and the sort of antiques that complete an elegant family home. The dining-room, with its whitewashed walls, polished parquet floor and marble fireplace, makes an elegant setting for the excellent Tuscan specialities that are served here ('spectacular – the best we had anywhere on our travels,' says one report). Bedrooms are beautifully and individually furnished – many of them in flowery fabrics and with fine antiques. In front of the house a simple terrace provides a haven after a hard day's sightseeing in Pistoia, Florence, Lucca or even Bologna.

Nearby cathedral, Ospedale del Ceppo and church of Sant'Andrea at Pistoia

Villa di Piteccio, 51030 Pistoia
Tel (0573) 42031
Location 6 km N of Pistoia on hillside, in private garden, with car parking
Food & drink breakfast, lunch, dinner
Prices rooms L80,000 with breakfast; DB&B L70,000 (minimum 3 days)
Rooms 8 double with bath
Facilities 2 sitting-rooms, games room, 2 dining-rooms
Credit cards AE (5% surcharge)
Children not very suitable
Disabled no special facilities
Pets not accepted
Closed never
Proprietor Maria-Rosa Vannini

Tuscany

Seaside hotel, Porto Ercole

Il Pellicano

Porto Ercole is one of those fashionable little harbours where wealthy Romans moor their boats at weekends. Il Pellicano is a russet-coloured vine-clad villa with gardens tumbling down to the rocky shoreline, where the flat rocks have been designated the hotel's 'private beach'. It was built in the mid-1960s with only nine rooms. Today it has grown to over three times the size, and provides all the luxuries you might expect from a very expensive four-star seaside hotel. However, it manages at the same time to preserve the style of a private Tuscan villa – and the exposed beams, stone arches and antique features make it feel much older than it really is. Antique country-house furnishings are offset by whitewashed walls, brightly coloured stylish sofas and large vases of flowers. Fish and seafood are the best things in the restaurant – if you can stomach the prices. Meals in summer are served on the delightful open-air terrace in the garden, or beside the pool where the spread of *antipasti* is a feast for the eyes.

Peaceful bedrooms, many of them in two- or three-storey cottages, combine antiques and modern fabrics. The majority are cool and spacious, and all of them have a terrace or balcony.
Nearby Orbetello (16 km).

Cala dei Santi, Porto Ercole 58018 Grosseto
Tel (0564) 833801 **Fax** 833418
Location 4 km from middle of resort, in own gardens overlooking the sea; private car parking
Food & drink breakfast, lunch, dinner
Prices rooms L210,000-L580,000; DB&B L220,000-L405,000; suites L520,000-L1,100,000; extra bed in room L100,000-L130,000

Rooms 30 double, 4 suites, all with bath and shower; all rooms have central heating, air-conditioning, minibar, phone **Facilities** restaurants, bars, sitting area, terrace; swimming-pool, private beach, tennis, riding, water-skiing, clay-pigeon shooting **Credit cards** AE, DC, V **Children** accepted over 14 **Disabled** access difficult **Pets** not accepted **Closed** Nov to Mar **Managers** Sg. and Sga. Emili

Tuscany

Country villa, Prato

Villa Rucellai

Industrialized Prato makes an off-putting approach to this mellow old villa, and rather spoils the views from its green, hillside setting. But the attractions of the house and gardens, the welcoming atmosphere and the modest prices compensate.

The rambling, red-roofed villa steps down the hillside, as do the surrounding terraced gardens and olive groves. Inside, the time-worn floors of the high-ceilinged rooms gleam with polish. The furnishings are a mixture of the antique and the comfortable, with something of the style of an English country house. The sitting-room and library are comfortably furnished with chintz sofas, flower arrangements, plenty of books and magazines dotted around and pictures lining the walls.

Bedrooms are large and simply furnished, often with antiques, and many have views up or along the hillside. Breakfast is served at large dining-tables in a home-like room with Isabel Piqué's collection of colourful ceramics on display.

More than one visitor has commented on the 'relaxed and easy-going atmosphere' that the proprietors manage to preserve – aided by the household's geese, hens and dogs.

Nearby Prato; Florence (20 km).

Via di Canneto 16, 50047 Prato (Florence)
Tel (0574) 460392
Location in Bisenzio river valley, 4 km NE of Prato; with car parking and grounds
Food & drink breakfast
Prices rooms L60,000-L110,000
Rooms 12 double, one single, one family room; 10 rooms have bath; all have central heating; some have phone
Facilities dining-room, sitting-room, TV room, gymnasium, terrace; swimming-pool
Credit cards not accepted
Children welcome; cots and high chairs by arrangement
Disabled 2 suitable bedrooms
Pets not usually accepted
Closed never
Proprietors Rucellai Piqué family

Tuscany

Country bed-and-breakfast, Pugnano

Casetta delle Selve

Yet another elevated Tuscan farmhouse – but this one, first drawn to our attention by a French reader who summarized it as a 'petit paradis', has a personality all its own. The gleaming white house, the peaceful surroundings, the flower-filled garden and the red-tiled terrace with wonderful views towards the sea are all there, as you would hope – but the interior is stunningly different from the norm.

Not only is the whole house exceptionally well maintained, with varnished beams standing out against immaculate white paintwork, but also the bedrooms have bold, bright colour schemes, involving bedheads, rugs, bedspreads (some handmade by Signora Menchi) and pictures (lots of them) – all happily rubbing along with the antique furniture. Public areas are more sober, but still full of pictures and ornaments, and gleaming antiques.

Nicla Menchi is no ordinary hotelier either – 'the most unusual hostess of any on our trip, and quite understanding of our American inability to speak Italian or French' says our most recent report – and many visitors leave as her friend.

Nearby Lucca (10 km); Pisa (12 km).

Pugnano 56010 Pisa
Tel (050) 850359
Location in countryside 2 km off SS12, E of Pugnano, 10 km SW of Lucca; with ample car parking
Food & drink breakfast
Prices rooms L80,000; breakfast L10,000
Rooms 5 double, one family room, all with bath; all rooms have central heating
Facilities breakfast room, terrace

Credit cards not accepted
Children accepted
Disabled no special facilities
Pets accepted
Closed never
Proprietor Nicla Menchi

Tuscany

Country hotel, Radda in Chianti

Relais Fattoria Vignale

This is a rare example of the hotel-guide editor's dream: an exquisite new establishment, entirely undiscovered by rival publications when, in 1987, our inspector came upon it by chance. He was immediately captivated by the taste and style with which this manor-house has been converted to a hotel. Subsequent visits have not dimmed our enthusiasm.The house is built on a slope down from the middle of the village. On the main 'ground' floor are four interconnecting sitting-rooms, each on a domestic scale and beautifully furnished with comfy sofas, antiques, muted rugs on polished terracotta floors, walls either white and dotted with paintings or covered by murals – and one or two grand stone fireplaces. The bedrooms above are similarly classy, with waxed wooden doors, white walls, antique beds.

There is a neat breakfast-room in a brick vault beneath the hotel, where an excellent buffet is set out, and coffee and extras are served by friendly waitresses. The best-known local restaurant (also called Vignale) is only 300m away; the hotel will make reservations for you. The sitting-rooms, the back bedrooms and the pool all share a grand view across the Radda valley.
Nearby Siena, Florence, Arezzo all within reach.

Via Pianigiani 15, Radda in Chianti 53017 Siena
Tel (0577) 738300 **Fax** 738592
Location in middle of village, 31 km N of Siena, with private gardens and ample car parking
Food & drink breakfast, snacks
Prices rooms L150,000-L300,000 with breakfast
Rooms 17 double, 4 with bath, 15 with shower; 4 single, all with shower; 3 family rooms, all with bath; all rooms have central heating, phone, minibar
Facilities 3 sitting-rooms, breakfast room, indoor and pool bars, 2 conference rooms
Credit cards AE, V
Children accepted, but prefer quiet ones **Disabled** access difficult
Pets not accepted
Closed Nov to Mar
Manager Silvia Kummer

Tuscany

Hilltop villa, Reggello

Villa Rigacci

This creeper-covered 15thC farmhouse, opened as a hotel for just over a decade, is in a beautiful secluded spot – on a hilltop surrounded by olive groves, pines, chestnut trees and meadows – yet only a few kilometres from the Florence-Rome autostrada, and a short drive from Florence and Arezzo.

Many of the original features of the house have been preserved – arched doorways, beamed bedrooms, tiled or stone-flagged floors – and it is furnished as a cherished private house might be. The sitting-room has an open fire in chilly weather. The bedrooms – the best (though not all) of them gloriously spacious – are full of gleaming antiques, and overlook the gardens or swimming-pool, which is of fair size, with a pleasant tile-and-grass surround and woodland views. For relaxation, there are plenty of quiet, shady spots in the park, which contains some magnificent trees.

An otherwise satisfied visitor who 'enjoyed a lovely holiday here' asks us to point out that the food is predominantly 'sophisticated French' in style, with few traditional Italian dishes offered – though he has no quibble with its quality.

Nearby Florence (35 km); Arezzo (45 km).

Vággio 76, Reggello 50066
Tel (055) 865 6718 **Fax** 6537
Location 300m N of Vággio, 30 km SE of Florence; exit Incisa from A1; with car parking and gardens
Food & drink breakfast, lunch, dinner
Prices DB&B L152,000-L185,000
Rooms 13 double, 3 suites; 13 with bath, 3 with shower; 2 single with bath; all rooms have central heating, air-conditioning, phone, TV, radio, minibar
Facilities dining-room, sitting-rooms, library; swimming-pool
Credit cards AE, DC, V
Children tolerated
Disabled access easy
Pets accepted if small and well-behaved
Closed restaurant only, Nov and Jan
Proprietors Frederic and Odette Pierazzi

Tuscany

Villa di Corliano

A sweeping, tree-lined drive leading through lawns with lofty palms to a fine late Renaissance mansion set against thickly wooded hills; then, an interior no less splendid – frescoes embellishing every inch of wall and ceiling, handsome classical busts on ornate stands, antiques, chandeliers and, from the 16thC salon and its balcony, a beautiful view of the sloping lawns below. Ruinously expensive? For once, no: all this comes for less than you pay for a room in some seedy station hotel in Pisa.

The bedrooms are not quite so grand; the cheapest border on the basic, with a basin and portable bidet (hidden discreetly behind decorative screens), creaky beds and possibly a long walk to the public bathroom. But there is compensation in the sheer size of the bedrooms (most are huge, with big 1920s wardrobes). The best doubles have touches of grandeur, and their own bathrooms; and the only rooms that could be described as small are the three in the 'tower' at the top. The old cellars serve as the breakfast room, and one of the buildings next to the main house is the restaurant. A recent visitor comments: 'Really special, unique atmosphere, and particularly friendly staff.'

Nearby Pisa (10 km); Lucca (15 km).

Rigoli, San Giuliano Terme 56010 Pisa **Tel** (050) 818193
Location 2.5 km NW of San Giuliano Terme at Rigoli; in large park with ample car parking
Food & drink breakfast, dinner
Prices rooms L70,000-L100,000; suite L170,000; breakfast L15,000; meals L40,000
Rooms 18 double, 6 with bath, 4 with shower; all rooms have central heating; 6 have phone
Facilities sitting-rooms, bar, breakfast room, tea room, TV room, conference room
Credit cards MC, V **Children** acccepted **Disabled** no special facilities **Pets** accepted **Closed** never
Proprietor Conte Ferdinando Agostini Venerosi della Seta

Tuscany

Country hotel, San Gimignano

Pescille

The Pescille used to be difficult to recommend wholeheartedly. It is a rambling hilltop manor house, converted with great taste and care, and with sufficient diversions to keep you there all day if sightseeing seems too strenuous – and yet it lacked a restaurant. This problem was remedied in 1987 by the creation of a big, independently run restaurant, the Cinque Gigli, decorated in a cool, modern, grey-and-white style with cane chairs on a tiled floor. The food is reported to be 'excellent', service 'perfect'.

Meanwhile, the hotel in general remains a peaceful and relaxing haven. The rustic terraced garden has plenty of secluded spots, while indoors there are several little sitting areas, trendily mixing smart modern furniture and antique agricultural clutter. Bedrooms are simple, stylish and moderately spacious, with enchanting views of open countryside or towards the distinctive skyline of San Gimignano. The swimming-pool is less than ideal – it has a raised lip about a foot high, which makes it seem utilitarian. What's more, complains an annoyed visitor (who also suffered a 'disagreeable' welcome), both the pool and the garden are closed in the middle of the evening.

Nearby San Gimignano; Florence, Siena, Pisa all within reach.

Localita Pescille, San Gimignano 53037 Siena
Tel and Fax (0577) 940186
Location 3 km SW of San Gimignano, in large gardens with private car parking
Food & drink breakfast, lunch, dinner
Prices rooms L60,000-L120,000, suites L160,000
Rooms 28 double, 4 single, one family room, 7 suites; all with bath; all rooms have central heating, phone

Facilities sitting-room, TV room, breakfast room, 2 bars, dining-room; swimming-pool, tennis, bowls
Credit cards AE, DC, MC, V
Children accepted, provided they are quiet
Disabled access difficult
Pets not accepted
Closed Jan and Feb
Proprietors Gigli brothers

Tuscany

Country hotel, San Gimignano

Le Renaie

A simple, well-run country hotel – built up over the years by the present owners from a simple bar and restaurant – which makes a respectable base within a short drive of San Gimignano. Outside, Le Renaie looks fairly unprepossessing: just a modern villa set back from a rural lane. Inside, it is cool and pretty with freshly painted walls, rattan furniture and traditional polished brick floors; bedrooms are spacious and immaculate, some with individual terraces. The restaurant, Da Leonetto, is popular with locals but gets mixed notices from reporters; on fine days you can eat outside on the veranda. For most holidaymakers the chief attractions are the small swimming-pool, the tranquil location ('a guest can live peaceful hours of repose', promises the brochure) and the reasonable prices.

Nearby sights of San Gimignano; hills and vineyards of Chianti; Volterra, Siena, Florence within reach.

Localita Pancole, San Gimignano 53037 Siena
Tel (0577) 955044
Location 6 km N of San Gimignano off road to Certaldo; private car parking
Food & drink breakfast, lunch, dinner
Prices rooms L70,000-L97,000; DB&B L90,000
Rooms 25 double, one single; all with bath; all rooms have phone
Facilities hall, TV room, dining-room, bar; swimming-pool, tennis
Credit cards AE, DC, MC, V
Children accepted, but must be accompanied by parents at swimming-pool
Disabled access difficult
Pets accepted in bedrooms
Closed last 3 weeks Nov
Proprietor Leonetto Sabatini

Tuscany

Country hotel, Scansano

Antico Casale di Scansano

Two widely travelled readers wrote in enthusiastic terms to draw our attention to this captivating hotel in the coastal region of Tuscany known as the Maremma, south-east of Grosseto. We can scarcely improve on their verdicts: 'Rooms sweetly decorated with country antiques and a lovely restaurant with terrace overlooking a spectacular green valley with vineyards and olive groves; a truly relaxing experience.' And: 'In four months touring the country, we thought this hotel number one; we were impressed by the welcome and hospitality, the cuisine, the surroundings – even the beds were the best we encountered in Italy.'

The Antico Casale is a beautifully restored, 200-year-old farmhouse which retains more of its origins than most such places. The Macereto estate of which it is part produces a range of *grappas* and wines (including the Morellino di Scansano DOC); many surrounding farms produce olive oil, and the Casale's stables are in very active use: riding holidays are offered (with instruction if you need it), and the hotel even offers special 'DB&B and horse' rates. Pottery and wine-tasting courses are also offered.

Nearby thermal spa of Saturnia, Argentarian coast.

Scansano, 58054 Grosseto
Tel (0564) 507219 **Fax** 507805
Location in countryside 22 km SE of Grosseto; with garden and car parking
Food & drink breakfast, lunch, dinner, snacks
Prices L95,000-L150,000; 20% reduction for children under 12 in parents' room
Rooms 11 double, 3 single, one family room, all with bath and shower; all rooms have central heating, air-conditioning, phone, TV, minibar, hairdrier
Facilities bar, sitting-room, dining-room, terrace; small swimming-pool, horse-riding, mountain bikes
Credit cards AE, MC, V
Children accepted
Disabled no special facilities
Pets accepted if well behaved
Closed mid-Jan to end-Feb
Proprietor Massimo Pellegrini

Tuscany

Town villa, Sesto Fiorentino

Villa Villoresi

The aristocratic Villa Villoresi looks rather out of place in what is now an industrial suburb of Florence, but once in the house and gardens you suddenly feel a million miles away from modern, bustling Florence. Contessa Cristina Villoresi is a warm hostess who has captured the hearts of many transatlantic and other guests. It is thanks to her that the villa still has the feel of a private home – all rather grand, if a little faded.

As you make your way through the building, each room seems to have some curiosity or feature of the past. The entrance hall is a superb gallery of massive chandeliers, frescoed walls, antiques and lofty potted plants. Then there are the beautiful frescoes on the first-floor landing, the family tree in reception, the sober looking Tuscan nobility in the dining-room, and the leather-bound novels in the sitting-room. Bedrooms are remarkably varied – from the small and quite plain to grand apartments with frescoes and Venetian chandeliers. Some overlook an inner courtyard, others look out on to the pool and garden. Half- or full-board terms at the Villa Villoresi are still quite reasonable; and we are assured that the food is now better than it once was.
Nearby Florence (8 km).

Via Ciampi 2, Colonnata di Sesto Fiorentino, Florence 50019
Tel (055) 443692 **Fax** 442063
Location 8 km NW of Florence; adequate car parking
Food & drink breakfast, lunch, dinner
Prices rooms L150,000-L330,000; DB&B L175,000-L260,000; meals L50,000-L55,000; 20% reductions out of season

Rooms 18 double, 3 single, 7 suites, all with bath or shower; all rooms have central heating, phone **Facilities** sitting-rooms, bar, dining-room, veranda; swimming-pool, ping-pong **Credit cards** AE, DC, MC, V **Children** welcome **Disabled** no special facilities
Pets not accepted in public rooms **Closed** never
Proprietor Contessa Cristina Villoresi

Tuscany

Converted monastery, Siena

Certosa di Maggiano

If you are looking for an exclusive but unostentatious hotel in Siena, this is probably it: a former Carthusian monastery – the oldest in Tuscany – secluded in a large park (yet only minutes from the enchanting old city) with just 17 bedrooms of which the majority are suites. Although it is extremely expensive, this is not a swanky place: the calm good taste, the atmosphere of a delightful country house and the discreet service appeal mainly to those in search of peace and privacy.

Meals are served in an exquisite dining-room, in the tranquil 14thC cloisters or under the arcades by the swimming-pool. Guests can help themselves to drinks in the book-lined library, play backgammon or chess in a little ante-room, or relax in the lovely sitting-room. Flower arrangements are just about everywhere and bowls of fresh fruit in the bedrooms add a personal touch. Bear in mind that exploration of Siena will have to be by taxi or bus – it's too far to walk, and parking is almost impossible in the centre. You may, however, wish to stay put and enjoy the beauty of the place – you will have paid for the privilege, after all.
Nearby sights of Siena; hills and vineyards of Chianti; San Gimignano, Florence, Arezzo within reach.

Via Certosa 82, Siena 53100
Tel (0577) 288180 **Fax** 288189
Location 1 km SE of middle of city and Porta Romana; in gardens, with car parking opposite entrance and garage available
Food & drink breakfast, lunch, dinner
Prices rooms L460,000-L620,000 with breakfast; suites L750,000; meals about L100,000
Rooms 5 double, 12 suites; all with bath; all have central heating, TV, phone, radio
Facilities dining-room, bar, library, sitting-room; tennis, heated outdoor swimming-pool, heliport
Credit cards AE, DC, MC, V
Children accepted
Disabled access possible – 3 rooms on ground floor
Pets small dogs accepted, but not in dining-room
Closed never
Manager Anna Recordati

Tuscany

Town guest-house, Siena

Palazzo Ravizza

We found the welcome here *sotto* to say the least, but when you see your room and begin to let the Ravizza's atmosphere sink in, even the deadpan nature of the staff seems in keeping – and a more recent visitor was received 'with great charm and good humour'. Owned by the same noble Siennese family for the past 200 years, it has been a hotel for most of this century (the card table was their undoing) and it positively oozes that elusive, faded charm which makes for a memorable stay.

Bedrooms vary but the best have views over the Tuscan countryside, quirky pieces of period furniture, comfy beds and huge modern bathrooms. (The thin bath towels, like table-cloths, apparently suit many guests though they don't suit us.) Downstairs there is a little sitting-area with bookshelves or the leather-bound visitors' books to browse through, as well as a large shady terrace and a well-kept dining-room with a ravishingly pretty ceiling. The food fits exactly – unpretentious but perfect home cooking (*pasta in brodo*, roast veal with artichokes and so on). For breakfast there are croissants filled with apricot jam, a welcome change from the usual hard rolls.

Nearby cathedral, Piazza del Campo.

Pian dei Mantellini 34, Siena 53100
Tel (0577) 280462 **Fax** 271370
Location inside city walls, close to heart of city; public car parking opposite
Food & drink breakfast, optional picnic lunch, dinner
Prices rooms L155,000 (double); DB&B L115,000
Rooms 25 double, 15 with bath, 3 with shower; 2 single; 3 family rooms; all rooms have central heating, phone

Facilities dining-room, library, bar, garden terrace; sightseeing mini-bus
Credit cards AE, DC, MC, V
Children welcome
Disabled level access to ground floor, small lift/elevator to bedrooms
Pets small dogs and cats only
Closed restaurant only, Jan and Feb
Proprietor Giovanni Iannone

Tuscany

Town villa, Siena

Villa Scacciapensieri

This modest hilltop villa dating from the early 1900s has been in the Nardi family since it ceased to be a private house in the 1930s. In that time the tentacles of suburban Siena have reached out to surround it; but if the villa can no longer claim to be in the country it is certainly on the edge of it, and it is still a calm retreat from the bustle of the city.

The garden is a great asset – a neat, formal, flowery area in front of the house, and a more rustic area to the side including the swimming-pool and a leafy terrace where meals are served in summer. Inside, beyond the cool entrance hall, the dining-room is smartly traditional in style; the sitting-room is something of a disappointment, with modern furniture which is neither stylish nor comfortable – though in cooler weather there is the attraction of a roaring log fire in the grand modern fireplace.

Bedrooms are unremarkably furnished but spacious, with views either of the roof-tops and towers of Siena or, in the opposite direction, of vineyards, olive groves and the hills beyond. We lack recent reports of the Tuscan and international cooking, but 'breakfast is simple and good,' says a recent reporter.

Nearby sights of Siena; Florence within reach.

Via di Scacciapensieri 10, Siena 53100
Tel (0577) 41442 **Fax** 270854
Location 2 km NE of middle of city, on hill; in private gardens with car parking
Food & drink breakfast, lunch, dinner
Prices rooms L120,000-L370,000; suites L360,000; DB&B L125,000-L220,000
Rooms 22 double, 4 single, 2 suites, all with bath or shower; all rooms have central heating, minibar, colour TV, phone, air-conditioning
Facilities dining-room, hall, bar, TV room; open air swimming-pool, tennis
Credit cards AE, DC, MC, V
Children welcome **Disabled** lift/elevator **Pets** small ones accepted, but not in public rooms or at pool
Closed Jan to mid-Mar; restaurant only, Wed
Proprietors Emma, Riccardo and Emanuele Nardi

Tuscany

Country inn, Sinalunga

Locanda dell'Amorosa

The Locanda dell'Amorosa is as romantic as it sounds. An elegant Renaissance villa-cum-village, within the remains of 14thC walls, has been converted into a charming country inn. The old stables, beamed and brick-walled, have been transformed into a delightful rustic restaurant serving refined versions of traditional Tuscan recipes, using ingredients from the estate, which also produces wine. The restaurant, which has earned a coveted array of chefs' hats in several Italian guides, can serve up to 80 people and is often full.

Only a fortunate few can actually stay at the Locanda – either in apartments in the houses where peasants and farmworkers once lived, or in ordinary bedrooms in the old family residence. The bedrooms we saw were cool, airy and pretty, with white-washed walls, wood-block floors, wrought-iron beds and flowery cotton curtains and bedspreads – and immaculate modern bathrooms. To complete the village there is a little parish church with lovely 15thC frescoes of the Sienese school. The Locanda is a paradise for connoisseurs of Tuscany, for gourmets and for all romantics.

Nearby Siena (45 km); Arezzo (45 km); Chianti wine country.

Sinalunga 53048 Siena
Tel (0577) 679497 **Fax** 678216
Location 2 km S of Sinalunga; ample car parking
Food & drink breakfast, lunch, dinner
Prices rooms L210,000-L350,000; suites L380,000-L480,000; meals from L70,000
Rooms 10 double, 5 suites, all with bathroom; all rooms have central heating, phone, colour TV, minibar, air-conditioning
Facilities dining-room, sitting-room, bar; swimming-pool
Credit cards AE, DC, MC, V
Children accepted
Disabled access difficult
Pets not accepted
Closed mid-Jan to end Feb; restaurant only, Mon, Tue
Manager Carlo Citterio

Tuscany

Country villa, Vicchio di Mugello

Villa Campestri

Get clear directions before you set off for this hilltop villa; it is in an isolated location, some way south of the village of Vicchio di Mugello.

The house looks classically Renaissance, but actually dates back to the 13thC. It overlooks sloping hillsides of mown grass, and miles of unspoilt countryside – much of it part of the villa's own estate. Inside, many original features remain: an old chapel, 14thC frescos, massive interior doors, and timbered ceilings. Furnishings blend with this venerable setting, including some valuable antiques, notably a vast and regal four-poster bed and an 18thC sofa. Plain white walls offset the dark wood of beams and furniture.

The bedrooms are handsomely furnished and wonderfully spacious – though some might find them too grand for comfort. Bathrooms are beautifully tiled in blue and white. The open-plan sitting-room and dining-room are traditionally furnished and fairly formal; the restaurant is renowned, and local dignitaries make the long trek to sample its offerings. If you're lucky the owner may regale you with a little piano music after dinner.

Nearby Florence (35 km).

Via di Campestri 19, 50039 Vicchio di Mugello (Firenze)
Tel (055) 849 0107
Fax (055) 849 0108
Location 3 km S of Vicchio, 35km NE of Florence, in countryside
Food & drink breakfast, dinner, snacks
Prices rooms L150,000 suites L270,000 with breakfast; meals from L40,000
Rooms 3 double, 4 suites; all rooms have central heating, phone, TV, minibar
Facilities swimming-pool, horse riding
Credit cards MC, V
Children not accepted
Disabled no special facilities
Pets accepted
Closed Jan to Mar
Proprietor Paolo Pasquali

Tuscany

Country villa, Balbano

Villa Casanova

An idiosyncratic place, dropped from the guide a couple of years ago but restored now on the strength of reports from readers. Spacious, simply-furnished rooms in an unaffected and atmospheric old country house (plus outbuildings); satisfying country food. Some reports mention noise from a nearby quarry.

■ Via di Casanova, 55050 Balbano (Lucca) **Tel** (0583) 548429 **Meals** breakfast, lunch, dinner **Prices** rooms L98,000 with breakfast; DB&B L75,000 **Rooms** 50, all with bath or shower, central heating **Credit cards** not accepted **Closed** Nov to Mar

---

Country hotel, Castellina in Chianti

Belvedere di San Leonino

This 600 year-old farmhouse, about equidistant from Castellina and Siena, has made a captivating little hotel. Inside, all is in simple, elegant taste, and the best of the rooms are gloriously spacious. The modest pool enjoys good views over the surrounding vineyards and olive groves.

■ San Leonino, 53011 Castellina in Chianti (Siena) **Tel** (0577) 740887 **Fax** (0577) 741034 **Meals** breakfast, dinner **Prices** rooms L105,000; dinner L25,000 **Rooms** 28, all with bath, central heating, phone **Credit cards** MC, V **Closed** never

---

Country villa, Castellina in Chianti

Villa Casafrassi

A gracious 17thC villa in rolling countryside on the way to Siena, carefully restored and opened as a hotel in 1986. The sitting-room opens on to the lawned gardens, which contain a tennis-court as well as a fair-sized swimming-pool. Bedrooms are in the main house and a separate outbuilding.

■ Via Chiantigiana 40, 53011 Castellina in Chianti (Siena) **Tel** (0577) 740621 **Fax** (0577) 741047 **Meals** breakfast, light lunch, dinner, snacks **Prices** rooms L192,000-L220,000 with breakfast **Rooms** 22, all with bath or shower, central heating; practically all have phone **Credit cards** DC, MC, V **Closed** mid-Nov to mid-Mar

---

Country inn, Certaldo

Osteria del Vicario

The basic structure of the 13thC monastery that underlies this simple inn remains, with a garden enclosed in a Romanesque cloister. Bedrooms have abundant charm, with leaded windows and old terracotta floors. Lovely flowered terrace in summer; game and wild mushrooms on the menu in autumn.

■ Via Rivellino 3, 50052 Certaldo (Firenze) **Tel** (0571) 668228 **Meals** breakfast, dinner; vegetarian meals **Prices** DB&B L87,000 (3 nights' stay preferred) **Rooms** 14, all with shower, TV on request **Credit cards** AE, DC, V **Closed** mid-Jan to end Feb

Tuscany

Country villa, Colle di Val d'Elsa

Villa Belvedere

An elegant restaurant-with-rooms – the smart dining-room is very much the heart of this handsome, weathered villa a few miles from Siena, and its food enjoys a high reputation in the locality. Bedrooms are also stylish, though with some amusingly ornate antique furniture.

■ Localita Belvedere, 53034 Colle di Val d'Elsa (Siena) **Tel** (0577) 920966 **Fax** (0577) 924128 **Meals** breakfast, dinner **Prices** rooms L124,000; DB&B L230,000 **Rooms** 15, all with bath, phone **Credit cards** AE, DC, MC, V **Closed** never

Resort village, Elba

Capo Sud

A complex of little villas in a quiet, rather remote spot, behind a beach. Rooms are modern and quite simple, scattered among trees and macchia, none of them very far away from the restaurant, bar, sitting area and terrace (with fine views of the bay). Fruit comes from local orchards.

■ Lacona, 57037 Elba (Livorno) **Tel** (0565) 964021 **Fax** (0565) 964263 **Meals** breakfast, lunch, dinner **Prices** DB&B L70,000-L105,000; FB L80,000-L115,000; reductions for children **Rooms** 39, all with bath or shower, phone; 20 rooms have minibar **Credit cards** DC **Closed** Oct to Apr

Town guest-house, Fiesole

Villa Bonelli

An appealing little hotel run by the friendly and helpful Boninsengi brothers who offer excellent and varied food. Bedrooms are simple but pleasant, the public rooms rather cramped, except for the restaurant. The road to the hotel is narrow and steep, but well signposted.

■ Via Francesco Poeti 1, 50014 Fiesole (Florence) **Tel** (055) 59513 **Fax** (055) 598942 **Meals** breakfast, dinner **Prices** rooms L55,000-L110,000; DB&B L110,000-L121,000 **Rooms** 21, all with shower, central heating, phone **Credit cards** AE, DC, MC, V **Closed** restaurant only, Nov to mid-Mar

Town hotel, Florence

Alba

This bright, neat hotel is handy for the station and only a few minutes from the heart of the city. It lacks the antique look of several nearby competitors, but its staff are friendly and bedrooms are well equipped.

■ Via della Scala 22-38, 50123 Florence **Tel** (055) 211469 **Fax** (055) 294041 **Meals** breakfast **Prices** rooms L125,000-L260,000 **Rooms** 24, all with bath or shower, air-conditioning, central heating, double glazing, phone, TV, minibar **Credit cards** MC, V **Closed** never

Tuscany

Town hotel, Florence

Aprile

The elegant lines of the original 15thC Medici palace are clearly visible in this attractive little hotel, furnished appropriately in a traditional but highly individual style. Guests may enjoy a fine breakfast by the shady terrace downstairs, or views of the striking church of Santa Maria Novella from upper rooms.

■ Via della Scala 6, 50123 Florence **Tel** (055) 216237 **Fax** (055) 280947 **Meals** breakfast **Prices** L55,000-L58,000 **Rooms** 29, all with most with bath, all with central heating, phone, minibar **Credit cards** AE, MC, V **Closed** never

---

Town hotel, Florence

Ariele

In the garden of this home-like hotel you may be able to hear music from the nearby Teatro Communale. It has a pleasantly old-fashioned and distinctly Italian atmosphere, and public areas that are more generous and elegant than the norm. Bedrooms are rather austere, but generally spacious.

■ Via Magenta 11, 50123 Florence **Tel** (055) 211509 **Fax** (055) 26852 **Meals** breakfast **Prices** rooms L95,000-L145,000 **Rooms** 40, all with bath or shower, central heating **Credit cards** AE, MC, V **Closed** never

---

Town hotel, Florence

Hotel Casci

A relatively busy setting some way north of San Lorenzo, but this simple place is unusually welcoming and well run. The building has some antiquity; there are intact original frescos. Rooms are fairly spartan, but clean; those at the rear very peaceful.

■ Via Cavour 13, 50129 Florence **Tel** (055) 211686 **Fax** (055) 239 6461 **Meals** breakfast **Prices** rooms L50,000-L105,000 with breakfast, family rooms more **Rooms** 25, all with bath or shower, central heating, phone **Credit cards** MC, V **Closed** never

---

Town guest-house, Florence

Cestelli

It is soon obvious that this small hotel on the upper floors of an ancient *palazzo* is a private family home, furnished over many years with care and taste. Some of its contents are a little battered now, but bedrooms are all full of character, and one or two are very spacious.

■ Borgo SS Apostoli 25, 50123 Florence **Tel** (055) 214213 **Meals** breakfast **Prices** rooms L68,000-L82,000 with breakfast **Rooms** 7, all with one with bath **Credit cards** not accepted **Closed** never

Tuscany

Town hotel, Florence

Hotel City

The interior is more smartly urban than the unassuming exterior suggests, with a mix of shiny black and bamboo furniture in the bar-lounge areas, and efforts made with rugs, urns and plants. Bedrooms are neat and attractive, and have excellent bathrooms.

■ Via S Antonio 18, 50123 Florence (Firenze) **Tel** (055) 211543 **Fax** (055) 295451 **Meals** breakfast **Prices** rooms L135,500-L185,000 **Rooms** 18, all with bath or shower, central heating, air-conditioning, TV, minibar, phone; most have hairdrier **Credit cards** AE, CD, MC, V **Closed** never

---

Town hotel, Florence

Hotel Principe

A graciously proportioned but somewhat faded mansion overlooking the Arno. Rooms with the view may suffer traffic noise, and rear rooms have the compensating prospect of a charming garden. Cosy rooms at the top of the house are more appealing than the high-ceilinged, old-fashioned ones on lower floors.

■ Lungarno Amerigo Vespucci 34, 50123 Florence **Tel** (055) 284848 **Fax** (055) 283458 **Meals** breakfast, snacks **Prices** rooms L200,000-L330,000 with breakfast **Rooms** 21, all with bath, central heating, air-conditioning, phone, hairdrier, TV, radio, minibar **Credit cards** AE, DC, MC, V **Closed** never

---

Town hotel, Florence

Quisisana e Pontevecchio

This elderly pensione was used as one of the sets for 'A Room with a View'; the view is of the Ponte Vecchio, though not many rooms enjoy it. Bedrooms, like the rest of the house, are still very old-fashioned, with flowery wallpapers and weighty mahogany furnishings; but one or two are grand and spacious.

■ Lungarno degli Archibusieri 4, 50122 Florence **Tel** (055) 216692 **Fax** (055) 268303 **Meals** breakfast **Prices** rooms L96,000-L156,000 with breakfast **Rooms** 37, all with bath or shower, central heating, phone **Credit cards** AE, DC, MC, V **Closed** never

---

Town hotel, Florence

Hotel Regency

Sister hotel of the Lord Byron in Rome, the Regency follows the same formula of intimate five-star luxury and personal service for the super-rich. Public rooms are elegantly formal; bedrooms are predictably opulent. The location is peaceful, and the garden a plus point in central Florence.

■ Piazza Massimo d'Azeglio 3, 50121 Florence **Tel** (055) 245247 **Fax** (055) 245247 **Meals** breakfast, lunch, dinner **Prices** rooms L300,000- L540,000 with breakfast **Rooms** 35, all with bath, phone, TV, minibar, air-conditioning, safe, hairdrier **Credit cards** AE, DC, MC, V **Closed** never

Tuscany

Town hotel, Florence

La Residenza

The homely feel of this friendly place is instantly appealing, even if it is not especially smart. Upstairs the flowery roof garden and sitting-room are restfully sunny havens. Rooms are simple and cheerful, with lots of pictures.

■ Via Tornabuoni 8, 50123 Florence **Tel** (055) 284197 **Fax** (055) 284197 **Meals** breakfast, dinner **Prices** rooms L90,000-L175,000 with breakfast; DB&B L136,000-L166,000; children under three years free **Rooms** 25, all with central heating, phone; 7 rooms have air-conditioning, most have bath or shower **Credit cards** AE, DC, MC, V **Closed** never

---

Town guest-house, Florence

Silla

The imposing lower courtyard and terrace overlooking the Arno are the main features of interest in this solid Florentine *palazzo*. Bedrooms are rather conventional and dark, and some other furnishings have become unnecessarily solemn of late, but the welcome remains courteous and unstuffy.

■ Via dei Renai 5, 50125 Florence **Tel** (055) 234 2888 **Fax** (055) 234 1437 **Meals** breakfast **Prices** rooms L100,000-L145,000 with breakfast **Rooms** 32, all with central heating, TV, phone; most with bath or shower **Credit cards** AE, DC, MC, V **Closed** 2 weeks Dec

---

Town guest-house, Florence

Splendor

A peaceful and still affordable *pensione* a little way out of the centre. It has a sunny terrace full of plants and several historic features; furnishings and some modern additions are not entirely harmonious.

■ Via San Gallo 30, 50129 Florence **Tel** (055) 483427 **Fax** (055) 461276 **Meals** breakfast buffet **Prices** rooms L76,000-L140,000 with breakfast **Rooms** 31, all with central heating; most with bath or shower **Credit cards** MC, V **Closed** never

---

Town hotel, Florence

Unicorno

Pleasant, simple, central hotel recreating something of a Florentine *palazzo* atmosphere with rag-rolled walls, vaulting and antique-look Italianate furnishings. Upstairs is a modern dining-room where 'American breakfasts' are served (a more elaborate buffet than usual).

■ Via dei Fossi 27, 50123 Florence **Tel** (055) 287313 **Meals** breakfast **Prices** rooms L105,000-L160,000 with breakfast **Rooms** 28, all with bath or shower, central heating, air-conditioning, phone, hairdrier, TV, minibar **Credit cards** AE, DC, MC,V **Closed** never

Tuscany

Town villa, Florence

Villa Carlotta

A gracious 19thC mansion standing on a hilly, tree-lined street on the south-eastern slopes of the city, now a quietly desirable residential area. Inside, style and furnishings aspire to formal elegance; many of the building's original features have been preserved. Better-than-average breakfasts are served in a plain, modern addition, or on an attractive terrace.

■ Via Michele di Lando 3, 50125 Florence **Tel** (055) 220530 **Meals** breakfast, dinner **Prices** L122,500-L175,000; DB&B L162,000-L215,000 **Rooms** 26, all with bath or shower, central heating, air-conditioning, minibar, safe, colour TV, phone **Credit cards** AE, DC, MC, V **Closed** never

---

Converted castle, Giglio

Castello Monticello

The pretty little island of Giglio attracts many day-trippers; if you fancy an overnight stay, this 'castle' is your best bet – built as a private house, and less austere within than without. Good views of the coast from the terrace, gardens and simple rooms.

■ Giglio Porto, 58013 Giglio (Grosseto) **Tel** (0564) 809252 **Meals** breakfast, lunch, dinner **Prices** rooms L85,000-L145,000 with breakfast; meals L30,000 **Rooms** 37, all with shower, central heating, phone, TV, fridge **Credit cards** AE, DC, MC, V **Closed** mid-Nov to mid-Mar

---

Seaside villa, Giglio

Pardini's Hermitage

A real retreat: Federigo Pardini's white villa, perched on a cliff above the sea, is reached only by boat from Giglio Porto (or an hour's walk). The villa is smartly modern and the bedrooms have balconies, but you will be hoping to spend most of your time on the terraces or swimming from the rocks.

■ 58013 Giglio (Grosseto) **Tel** (0564) 809034 **Fax** (0564) 809177 **Meals** breakfast, lunch, dinner **Prices** BD&B L85,000-L130,000; FB L100,000-L150,000 **Rooms** 11, all with bath, phone, hairdrier, TV **Credit cards** V **Closed** Oct to Mar

---

Village hotel, Greve in Chianti

Albergo del Chianti

Across Greve's central piazza from the Giovanni da Verrazzanoo is this very different place – a cool, calm, neatly restored and well run bed-and-breakfast hotel, with the unusual feature for such a modest village hotel of an attractive swimming-pool in the back garden.

■ Piazza Matteotti 86, 50022 Greve in Chianti (Firenze) **Tel** (055) 853763 **Fax** (055) 853763 **Meals** breakfast **Prices** rooms L90,000 **Rooms** 16, all with shower, central heating, air-conditioning, phone **Credit cards** AE, DC, MC, V **Closed** Nov

Tuscany

Village hotel, Greve in Chianti

Giovanni da Verrazzano

To call this a town hotel would be quite misleading. Above all else it is a bustling restaurant, its first-floor terrace overlooking the unusual triangular piazza around which Greve revolves. Bedrooms are no more than adequate, but sound value.

■ Piazza Matteotti 28, 50022 Greve in Chianti (Firenze) **Tel** (055) 853189 **Fax** (055) 853648 **Meals** breakfast, lunch, dinner **Prices** rooms L45,000-L85,000; DB&B L70,000 **Rooms** 11, all with shower, phone, minibar, TV, hairdrier **Credit cards** AE, DC, MC, V **Closed** for a period in winter; restaurant only, Sun dinner and Mon

---

Converted fortress, Lecchi in Chianti

San Sano

The German/Italian Matarazzos have converted this solid, rambling farmhouse-fortress with a sure hand. It is all gloriously simple and stylish: mellow stone arches, white walls, exposed wooden beams, tiled floors, iron bedsteads, austere modern bathrooms. 'Bountiful' buffet breakfasts, long Chianti views.

■ Localita San Sano 21, 53010 Lecchi in Chianti (Siena) **Tel** (0577) 746130 **Fax** (0577) 746156 **Meals** breakfast, dinner **Prices** rooms L120,000- L130,000 with breakfast; dinner L28,000 **Rooms** 10, all with bath, central heating, phone **Credit cards** AE, MC, V **Closed** Nov to mid-Mar

---

Country villa, Lucca

Villa San Michele

An impressive 14thC/17thC villa set among woods and olive groves only 2 km from downtown Lucca, off the road to Pisa. Unlike the public areas, the bedrooms are furnished more for comfort than period style, but they are beautifully decorated in sympathy with the house. Neat breakfast room.

■ Via della Chiesa 462, S Michele in Escheto, 55050 Lucca **Tel** (0583) 370276 **Fax** (0583) 370277 **Meals** breakfast **Prices** rooms L115,000-L280,000, suites L240,000-L380,000; buffet breakfast L20,000 **Rooms** 22, all with bath, central heating, phone, TV, radio, minibar **Credit cards** AE, DC, MC, V **Closed** never

---

Restaurant-with-rooms, Montefollonico

La Chiusa

La Chiusa has lost its Michelin star, but its reputation for outstanding pasta remains, as does its appeal as a place to stay. It is a stylishly renovated farmhouse, with views of Montepulciano from the simple, tasteful rooms with spectacularly swish bathrooms.

■ Via della Madonnina 88, 53040 Montefollonico (Siena) **Tel** (0577) 669668 **Fax** (0577) 669593 **Meals** breakfast, dinner **Prices** rooms L240,000-L340,000 with breakfast; suite L390,000 **Rooms** 12, all with bath or shower, phone, TV, minibar, hairdrier **Credit cards** AE, DC, MC, V **Closed** Nov to Mar except Christmas/New Year

Tuscany

Seaside hotel, Punta Ala

Piccolo Hotel Alleluja

The smallest and most inviting of the smart hotels of exclusive, sporty Punta Ala. Inside and out it is stylish and well cared for. Designs are simple, colours light and the atmosphere cheerful. Some bedrooms have their own sitting-rooms.

■ 58040 Punta Ala (Grosseto) **Tel** (0564) 922050 **Fax** (0564) 920734 **Meals** breakfast, lunch, dinner **Prices** DB&B L310,000-L590,000; FB L203,000-L393,000 **Rooms** 42, all with bath or shower, air-conditioning, phone, TV, minibar, radio **Credit cards** AE, DC, MC, V **Closed** never

---

Country inn, Radda in Chianti

Villa Miranda

This roadside inn has been in the same family for over 150 years, its reputation for wholesome Tuscan food as strong as ever. There are prettily decorated bedrooms above the restaurant – all stone walls and heavy beams – and more over the road in the modern Residence S. Cristina, with swimming-pool and tennis.

■ 53017 Radda in Chianti (Siena) **Tel** (0577) 738021 **Fax** (0577) 738668 **Meals** breakfast, lunch, dinner, **Prices** rooms L69,000-L120,000 **Rooms** 32, all with bath or shower, central heating, minibar, radio, phone **Credit cards** MC, V **Closed** never

---

Country guest-house, Radda in Chianti

Podere Terreno

An old farmhouse, surrounded only by fields, vineyards and woods, and run as a family home taking guests by a Franco-Italian couple. You eat together at a refectory table in the jolly beamed living room, with open fireplace. Bedrooms are simple but satisfactory.

■ Localita Volpaia, 53017 Radda in Chianti (Siena) **Tel** (0577) 738312 **Fax** (0577) 738312 **Meals** breakfast, dinner **Prices** DB&B 95,000-L100,000 **Rooms** 7, all with shower, central heating **Credit cards** MC, V, **Closed** never

---

Country estate, Radda in Chianti

Vescine – Il Relais del Chianti

Opened in 1990, this new arrival midway between Castellina and Radda is enthusiastically recommended by a reader, and seems set for a full entry next year. Three old hilltop houses contain the tastefully simple rooms and welcoming public areas. Swimming-pool with views, tennis-courts. Associated restaurant 700m away.

■ Localita Vescine, 53017 Radda in Chianti (Siena) **Tel** (0577) 741144 **Fax** (0577) 740263 **Meals** buffet breakfast **Prices** rooms L110,000-L230,000 with breakfast; suites L240,000-L280,000 **Rooms** 25, all with shower, minibar, phone; TV on request **Credit cards** AE, MC, V **Closed** Feb, Nov

Tuscany

Restaurant-with-rooms, Sambuca Val di Pesa

La Scuderia

This modest, creeper-covered restaurant-with-rooms is a pleasant find, in a delightful village of monumental buildings reached via a long avenue of olive and cypress trees. Inside, the bar and dining-room walls are cluttered with a cheerful collection of bottles and kitchen utensils; outside, the terraces overlook classic Tuscan coutryside.

■ Badia a Passignano, 50020 Sambuca Val di Pesa (Firenze) **Tel** (055) 807 1623 **Meals** breakfast, lunch, dinner **Prices** rooms L60,000 **Rooms** 3, all with bath or shower **Credit cards** AE, DC, MC, V **Closed** never

---

Town hotel, San Gimignano

L'Antico Pozzo

Recently recommended to us, and clearly a strong candidate for a full entry next year, the Antico Pozzo brings much-needed new blood to the San Gimignano scene. A 15thC town house, beautifully restored in 1990 and furnished with fine, simple taste – quite possibly the best in town.

■ Via S Matteo 87, 53037 San Gimignano (Siena) **Tel** (0577) 942014 **Fax** (0577) 942117 **Meals** breakfast, dinner **Prices** rooms L100,000-L180,000 **Rooms** 18, all with bath, central heating, fan-cooling, phone, TV, radio, hairdrier **Credit cards** AE, DC, MC, V **Closed** never

---

Town hotel, San Gimignano

Bel Soggiorno

Just inside the walls of San Gimignano, this 13thC house has made a very appealing small hotel. The main attraction is the restaurant, with panoramic windows and satisfying food. Rooms are modernized and lacking character, but are pleasant; some share the views.

■ Via San Giovanni 91, 53037 San Gimignano (Siena) **Tel** (0577) 940375 **Fax** (0577) 940375 **Meals** breakfast, lunch, dinner **Prices** rooms L85,000-L150,000 **Rooms** 21, all with bath, central heating, phone, TV; 8 rooms have air-conditioning **Credit cards** AE, DC, MC, V **Closed** restaurant only, Mon

---

Farmhouse hotel, San Gimignano

Il Casolare di Libbiano

Three enterprising young citizens of San Gimignano have restored this captivating old house 8 km from the town. Its hallmarks are simplicity, good taste and honesty. Everything from the furniture to the cooking is carefully considered. Splendid living room, peaceful garden with fair-sized pool.

■ Localita Libbiano 3, 53037 San Gimignano (Siena) **Tel** (0577) 955102 **Fax** (0577) 955102 **Meals** breakfast, dinner **Prices** DB&B L110,000-L150,000 **Rooms** 6, all with bath or shower, central heating; most have TV **Credit cards** not accepted **Closed** Nov to Mar

Tuscany

Town hotel, San Gimignano

La Cisterna

This popular hotel on San Gimignano's central square generates conflicting reports from readers: don't accept a room beneath the kitchens. Excellent views from the better rooms and Terrazze restaurant. Small but splendid stone-arched sitting-room.
■ Piazza della Cisterna 24, 53037 San Gimignano (Siena) **Tel** (0577) 940328 **Fax** (0577) 942080 **Meals** breakfast, lunch, dinner **Prices** rooms L72,000-L144,000 with breakfast; DB&B L107,000-L214,000; FB L142,000-L284,000; suite L140,000 **Rooms** 57, all with bath or shower, central heating, phone, TV **Credit cards** AE, DC, MC, V **Closed** 10 Nov to 10 March; restaurant only, Tue and midday Wed

Town hotel, San Gimignano

Hotel Leon Bianco

Directly opposite the better-known Cisterna on San Gimignano's main square, this spick-and-span hotel offers rather better value. Rooms are generally spacious, and furnished with a bit of panache. 'Copious' buffet breakfasts are to be had on the enclosed terrace, says a reporter.
■ Piazza del Cisterna, 53037 San Gimignano (Siena) **Tel** (0577) 941294 **Fax** (0577) 942123 **Meals** breakfast **Prices** rooms L80,000-L110,000 with breakfast; suites L130,000 **Rooms** 25, all with bath or shower, phone, air-conditioning **Credit cards** AE, DC, MC, V **Closed** Jan and Feb

Country villa, San Gimignano

Villa San Paola

A French reader draws our attention to this smartly restored villa 4 km from San Gimignano, opened to guests only since 1989. Decoration is light, confident and fresh, and the rooms are well equipped. There is tennis, and a pool served by a special bar.
■ Strada Certaldo, 53037 San Gimignano (Siena) **Tel** (0577) 955100 **Fax** (0577) 955113 **Meals** breakfast, snacks **Prices** rooms L150,000-L180,000 with breakfast **Rooms** 15, all with bath, central heating, air-conditioning, phone, hairdrier, satellite TV, minibar **Credit cards** AE, DC, MC, V **Closed** early Jan to mid-Feb

Country villa, San Gusmè

Villa Arceno

A handsome 17thC villa on an extensive wooded estate half-way between Siena and Arezzo. Vaulted public rooms with light decoration and comfortable reproduction furniture, gloriously spacious bedrooms, some with terraces. Immaculate swimming-pool in a secluded courtyard.
■ Localita Arceno, 53010 San Gusmè (Siena) **Tel** (0577) 359292 **Fax** (0577) 359276 **Meals** breakfast, lunch, dinner **Prices** rooms L180,000-L374,000 with breakfast; suite L474,000 **Rooms** 16, all with bath, central heating, air-conditioning, phone, TV, minibar, hairdrier **Credit cards** AE, DC, MC, V **Closed** at times from Nov to Feb

Tuscany

Town hotel, Siena

Santa Caterina

An 18thC house just outside the city walls, carefully converted, furnished in rustic style and in keeping with its age, and heartily recommended by readers. Bedrooms vary in style and size, but all are pleasantly furnished, some with antiques. The breakfast room looks on to the flowery garden.

■ Via Enea Silvio Piccolomini 7, 53100 Siena **Tel** (0577) 221105 **Fax** (0577) 271087 **Meals** breakfast **Prices** rooms L75,000-L165,000 **Rooms** 19, all with bath or shower, central heating, air-conditioning, phone **Credit cards** AE, DC, MC, V **Closed** early Jan to early Mar

---

Town villa, Siena

Villa Patrizia

This plain-looking villa just misses being a truly excellent little hotel: it has aristocratic style and is relaxed and dignified, but the bedrooms are routine in their furnishings, and there is no sitting-room. Breakfast is an adequate self-service buffet.

■ Via Fiorentina 58, 53100 Siena **Tel** (0577) 50431 **Meals** breakfast, lunch, dinner **Prices** L215,000-L324,000 **Rooms** 33, all with central heating, phone, minibar, TV, air-conditioning **Credit cards** AE, DC, MC, V **Closed** never

---

Country estate, Sovicille

Torre Pretale

The 'Torre' is a severe, tower-like building forming part of the hamlet of Borgo Pretale, immersed in the countryside south-west of Siena. It has been restored and furnished in the best of taste, blending old and new with success. The grounds include a big, secluded swimming-pool.

■ Localita Pretale, 53018 Sovicille (Siena) **Tel** (0577) 345401 **Fax** (0577) 345625 **Meals** breakfast, lunch, dinner, snacks **Prices** rooms L300,000-L350,000 with breakfast; DB&B L220,000-L240,000 **Rooms** 30, all with bath or shower, central heating, air-conditioning, phone, TV, minibar **Credit cards** AE, DC, MC, V **Closed** mid-Nov to Feb

---

Village hotel, Strove

Casalta

This stylish and intimate little hotel is tucked away in the middle of the sleepy hilltop village of Strove. The cool white-walled restaurant specializes in fish. Above it is a civilized sitting-room, and off this the tastefully simple bedrooms. Gently good-humoured padrone.

■ 53035 Strove (Siena) **Tel** (0577) 301002 **Meals** breakfast, lunch (Sun only), dinner **Prices** rooms L60,000-L110,000 with breakfast; DB&B L80,000 **Rooms** 12, all with bath, central heating **Credit cards** not accepted **Closed** mid-Nov to Feb; restaurant Wed

Tuscany

Country hotel, Strove

San Luigi Residence

An unusual formula, appealing to families: the San Luigi is a polished conversion of a sizeable old house and its outbuildings, which are separated by expansive lawns from a very large pool. With its adjacent restaurant, this can be a hubbub of activity – though there is plenty of space to escape from the fun.

■ Via della Cerreta 38, Monteriggioni, 53030 Strove (Siena) **Tel** (0577) 301055 **Fax** (0577) 301167 **Meals** breakfast, lunch, dinner **Prices** DB&B L120,000-L280,000 **Rooms** 44, all with bath or shower, central heating, kitchenette, fridge, dishwasher, phone, radio **Credit cards** AE, MC, V **Closed** Nov to mid-Mar

---

Country guest-house, Terontola di Cortona

Residenza di San Andrea

A home, not a hotel: Patrizia Nappi takes guests in only four rooms in her mellow stone-and-brick 13thC manor house, among wooded hills 8 km from Cortona and close to Lago Trasimeno. A house-party atmosphere prevails, and Patrizia serves authentic Tuscan food. She has four dogs.

■ 52044 Terontola di Cortona (Arezzo) **Tel** (0575) 677736 **Meals** breakfast, dinner, snacks **Prices** rooms L120,000-L150,000 with breakfast; dinner L35,000 inclusive of wine **Rooms** 4, all with bath or shower, central heating, hairdrier, radio, fans **Credit cards** not accepted **Closed** Feb

---

Country villa, Trespiano

Villa le Rondini

The secluded grounds and the views of the city and the Arno valley are the main attractions here. Rooms in the main house can be spacious and beautifully furnished, those in the two annexes rather simpler.

■ Via Bolognese Vecchia 224, 50010 Trespiano (Florence) **Tel** (055) 400081 **Fax** (055) 268212 **Meals** breakfast, lunch, dinner, snacks **Prices** rooms L145,000-L230,000; suites L323,000; DB&B L137,500-L190,000 **Rooms** 43, all with central heating, minibar, phone; most with bath or shower **Credit cards** AE, MC, V **Closed** never

---

Country hotel, Volterra

Villa Nencini

Set just outside the hilltop town of Volterra, this captivating, mellow stone house offers impressive views of the glorious sweeping countryside. Recently, some of its charm has been lost through the construction of a large annexe which leaves little of the previous garden.

■ Borgo Santo Stefano 55, 56048 Volterra (Pisa) **Tel** (0588) 86386 **Meals** breakfast **Prices** rooms L59,000-L113,000 **Rooms** 14, all with central heating, phone; TV on request; most with bath or shower **Credit cards** MC, V **Closed** never

Umbria and Marche

Hotels in Umbria and Marche

Visitors are increasingly discovering that there is more to Umbria than Assisi; but it remains the main tourist highlight of the region. Choice of hotel is tricky: there are many that are mediocre, and some of the more comfortable hotels are too big for a full entry here; of these, the Subasio (Tel (075) 812206, fax 816691) is a 70-room, polished, rather formal place, but notable for the views from its better bedrooms and beautiful flowery terraces. If you would rather see the sights from a base outside town, the Poppy Inn-Locanda del Papavero (Tel (075) 803 8041) is a restaurant with 9 bedrooms at Petrignano, 9 km away.

Perugia is not nearly so well known as Assisi, but well worth a visit if you can penetrate the infuriating defences of its traffic system. The Brufani (page 164) lies at one end of its lively central Corso Vannucci, and just along it is another hotel worth knowing about – La Rosetta (Tel and fax (075) 20841); it is much bigger, but not worryingly impersonal, and indisputably better value.

Marche's coast, like the rest of the Adriatic, offers large resorts with plenty of hotels, but not many to suit our requirements. Pesaro, though a big town, is a more interesting mixture of old town and beach resort than many along this coastline; the Villa Serena on page 158 is our main recommendation for this area, but the Vittoria, a stylish, well-equipped hotel on the seafront in the town itself (Tel (0721) 34343, fax 68874) is another possibility. Ancona, regional capital of the Marches and a big seaport, is definitely not the place to stay but 12 km down the coast, at the popular resort of Portonovo, we have two full recommendations and can also suggest the Internazionale (Tel (071) 801001). Further south at Numana, the Eden Gigli (Tel (071) 936182, fax 936500, 30 rooms) is a smart, modern hotel in a beautiful setting overlooking the sea.

Inland from Pesaro, the Renaissance art city of Urbino is an essential visit, but there is no hotel to which we can wholeheartedly give a full recommendation. Our best suggestion is the Raffaello (Tel (0722) 4896, fax 328540), a straightforward 19-room hotel; it has no restaurant but this is not a problem since it is right in the middle of the town.

Gubbio is an equally compelling place to visit, and an extravagant alternative to our main recommendation – the Bosone, on page 163 – is the recently rebuilt Park Hotel ai Cappuccini, slightly out of the town (Tel (075) 9234, fax 9220323).

This page acts as an introduction to the features and hotels of Camapnia, and gives brief recommendations of reasonable hotels that for one reason or another have not made a full entry. The long entries for this region – covering the hotels we are most enthusiastic about – start on the next page. But do not neglect the shorter entries starting on page 194: these are all hotels that we would happily stay at.

Umbria and Marche

Le Silve

Even if you are not planning to stay at this rustic gem, the road up to Le Silve is worth exploring for its own rewards – or perhaps avoiding if you are the nervous sort. It winds up over a series of hills and passes until you reach the house, set on its own private hill-ridge, 700m above sea level. The views are simply wonderful.

Le Silve is an old farmhouse (parts of it very old indeed – 10thC) converted to its new purpose with great sympathy and charm. There is a delightfully rambling feel to the place, with rooms on a variety of levels. The rustic nature of the building is preserved perfectly – all polished tile floors, stone or white walls, beamed ceilings, the occasional rug – and it is furnished with country antiques. Public rooms are large and airy, bedrooms stylishly simple. The self-contained suites are in villas about 1.5 km from the main house.

Food is wholesome and satisfying, using oil, cheese and meat from the associated farm. Le Silve is close enough to Assisi for sightseeing expeditions but remote enough for complete seclusion – and with good sports facilities immediately on hand (fair-sized pool). But it's not for vertigo sufferers.

Nearby sights of Assisi.

Località Armenzano, Assisi 06081 Perugia
Tel (075) 801 9000
Location in countryside 12 km E of Assisi, between S444 and S3; ample car parking
Food & drink breakfast, lunch, dinner
Prices rooms L120,000- L230,000 with breakfast; DB&B L160,000; FB L200,000; reductions for children
Rooms 11 double, 3 single, 4 self-contained suites; all with bath; all rooms have central heating, phone, TV
Facilities dining-room, 2 sitting-rooms, bar; swimming-pool, tennis, sauna, riding, archery, mini-golf, motor-bike
Credit cards AE, DC, V
Children welcome
Disabled no special facilities
Pets not accepted
Closed mid-Jan to mid-Feb
Manager Daniela Taddia

Umbria and Marche

Umbra

Tucked away down a little alley off the main square of Assisi is this delightful little family-run hotel, with a restaurant worth a visit in its own right.

The Umbra consists of several small houses – parts date back to the 13th century – with a small gravelled courtyard garden shaded by a pergola. The interior is comfortable and in parts more like a private home than a hotel; there is a bright little sitting-room with Mediterranean-style tiles and brocaded wing armchairs, and a series of bedrooms, mostly quite simply furnished but each with its own character and some with lovely views over the Umbrian plain. We like the elegant dining-room, where imaginative regional dishes triumph over the bland cooking you so often find in hotel restaurants. Reporters generally agree, but one complains of a sombre atmosphere and poor food. In fine weather, meals are served outside. The Umbra offers all the peace and tranquillity which you might hope to find in Assisi, and nothing is too much trouble for Alberto Laudenzi, whose family has run the hotel for more than 50 years.
Nearby basilica of St Francis, church of Santa Chiara, cathedral; medieval castle

Via degli Archi 6, Assisi 06081 Perugia
Tel (075) 812240 **Fax** 813653
Location in middle, off Piazza del Comune, with small garden; nearest car park some distance away
Food & drink breakfast, lunch, dinner
Prices rooms L85,000-L155,000 with breakfast; suites L190,000
Rooms 16 double, 5 single, 4 suites, all with bath; all rooms have phone, central heating, TV
Facilities 3 sitting-rooms, bar, dining-room
Credit cards AE, DC, MC, V
Children tolerated
Disabled access difficult
Pets not accepted
Closed mid-Nov to mid-Dec, mid-Jan to mid-Mar
Proprietor Alberto Laudenzi

Umbria and Marche

Restaurant with rooms, Campello sul Clitunno

Le Casaline

Here is one of those restaurants out in the country which attract families from miles around on holidays; no further testimony to the quality of the food (especially the charcoal grills) is necessary. The bedrooms are very much a sideline – so much so that the *padrone* has been known to throw a room in with the price of a good meal (in the days before he realised that he could charge substantial amounts for them). The simple bedrooms are in converted outbuildings a little way from the restaurant. 'Wished we could have stayed longer' commented one visitor.

Nearby Spoleto (14 km); Assisi (35 km).

Località Poreta, Campello sul Clitunno 06042 Perugia
Tel (0743) 521113 **Fax** 275099
Location 3 km E of Campello, isolated in countryside; in gardens, with ample car parking
Food & drink breakfast, lunch, dinner
Prices rooms L55,000-L68,000; breakfast L8,000; meals from L35,000
Rooms 7 rooms, 2 with bath, 5 with shower

Facilities dining-room terrace, TV room **Credit cards** AE, DC, V **Children** welcome **Disabled** access to 2 bedrooms possible **Pets** accepted
Closed restaurant only, Mon
Proprietor Benedetto Zeppadoro

Umbria and Marche

Converted monastery, Orvieto

La Badia

This marvellously preserved former Benedictine abbey (*badia*) dating from the 12th century is probably the best place from which to visit Orvieto, with its splendid cathedral. It is a sight worth seeing in its own right, with its 12-sided tower and beautifully harmonious Romanesque arches. The mellow stone buildings, the view across to the dramatically sited town, and the swimming-pool are powerful attractions.

An inspection visit confirmed other favourable reports, finding the rooms thoroughly comfortable, the suites notably spacious and restful; the Umbrian food excellent (grills on an open fire the speciality); and the service courteous and efficient, with English, French, German and Spanish spoken.

However, a more recent guest, while agreeing that the situation was 'beautiful' and the suite 'really excellent', judged the public rooms gloomy and uncomfortable and the staff impersonal.

Nearby cathedral in Orvieto; Lake of Bolsena; Todi (40 km).

La Badia, Orvieto Scalo 05019 Terni
Tel (0763) 90359 **Fax** 92796
Location 1 km S of Orvieto, off Viale 1 Maggio towards Viterbo; in large park with parking for 200 cars
Food & drink breakfast, lunch, dinner
Prices rooms L211,000-L246,000; suites L353,000-L388,000
Rooms 16 double, 14 with bath, one with shower; 3 single, 2 with bath, one with shower; 7 suites, 2 with bath, 2 with shower; all rooms have phone, air-conditioning, central heating **Facilities** dining-room, bar, sitting-room with TV, conference hall; swimming- pool, 2 tennis courts **Credit cards** AE, V
Children welcome
Disabled access difficult
Pets no dogs **Closed** Jan and Feb; restaurant only, Wed
Proprietor Luisa Fiumi

Umbria and Marche

Villa Ciconia

Until a couple of years ago, Villa Ciconia was run mainly as a restaurant, with a few simple rooms above. When we first encountered it, we were doubtful about its inclusion in these pages. Now, all such doubts are banished: the genial Petrangeli family have re-established their 16thC home as a comfortable and welcoming country hotel, refurbished in keeping with the villa's original style.

The solid old house sits in a leafy, park-like garden watered by two streams that meet nearby, with tall pines giving plenty of shade. The bedrooms are simply but tastefully furnished, with elegant iron-framed canopy beds and antique country furniture; all the ones we have seen have been spacious. The air-conditioning is not totally effective in all of them, though.

The lofty dining-room is as splendid as ever, with its coffered ceiling and surrounding murals, and enormous fireplace. Cooking is distinctly Umbrian, using oil and wine from the adjacent family farm as well as fresh trout and shellfish. Dr Valentino Petrangeli is a wine enthusiast, always keen to share his knowledge of Orvieto and its wines with interested guests.

Nearby cathedral at Orvieto; Todi (40 km); Lake Bolsena.

Via dei Tigli 69, 05019 Orvieto
Tel (0763) 92982 **Fax** 90677
Location set in its own 5-acre park, about 2 km from Florence- Rome motorway; with private car parking
Food & drink breakfast, lunch, dinner
Prices rooms L110,000-L190,000
Rooms 8 double, one single, all with bath (one with jacuzzi); all have central heating, TV, phone, minibar

Facilities dining-room, sitting-room, bar, conference room
Credit cards AE, DC, MC, V
Children accepted
Disabled no special facilities
Pets not encouraged
Closed mid-Jan to mid-Feb; restaurant only, Mon
Proprietor Dr Valentino Petrangeli

Umbria and Marche

Medieval manor, Ospedalicchio de Bastia

Lo Spedalicchio

Despite the attractions of Assisi, for the touring motorist there is much to be said for staying out of town in an hotel easily accessible by car. This one is the best around: a four-square manor house on the road to Perugia. The ground-floor public rooms have high, vaulted brick ceilings and tiled floors with the occasional rug – whether you approach from the 'back' door as most drivers do or from the 'front' door opening on to the village square, the immediate impression is of centuries of calm living. The restaurant (which enjoys a high local reputation) is on one side – stylishly set out with bentwood chairs and pink napery; in contrast, the sitting-room bar area, which occupies much of the ground floor, is traditionally sparse with exposed stone walls. Bedrooms vary widely – some high-ceilinged, some two-level affairs with sitting space (an attractive possibility, given the poor public sitting area) – but all those we have seen are spacious and inviting. The staff are courteous and helpful; their French is better than their English. Ask for a room away from the church bells, say reporters, most of whom are otherwise content.
Nearby Assisi (10 km); Perugia (10 km); Gubbio, Orvieto, Todi and Spoleto all within reach.

Piazza Bruno Buozzi 3,
Ospedalicchio di Bastia 06080
Perugia
Tel and fax (075) 801 0323
Location between Assisi and Perugia on S147; in garden with ample car parking
Food & drink breakfast, lunch, dinner
Prices rooms L80,000-L110,000; meals from L37,000-L55,000
Rooms 20 double, 2 single, 3 family rooms; all with shower; all rooms have central heating, phone, colour TV
Facilities dining-room, American bar, TV room, conference rooms
Credit cards AE, DC, V
Children welcome; special meals, baby-sitter, small beds on request
Disabled no special facilities
Pets small ones only
Closed never
Manager Sg. G Costarelli

Umbria and Marche

Country villa, Pesaro

Villa Serena

The Adriatic coast south of Rimini is not short of hotels, but it is very short of our kind of hotel, which makes this one a real find – a handsome 17thC mansion with some token castellations, standing in a wooded park high above the hubbub of the coast.

The villa has always belonged to one family – the counts Pinto de Franca y Vergaes, who used it as a summer residence until, in 1950, they turned it into a small hotel to be run like a family home. Renato Pinto does the cooking and serves up some better-than-average dishes; Stefano and Filippo see to guests and reception; while their mother, Signora Laura, busies herself in the house and garden; all are reassuringly down-to-earth.

The emphasis in their house is on character, simplicity and tranquillity, not luxury. There are salons of baronial splendour, antiques and curiosities wherever you go, and corridors delight-fully cluttered with potted plants. A few faded corners reinforce the villa's appealing air of impoverished aristocracy.

No two bedrooms are alike but antiques and fireplaces feature in most. A couple could do with a lick of paint and some trees lopped to let in light, but at these prices, who can complain?
Nearby municipal museum, Ducal Palace at Pesaro.

Via San Nicola 6/3, 61100 Pesaro
Tel (0721) 55211
Location 4 km from Pesaro and beach, in a large wooded park on hillside with private car parking
Food & drink breakfast, lunch, dinner
Prices rooms L95,000-L130,000; meals from L55,000
Rooms 10 double, all with bath or shower; all rooms have central heating, phone

Facilities 4 sitting-rooms, dining-room, bar, terrace; swimming-pool
Credit cards AE **Children** accepted **Disabled** access difficult **Pets** accepted
Closed 1st 2 weeks in Jan
Proprietor Renato Pinto

Umbria and Marche

Seaside hotel, Portonovo

Emilia

Although the Emilia is a seaside hotel, it stands aloof from the beaches south of Ancona, on the flanks of Monte Conero above the little resort of Portonovo (which is a car-journey away for all but the most energetic). It is a modern building of no great architectural merit. But its proprietors some years ago hit on a clever way of giving the hotel a distinctive appeal: they invited artists to come and stay, and to pay their way in kind. The results continue to accumulate on the walls: score upon score of paintings (none, we are assured, has ever been sold). Among the Italian signatures, our inspector spotted the artist Graham Sutherland's.

Even without the extraordinary wall-covering, the hotel would have an attractive air. A long, low sitting-room with clusters of chunky modern armchairs links reception to the large, light, simply furnished dining-room, which has big windows looking on to a passable imitation of a *prato inglese* (a lawn). Bedrooms are thoroughly modern and snazzy. Most are in the older part of the hotel, ranged at an angle so as to give each room a sea-view and a small balcony. Food is taken seriously, although it no longer earns a Michelin star. Fish dominates the menu, and is competently cooked, though expensive.

Nearby church of Santa Maria (at Portonovo), Monte Conero; Ancona (12 km).

Via Poggio, 149/A Portonovo, Ancona 60020
Tel (071) 801145 **Fax** 801330
Location 2 km W of Portonovo on cliffs; ample private car parking
Food & drink breakfast, lunch, dinner
Prices rooms L100,000-L220,000
Rooms 23 double, 2 with bath, 21 with shower; 2 single, both with shower; 5 family rooms, one with bath, 4 with shower; all rooms have central heating, phone, colour TV, minibar
Facilities dining-room, TV room, conference room, bar, gazebo-bar; swimming-pool, tennis
Credit cards AE, DC, MC, V
Children accepted
Disabled some ground-floor rooms
Pets not accepted
Closed Nov to Mar
Proprietor Lamberto Fiorini

Umbria and Marche

Le Tre Vaselle

On paper, the Tre Vaselle sounds disturbingly impersonal – it has more than 50 bedrooms and several conference rooms. But the hotel is entirely without ostentation, its modest entrance on a narrow street scarcely detectable, and the conference areas have now been made entirely separate. Friendly and courteous staff make you feel instantly at home, while the maze of ground-floor sitting-rooms – with its massive arches, white walls, rustic beams, terracotta floors, shabby but colourful armchairs and sofas, card-table and stone fireplaces – is immediately captivating.

Bedrooms, some in a more modern building behind the main one and others in a new luxury annexe a short walk away, are smart and civilized. There are two pleasant dining-rooms but in warm weather the best place to eat is in the newly equipped outdoor courtyard. The food at the Tre Vaselle is excellent, and well complemented by the wines for which the owner, Dr Lunga-rotti, has made Torgiano well known (don't miss the fascinating wine museum a street away from the hotel). This is the sort of place which the touring visitor hesitates to leave, knowing for sure that the next night's hotel will be inferior.

Nearby Perugia; Assisi (25 km).

Via Garibaldi 48, Torgiano 06089 Perugia
Tel (075) 988 0447 **Fax** 0214
Location in side street of village, 12 km SE of Perugia; ample car parking nearby
Food & drink breakfast, lunch, dinner
Prices rooms L150,000-L280,000
Rooms 52 double, 2 singles, 7 suites, most with bath, others with shower; all rooms have central heating, air-conditioning, phone, minibar
Facilities sitting-rooms, dining-rooms, card and TV rooms, breakfast room, bar, conference rooms
Credit cards AE, DC, MC, V
Children accepted
Disabled access possible – lift/elevator to bedrooms
Pets not accepted
Closed never
Manager Romano Sartore

Umbria and Marche

Village hotel, Aquaviva Picena

Hotel O'Viv

A beautifully restored medieval *palazzo* in a hilltop village a little way inland from the Adriatic, opened as a hotel in 1976, and since 1984 in the hands of an Anglo-Italian couple who have made a great success of it. Simple dining-room, grand bedrooms, panoramic terrace for summer dining.

■ Via Marziale 43, 63030 Aquaviva Picena (Ascoli Piceno) **Tel** (0735) 764649 **Fax** (0735) 83697 **Meals** breakfast, lunch, dinner **Prices** rooms L80,000; meals L31,500 **Rooms** 12, all with bath, central heating, phone, TV **Credit cards** AE, MC, V **Closed** 3 weeks in Oct

---

Country hotel, Assisi

Castel San Gregorio

An eccentric place, occupying a small-scale castle-style building in an elevated position a few miles from Assisi. Decoration falls somewhere between Scottish baronial and chateau kitsch. Some interesting bedrooms. You eat communally at one enormous table.

■ San Gregorio, 06081 Assisi (Perugia) **Tel** (075) 8038009 **Fax** (075) 8038904 **Meals** breakfast, lunch, dinner **Prices** DB&B L90,000 **Rooms** 12, all with bath or shower, central heating, phone **Credit cards** AE, DC, MC, V **Closed** late Jan

---

Country guest-house, Assisi

Country House

An unassuming guest-house amid fields and orchards a short distance from the western gates of Assisi. Silvana Ciammarughi runs an antiques business on the ground floor, and furnishes the guest rooms from her stock. She strikes some visitors as jolly, others as unfriendly; more reports welcome.

■ San Pietro Campagna 178, 06081 Assisi (Perugia) **Tel** (075) 816363 **Fax** (075) 816363 **Meals** breakfast **Prices** rooms L75,000-L110,000 **Rooms** 15, all with bath, central heating **Credit cards** AE, V **Closed** never

---

Town hotel, Assisi

Hotel Fontebella

An immaculately kept hotel in an old *palazzo* on one of the well-worn routes from the central piazza to the basilica, with some late-night noise affecting front rooms. Some other rooms are said to be very small, but reporters speak well of the proprietors.

■ Via Fontebella 25, 06081 Assisi (Perugia) **Tel** (075) 812883 **Fax** (075) 812941 **Meals** breakfast, lunch, dinner **Prices** rooms L103,500-L236,000 with breakfast; suite L262,500-L350,000; DB&B L113,000-L156,000; FB L127,500-L180,000 **Rooms** 38, all with bath or shower, central heating, phone, TV **Credit cards** AE, DC, MC, V **Closed** never

Umbria and Marche

Town hotel, Assisi

Hotel dei Priori

A well-run hotel in the heart of Assisi, close to all the tourist sights and housed in an historic *palazzo*. Tastefully and comfortably furnished bedrooms, polished sitting-room and gracious, arched dining-room – don't be put off by the modernized lobby and bar.

■ Corso Mazzini 15, 06081 Assisi (Perugia) **Tel** (075) 812237 **Fax** (075) 816804 **Meals** breakfast, lunch, dinner **Prices** rooms L87,000-L159,000; lunch/dinner L38,000-L35,000 **Rooms** 34, all with bath or shower, central heating, phone; most with bath or shower **Credit cards** AE, DC, MC, V **Closed** mid-Nov to mid-Mar

Converted mill, Campello sul Clitunno

Il Vecchio Molino

An ancient mill set on an island in the middle of the river Clitunno, overlooked by and even more ancient (Roman) temple – of which the garden and terrace give a good view. Restrained decoration and harmonious furnishings in the spacious bedrooms.

■ Via del Tempio 34, Localita Pissignano, 06042 Campello sul Clitunno (Perugia) **Tel** (0743) 521122 **Fax** (0743) 275097 **Meals** breakfast **Prices** rooms L135,000-L185,000 **Rooms** 15, all with bath, central heating, phone; most have air-conditioning **Credit cards** AE, DC, MC, V **Closed** Nov to Mar

Converted castle, Deruta

Nel Castello

High above Deruta (famous for its ceramics) is the walled village of Castelleone, and higher still is this neatly crenellated castle, apparently of 11thC origin. Prettily furnished rooms above a stone-walled dining-room. Good views from the shady garden.

■ Castelleone, 06053 Deruta (Perugia) **Tel** (075) 971 1302 **Meals** breakfast, lunch, dinner **Prices** DB&B L127,000 **Rooms** 10, all with bath or shower, phone; some rooms have TV, minibar **Credit cards** AE, DC, V **Closed** Nov to Mar

Town villa, Folignano

Villa Pigna

Business-style hotel – breakfast means pastries and coffee from the bar, taken standing up at peak times – and the bedrooms lack character. But the ground-floor sitting-rooms are exceptionally welcoming and satisfactory food is served in the modern dining-room.

■ Viale Assisi 33, 63040 Folignano (Ascoli Piceno) **Tel** (0736) 491868 **Meals** breakfast, lunch, dinner **Prices** rooms L121,000-L193,000; suites L209,000; meals about L44,000 **Rooms** 52, all with phone, TV, minibar, balcony **Credit cards** AE, DC, V **Closed** restaurant only, 20 July to 23 Aug

Umbria and Marche

Restaurant-with-rooms, Foligno

Villa Roncalli

Foligno may not be much to write home about, but this smart little restaurant with rooms certainly is. Fine regional cooking, imaginatively prepared and using only the best quality local ingredients, is served in the light vaulted dining-room.

■ Via Roma 25, 06034 Foligno (Perugia) **Tel** (0742) 391091 **Meals** breakfast, lunch, dinner **Prices** rooms L70,000-L110,000; DB&B L120,000 **Rooms** 10, all with bath or shower, TV, phone **Credit cards** AE, DC, V **Closed** 2 weeks Aug; restaurant only, Mon

---

Town hotel, Gubbio

Hotel Bosone

The best place to stay to savour the atmosphere of historic Gubbio: the Bosone occupies a *palazzo* as old as some of the sights you have come to see. Two of the bedrooms are remarkably grand, with flamboyant decoration; the rest relatively ordinary. The Taverna del Lupo, where main meals are taken, is jolly.

■ Via XX Settembre 22, 06024 Gubbio (Perugia) **Tel** (075) 927 2008 **Fax** (075) 927 1269 **Meals** breakfast, lunch, dinner; meals taken in nearby Taverna del Lupo **Prices** rooms L90,000-L150,000; DB&B L71,000 **Rooms** 30, all with bath, phone **Credit cards** AE, DC, MC, V **Closed** Jan or Feb

---

Converted fortress, Monte Vibiano

Castello di Monte Vibiano

Despite its size, this hilltop castle, rebuilt in the 17thC, takes only 12 guests – so there is no risk of tripping over one another in the vaulted public rooms of the house or on the immaculate lawns outside. It is run on house-party lines; all drinks are included in the price.

■ Mercatello, 06050 Monte Vibiano (Perugia) **Tel** Florence booking office (055) 218112 **Fax** (055) 287157 **Meals** breakfast, lunch, dinner **Prices** DB&B L230,000; FB L260,000; single room supplement L40,000 **Rooms** 6, all with bath, central heating, air-conditioning, phone **Credit cards** not accepted **Closed** Oct to Jun

---

Country villa, Montecassiano

Villa Quiete

A substantial house of mixed merits: dreary sitting- rooms, smart café-style dining-room, bedrooms varying from ordinary to grand with antiques. Its key asset is the moderate-sized garden with its pines, palms and geraniums.

■ Vallecascia di Montecassiano, 62010 Montecassiano (Macerata) **Tel** (0733) 599559 **Meals** breakfast, lunch, dinner **Prices** rooms L75,000-L110,000 **Rooms** 38, all with central heating, phone, TV **Credit cards** AE, DC, V **Closed** never

Umbria and Marche

Town hotel, Orvieto

Virgilio

An engagingly shabby-looking building whose prime virtue is its position right at the heart of things. Inside, sadly, it has been left shiny but soulless by modernization, but it is comfortable and prices are modest.

■ Piazza del Duomo 5/6, 05018 Orvieto (Terni) **Tel** (0763) 41882
Meals breakfast **Prices** rooms L100,000-L140,000 **Rooms** 16, all with bath or shower, phone **Credit cards** not accepted **Closed** 20 days Jan-Feb

Town hotel, Perugia

Hotel Brufani

Calm and polished hotel with a splendid location atop one of the cliffs that define central Perugia, and at one end of the *corso*. Public areas particularly attractive, with a spacious central lobby and a glossy American bar.

■ Piazza Italia 12, 06100 Perugia **Tel** (075) 62541 **Fax** (075) 20210
Meals breakfast, lunch, dinner **Prices** rooms L150,000-L320,000; breakfast 16,800; suites L280,000-L500,000 **Rooms** 25, all with bath, central heating, phone, TV, hairdrier, minibar **Credit cards** AE, DC, MC, V **Closed** never

Town hotel, Perugia

Locanda della Posta

Perugia's oldest hotel, opened over 200 years ago, is now one of its most attractive, following a thorough renovation a couple of years ago. Bedrooms are smart and comfortable, public areas limited but elegant – and just outside the door is Perugia's famous pedestrian *corso*.

■ Corso Vannucci 97, 06100 Perugia **Tel** (075) 61345 **Fax** (075) 61345
Meals breakfast **Prices** rooms L150,000-L295,000, suite L300,000-L425,000 **Rooms** 40, all with bath, central heating, air-conditioning, phone, hairdrier, TV, minibar **Credit cards** AE, DC, MC, V **Closed** never

Seaside hotel, Portonovo

Fortino Napoleonico

An extremely unusual hotel, built within a single-storey seaside fortress, apparently dating (as the name suggests) from the early 19thC. The whole place is simple, clean and roomy, and suits families very well – many of the rooms (contained within the ramparts) can accommodate three or four.

■ 60020 Portonovo (Ancona) **Tel** (071) 801124 **Fax** (071) 801314
Meals breakfast, lunch, dinner **Prices** rooms L160,500; suites L267,500 **Rooms** 30, all with bath or shower, central heating, phone **Credit cards** AE, DC, MC, V **Closed** never

Umbria and Marche

Town hotel, Santa Vittoria in Matenano

Farfense

A friendly, simple, family-run hotel in a backwater hilltop town, surrounded by pretty and distinctive countryside with a patch-work of tiny fields. Spotless bedrooms (some with views) and a jolly little restaurant down in the brick-vaulted cellars.

■ Corso Matteoti 41, 63028 Santa Vittoria in Matenano (Ascoli Piceno) **Tel** (0734) 780171 **Meals** breakfast, lunch, dinner **Prices** rooms L38,000-L60,000; FB L65,000; meals L25,000 **Rooms** 10, all with bath or shower, central heating; 4 have balconies **Credit cards** AE, DC, MC, V **Closed** 2 weeks end Sep/early Oct; restaurant only, Mon

---

Converted monastery, Sirolo

Monteconero

Yet another religious house in a prime position – on the very summit of Monte Conero, 500 metres above the Adriatic, with superb views along the coast from the bar terrace. Bedrooms are simple, modern, adequate. There is an atmospheric little stone-vaulted restaurant on the lower floor.

■ Monte Conero, 60020 Sirolo (Ancona) **Tel** (071) 9330592 **Fax** (071) 9330365 **Meals** breakfast, lunch, dinner **Prices** rooms L80,000-L130,000 **Rooms** 47, all with shower, phone **Credit cards** AE, DC, MC, V **Closed** Nov to Easter

---

Converted mill, Spello

La Bastiglia

A comfortable recommendation for this picturesque little medie-val town – a smartly restored old mill-house, with its ancient character preserved, and panoramic views from practically all its rooms; 7 of them are suites with private garden-terraces.

■ Piazza Vallegloria, 06038 Spello (Perugia) **Tel** (0742) 651277 **Fax** (0742) 651277 **Meals** breakfast, lunch, dinner **Prices** rooms L75,000-L95,000; suites L130,000; DB&B L85,000-L105,000 **Rooms** 26, all with bath, air-conditioning, minibar, TV, phone **Credit cards** AE, DC, MC, V **Closed** restaurant only, mid-Jan to Feb

---

Town hotel, Spoleto

Hotel Gattapone

This smart little hotel is named after the architect of Spoleto's impressively high 14thC Bridge of Towers, of which guests get a grandstand view. The rooms are spacious and stylish, the position peaceful as well as panoramic.

■ Via del Ponte 6, 06049 Spoleto (Perugia) **Tel** (0743) 223447 **Fax** (0743) 223448 **Meals** breakfast **Prices** rooms L180,000-L260,000 with breakfast **Rooms** 13, all with bath or shower, minibar, TV **Credit cards** AE, DC, MC, V **Closed** never

Umbria and Marche

Country hotel, Todi

Hotel Bramante

Not the last word in character, but a pleasant stopover in an ideal position, just outside Todi and in the shadow of Bramante's church of Santa Maria. At the core of the hotel is an old stone house; the modern furnishings are restrained and comfortable.

■ Via Orvietana 46, 06059 Todi (Perugia) **Tel** (075) 894 8381 **Fax** (075) 894 8074 **Meals** breakfast, lunch, dinner **Prices** rooms L140,000-L190,000 with breakfast; FB L160,000-L190,000 **Rooms** 45, all with bath, phone, air-conditioning, TV; some rooms have minibar **Credit cards** AE, DC, MC, V **Closed** never

---

Converted monastery, Todi

Convento San Valentino

An extraordinary little hillside hotel, with some exceptional original features – one of the several sitting-rooms still feels like the church it once was. Bedrooms vary widely in shape and size, but all have abundant character and comfort. The suites are splendid. Get directions, and a map.

■ Fiore di Todi, 06059 Todi (Perugia) **Tel** (075) 894 4103 **Fax** (075) 894 8696 **Meals** breakfast, lunch, dinner **Prices** rooms L380,000 with breakfast; suites L460,000 **Rooms** 12, all with bath or shower, central heating, minibar, TV, phone, hairdrier **Credit cards** DC, MC, V **Closed** never

Lazio and Abruzzi

Hotels in Lazio and Abruzzi

Rome is a city of grand hotels rather than small and charming ones. Among the hotels we have looked at but not given an entry to are two simple but adequately comfortable places in the peaceful residential area of Aventino – the Domus Maximi (Tel (06) 578 2565) and the Sant'Anselmo (Tel (06) 574 3547, fax 578 3604). Other possibilities include the Cesari (Tel (06) 679 2386, fax 0882, 50 rooms, old-fashioned but comfortable). At the top end of the market (and of the Spanish Steps) is the luxurious 50-room Lord Byron (Tel (06) 322 0404, fax 0405) – certainly less impersonal than most smart Rome hotels, but still impressively ritzy and correspondingly expensive.

A few miles outside Rome is the Villa Fiorio at Grottaferrata (Tel (06) 945 92767, fax 941 3482), dropped from the guide a couple of years ago following a negative report, but still highly rated by some of our competitors. Reports welcome.

Palestrina (birthplace of the 16thC composer) and Tivoli (villas of Emperor Hadrian and the 16thC Cardinal d'Este) are within day-trip range of Rome, but if you want to stay overnight in Palestrina, go for the Stella – modern, excellent restaurant, clean spacious bedrooms (Tel (06) 955 8172, fax 957 3360). North of the capital is the pretty wooded countryside around Viterbo and Lago di Vico. The Rio Vicano (Tel (0761) 612339, fax 612338) is a modern 42-room hotel in a picturesque setting near the clifftop medieval village of Ronciglione and recommended for comfort, welcome and food. An average town hotel in the heart of Viterbo is the Leon d'Oro (Tel and fax (0761) 344444).

The Abruzzi is a wild and wooded mountainous region, forming part of the Apennine mountains. Charming small hotels are hard to find and you might do best to explore the area from a base nearer Rome. We do have a couple of short-entry recommendations though – at Balsorano (page 177) and Scanno (page 180), and another Scanno hotel worth considering is the Del Lago (Tel (0864) 71343), in a lakeside setting 3 km outside the town.

L'Aquila, the capital of the region, is a big town further north but still in the heart of the mountains. Though mainly a business centre today, the surrounding mountains and the imposing historical buildings within the town itself still make it an interesting place to stay. Try the Grand Hotel del Parco (Tel (0862) 413248, fax 65938, 36 rooms), smaller and less business-oriented than most of the hotels in the town.

This page acts as an introduction to the features and hotels of Lazio and Abruzzi, and gives brief recommendations of reasonable hotels that for one reason or another have not made a full entry. The long entries for this region – covering the hotels we are most enthusiastic about – start on the next page. But do not neglect the shorter entries starting on page 177: these are all hotels that we would happily stay at.

Lazio and Abruzzi

Town hotel, Rome

Hotel Carriage

This smart little hotel stands in one of the narrow streets near the Piazza di Spagna, renowned for their elegant boutiques dealing in impossibly-priced clothes. The Carriage matches the designer style of its surroundings, though its prices for this part of Rome are not at all unreasonable.

The reception area of fat-cushioned, expensive-looking sofas and chairs in gold and blue stripes, the pretty breakfast room of black bentwood and rattan and twirly gilt, the cool flower arrangements – all seem to await only the photographer and slinky models. Upstairs, bedrooms are less florid in blue and white, with fine, solid reproduction French-look furnishings. Bathrooms are clean and streamlined, with spotlit mirrors and all the usual trimmings.

At the top of the hotel there is a small roof terrace, slightly less orderly than the rest of the hotel, but allowing a breath of air along with your summer breakfast. From what we saw, breakfast is of above-average standard, with a range of hot and cold items. Reception was manned by a pleasantly professional English-speaker when we visited.

Nearby Piazza di Spagna, Via del Corso.

Via della Carrozze 36, 00187 Rome
Tel (06) 699 0124
Fax (06) 678 8279
Location between Via del Corso and Piazza di Spagna
Food & drink breakfast
Prices rooms L185,000-L235,000 with breakfast
Rooms 17 double, all with bath and shower, 3 single, all with shower, 2 suites; all rooms have central heating, air-conditioning, phone, hairdrier, TV, radio, minibar
Facilities breakfast room, seating in reception
Credit cards AE, DC, MC, V
Children accepted
Disabled no special facilities
Pets not accepted
Closed never

Lazio and Abruzzi

Town hotel, Rome

Hotel Condotti

Recently taken over and totally refurbished by new owners, this formerly modest hotel in a quiet side-street has been considerably improved without becoming too stiffly posed for comfort – and without losing its traditional shuttered façade.

The glossy little reception area is the only place to lounge, offering several squashy sofas liberally heaped with cushions. Downstairs in the basement is a limited but civilized little breakfast room decorated with displays of porcelain and neutral damask wallcoverings.

Bedrooms are reassuringly harmonious but modern, without a great deal of personality; unusually for a hotel of this category, there are no hairdriers in bathrooms. One or two have pleasant, spacious terraces – understandably in great demand among regular visitors.

Breakfast is more than minimal, with cheese and other extras. On the occasion of our inspection, the receptionist was a highly professional American, and the hotel seemed to be doing a thriving transatlantic trade. The location is excellent for exploring the posh little shops off the Corso.

Nearby Spanish Steps, Via del Corso.

Via Mario De'Fiori 37, 00187 Rome
Tel (06) 679 4661
Fax (06) 679 0457
Location between Via del Corso and Piazza di Spagna
Food & drink breakfast
Prices rooms L170,000-L220,000; suites L250,000-L280,000 with breakfast
Rooms 17 double, 12 with bath, 5 with shower; all rooms have central heating, air-conditioning, phone, TV, minibar
Facilities reception, breakfast room
Credit cards AE, MC, V
Children accepted
Disabled lift/elevator
Pets not accepted
Closed never
Manager Sig Massimo Funaro

Lazio and Abruzzi

Town hotel, Rome

La Residenza

The Via Vittorio Veneto is one of Rome's most fashionable addresses, and the location of some of its grandest hotels. The Residenza is not one of them, but its position only a block away from this sweeping tree-lined avenue gives it a head start.

The Residenza is part of the small Giannetti chain of hotels, concentrated in dreary Lido di Jesolo – not a good sign. But Signor d'Arezzo does a sound job as manager and the front desk staff are friendly and helpful.

Another key aspect of the hotel's appeal is its bar and sitting areas on the elevated ground floor, which are comfortable and welcoming, with a mixture of modern and antique furniture. A better-than-average help-yourself breakfast is served in a more ordinary, windowless room at the back of the hotel, with bright red café-style chairs. Bedrooms are comfortable and well equipped, but uniformly furnished with no great flair or character. Those at the back are quieter than those at the front, which despite their double glazing suffer from noise from a nearby nightclub. Some have fair-sized terraces, and there is also a communal roof-top terrace with interesting views.

Nearby Spanish Steps, Villa Borghese.

Via Emilia 22, Rome 00187
Tel (06) 488 0789 **Fax** 485721
Location in side-street off Via Veneto; limited car parking
Food & drink breakfast
Prices rooms L120,000-L260,000
Rooms 24 double, all with bath; 3 single, all with shower; all rooms have central heating, minibar, satellite TV, air-conditioning, hairdrier, phone
Facilities sitting-rooms, bar, breakfast room, patio, terrace
Credit cards not accepted
Children accepted
Disabled access difficult
Pets not accepted
Closed never
Manager Adriano d'Arezzo

Lazio and Abruzzi

Town guest-house, Rome

Scalinata di Spagna

The Spanish Steps are a favourite spot for visitors to Rome to sit around soaking up the atmosphere and the afternoon sun, and at the top of them are two hotels – the Hassler (where rooms typically cost L500,000) and, facing it across the piazza, this highly individual little *pensione* (now elevated to 3-star status).

The idiosyncratic character of the place is obvious as soon as you walk in the door, when you come face to face with Cacao, the resident parrot. Beyond the tiny reception area, a corridor dotted with antiques and paintings leads to old-fashioned bedrooms of varying size with bathrooms which by Italian standards are rather plain. For eight months of the year breakfast is served on the roof-top terrace, from which many of the famous sights of Rome can be spotted across the neighbouring roofs; but a recent visitor was worried by pigeons invading vacated tables. At other times, a tiny room off reception is brought into play.

Signor Bellia is charming and helpful. His prices are no longer low, yet demand for rooms continues to exceed supply. The rational response is to raise prices further; we hope the temptation can be resisted. Book early.

Nearby Spanish Steps, Villa Borghese, Via Veneto.

Piazza Trinita dei Monti 17, Rome 00187
Tel (06) 679 3006
Fax 684 0598
Location at the top of the Spanish Steps; car parking 50 m away
Food & drink breakfast
Prices rooms L200,000-L300,000 with breakfast
Rooms 15 double, all with bath or shower; all rooms have central heating, minibar, radio, phone, air-conditioning, safe; TV on request
Facilities breakfast room, roof garden
Credit cards AE, MC, V
Children accepted
Disabled no special facilities
Pets accepted
Closed never
Proprietor Giuseppe Bellia

Lazio and Abruzzi

Town hotel, Rome

Sole al Pantheon

Complete refurbishment in 1988 has at last given this ancient *albergo* the decoration and atmosphere which does justice to its privileged position – to one side of the square in front of the famous Pantheon, one of Rome's few perfectly preserved ancient Roman buildings. The Sole is now unquestionably one of Rome's most delightful small hotels; unfortunately for prospective guests, it is now also one of the most expensive.

Bedrooms – each named after some famous visiting worthy – feature fascinating coffered and painted ceilings, and are gorgeously furnished in imaginative and elegant styles. Each is different and distinctive, though all have restful colour schemes, fabric-framed mirrors, and fine antiques. Many have interesting views. Public areas are equally pleasant: a salon of white leather seating on terracotta-tiled floors straight from the pages of some glossy magazine, and a small, cosy bar downstairs. Breakfast is served either on an upper courtyard terrace, or in a pleasant little room leading off it. Italianate corners throughout the hotel are thoughtfully filled with plants, urns, statuary or dribbling fountains.

Nearby Pantheon, Villa Borghese.

Piazza della Rotonda 63,
00186 Roma
Tel (06) 678 0441
Fax (06) 684 0689
Location in piazza in front of the Pantheon
Food & drink breakfast
Prices rooms L250,000-L380,000; suites L450,000
Rooms 22 double, 3 single, all with bath; all rooms have central heating, air-conditioning, phone, TV, hairdrier, radio, minibar

Facilities breakfast room, bar
Credit cards AE, DC, MC, V
Children accepted
Disabled lift/elevator
Pets not accepted
Closed never
Proprietor A Giraudini

Lazio and Abruzzi

Town hotel, Rome

Valadier

The Valadier began its metamorphosis from gracious decay into its present slick form – something like the innards of a millionaire's yacht (or our image of one) – a year or two back. The refit continues with the recent construction of an elegantly intimate restaurant, adding to an already generous assortment of smallish but very smart public rooms. Marble, mirror-glass, and highly polished wood face every surface.

The cabin-like bedrooms are what really bring the yacht image to mind. Not only are they very cleverly fitted out to make the most of their compact dimensions, but also they bristle with electronic gadgetry. Bewildering consoles of instruments await the visitor by the bedside, so that switching a light on in the middle of the night can be a baffling process of trial and error. You can even check your bill on the TV screen in your room. The ritzy gin-palace feel is reinforced by the obedient hum of the air-conditioning system, like the purr of the engine room.

Charming? Well, no. But distinctive and exceptionally comfortable – and well run by a pleasant staff. A good location, too, close to the heart of things.

Nearby Spanish Steps, Villa Borghese.

Via della Fontanella 15, Rome 00187
Tel (06) 361 0559
Fax 320 1558
Location off Via del Corso, close to Piazza del Popolo; garage 100 m away
Food & drink breakfast, lunch, dinner
Prices rooms L230,000-L330,000; suites up to L510,000; meals about L50,000
Rooms 24 double, 12 single, 3 suites, all with bath and shower; all rooms have central heating, phone, minibar, TV, piped music, air-conditioning, electronic safe, hairdrier
Facilities piano/American bar, dining-room, sitting-room, conference rooms; solarium
Credit cards AE, DC, MC
Children welcome
Disabled entrance difficult, but 2 lifts/elevators
Pets small ones only
Closed never **Proprietor** Simonetta Battistini

Lazio and Abruzzi

Town villa, Rome

Villa Florence

On the broad Via Nomentana to the north-east of the middle of Rome, this well-run hotel has particular attractions for motorists reluctant to tangle with the worst of Rome's traffic (in addition to a convenient location, it has private parking in the garden behind the house).

The villa's other chief merit is the welcoming ambience of its public areas. Great efforts have been made to give the little sitting area (off reception) and the adjacent café-style breakfast room some interest and warmth. Dotted around all the public areas are interesting archaeological fragments which have been discovered on the site of the hotel.

There is a small, secluded terrace behind the house, with sun-beds as well as tables and chairs; smart white parasols provide shade. The bedrooms (some of them in outbuildings, with doors opening on to the garden) are simple and functional but comfortable.

The cheerful proprietor makes an effort to see that breakfast is more than usually satisfying, with yoghurt, cheese and ham as well as the standard fare.

Nearby Villa Borghese.

Via Nomentana 28, Rome
00161 (Porta Pia)
Tel (06) 440 3036
Fax (06) 440 2709
Location about one km NE of Via Veneto, with private car parking in garden
Food & drink breakfast
Prices rooms L150,000-L200,000; 30% reduction for children sharing parents' room
Rooms 32 double, one single, 4 family rooms, all with bath or shower; all rooms have colour TV, minibar, air-conditioning, phone, hairdrier
Facilities breakfast room, TV room, bar
Credit cards AE, DC
Children accepted
Disabled no special facilities
Pets not accepted
Closed never
Proprietor Tullio Cappelli

Lazio and Abruzzi

Villa del Parco

This mellow, early-20thC villa is about a 15-minute bus ride from the middle of Rome, but its peaceful setting – on a tree-lined street in a pleasant residential area with parks and gardens nearby – more than makes up for this. The villa is set back from the road, partly shielded from traffic by walled gardens to either side.

Inside, all is elegant and tranquil. From the welcoming reception lobby, steps lead down to a light and classily furnished two-part sitting-room, with a breakfast room at the far end. The ambience is both restful and tasteful: pale blue sofas, antiques, plants, a chessboard, and a mass of nicely framed pictures (*fin-de-siècle* theatrical memorabilia and sepia photographs of old Paris).

Bedrooms vary in size; some are quite small, others larger, with a touch of elegance. But all are well-furnished in quiet, restrained styles, with plain, softly textured wallcoverings and good modern fittings in bathrooms. On sunny days the little garden comes into its own, and tables are set for alfresco breakfasts beneath parasols.

Nearby Villa Torlonia, Villa Borghese

Via Nomentana, 110,
Roma 00161
Tel (06) 864115
Fax (06) 854 0410
Location in residential area, NE of the middle of the city; with gardens and car parking
Food & drink breakfast, snacks
Prices L127,000-L200,000
Rooms 12 double, 12 single, all with bath or shower; all rooms have central heating, air-conditioning, phone, TV, radio, minibar

Facilities 2 sitting-rooms, breakfast room, small bar
Credit cards AE, DC, V
Children accepted
Disabled no special facilities
Pets accepted
Closed never
Proprietor Elisabetta Bernardini

Lazio and Abruzzi

Seaside hotel, San Felice Circeo

Punta Rossa

San Felice is an amiable village at the foot of the 550-metre Monte Circeo, which is an isolated lump of rock at the seaward point of a flat area, once marshland but now drained except for zones which have been declared a national park to preserve the flora and fauna. The Punta Rossa lies around the mountain in a secluded setting above an exposed and rocky shore.

The hotel has the form of a miniature village. Reception is in a lodge just inside an arched gateway, and beyond that is a little piazza enclosed by white-walled buildings in rough Mediterranean style. Bedrooms are spread around in low buildings at or near the top of a garden beyond the piazza which descends steeply to the sea. They are pleasant, varying in size, many with colour schemes which look a bit dated; all have balconies with sea views. The main attraction of the suites is their admirable size. The restaurant is part-way down the garden (already bursting with colour when we visited in spring) towards the sea and pool, with views from its terraces.

Nearby Terracina (20 km); Circeo national park.

San Felice Circeo 04017 Latina
Tel (0773) 528085 **Fax** 528075
Location 4 km W of San Felice, isolated on rocky shore; in gardens, with ample car parking
Food & drink breakfast, lunch, dinner
Prices rooms L.220,000-L320,000 with breakfast; suites L420,000-L520,000
Rooms 27 double, 6 single, 7 suites; all with bath or shower; all rooms have phone, minibar, colour TV; all double rooms have sea-view balcony or terrace, air-conditioning
Facilities bar, dining-room, terrace, courtyard; outdoor swimming-pool, small beach
Credit cards AE, DC, V
Children welcome
Disabled access difficult
Pets small dogs accepted by arrangement
Closed never
Manager Maria Fiorella Battaglia

Lazio and Abruzzi

Converted fortress, Balsorano

Castello di Balsorano

After a period of closure, this fine-looking hilltop fortress has apparently re-opened in new ownership. As far as we know, the authentically medieval interior remains, with weapons and wall-hangings all around, and ornate antique beds. Reports on the new regime would be very welcome.

■ Piazza Piccolomini, 67025 Balsorano (L'Aquila) **Tel** (0863) 951236 **Meals** breakfast, lunch, dinner **Prices** rooms L120,000; suites L150,000 **Rooms** 6, all with bath, central heating **Credit cards** not accepted **Closed** Nov

Converted castle, Formia

Castello Miramare

This 19thC 'castle' (converted in the 1970s) stands high above Formia, with tremendous views of the vast, sweeping bay of Gaeta. Rooms are neatly furnished in Spanish style. In summer, drinks and breakfast can be enjoyed on the little garden terraces.

■ Balze di Pagnano, 04023 Formia (Latina) **Tel** (0771) 700138 **Fax** (0771) 700139 **Meals** breakfast, lunch, dinner **Prices** rooms L90,000-L180,000; meals about L65,000, breakfast L1600 **Rooms** 10, all with bath or shower, minibar, TV, hairdrier, air-conditioning **Credit cards** AE, DC, MC, V **Closed** Nov

Country villa, Palo Laziale

La Posta Vecchia

Start with the prices; count the noughts before you entertain thoughts of booking. This is the most expensive hotel in these pages, by quite a margin. It was restored and furnished by the late Paul Getty, and is as luxurious and tasteful as you would hope, but without formality. Close to perfection.

■ 00055 Palo Laziale (Rome) **Tel** (06) 994 9501 **Fax** (06) 994 9507 **Meals** breakfast, lunch, dinner **Prices** rooms and suites L1,200,000-L2,000,000 **Rooms** 12, all with bath or shower, phone, TV, air-conditioning **Credit cards** AE, DC, MC, V **Closed** never

Cottage complex, Poggio Catino

Borgo Paraelios

A reader recommends this immaculately executed rustic-style development in the hills half-way between Rome and Rieti. It is almost entirely single-storey, the individually furnished rooms and suites spread around grassy gardens and flowery courtyards. Smart little pool. You'll need detailed directions.

■ Localita Valle Collichia, 02040 Poggio Catino (Rieti) **Tel** (0765) 26267 **Fax** (0765) 26268 **Meals** breakfast, lunch, dinner **Prices** rooms L250,000-L350,000 with breakfast; DB&B L340,000-L530,000, FB L430,000-L660,000 **Rooms** 15, all with bath or shower, central heating, air-conditioning, private patio, phone, TV, hairdrier **Credit cards** AE, V **Closed** never

Lazio and Abruzzi

Town guest-house, Rome

Gregoriana

A courteous welcome and highly distinctive decoration more than compensate for the lack of public spaces in this pleasant, shuttered, 300-year-old house, on a street leading to the Trinita dei Monti church at the top of the Spanish Steps. Some rooms have leafy balconies and quiet rooftop views.

■ Via Gregoriana 18, 00187 Rome **Tel** (06) 679 7988 **Fax** (06) 678 4258 **Meals** breakfast **Prices** rooms L143,000-L218,000 **Rooms** 19, all with bath or shower, central heating, air-conditioning, TV, phone **Credit cards** not accepted **Closed** never

---

Town hotel, Rome

Internazionale

The interconnected dining- and sitting-rooms on the third floor display the venerable pedigree of this former convent most clearly; elsewhere the rooms of this rambling hotel vary greatly in size and style, though all are comfortable – some exceptionally elegant and spacious.

■ Via Sistina 79, 00187 Rome **Tel** (06) 679 3047 **Fax** (06) 678 4764 **Meals** breakfast **Prices** rooms L180,000-L250,000 with breakfast **Rooms** 42, all with bath or shower, central heating, air-conditioning, TV, phone, minibar; most rooms have hairdrier **Credit cards** AE, MC, V **Closed** never

---

Town hotel, Rome

Locarno

Recent improvements should further heighten the attractions of this stylish, wisteria-covered building with fine *fin de siècle* doors, in particular its delightful sheltered terrace where breakfast can be served. In contrast to the slightly dark and dispiriting lounge, the bedrooms are easeful and interestingly furnished.

■ Via della Penna 22, 00186 Rome **Tel** (06) 321 6030 **Fax** (06) 321 5249 **Meals** breakfast **Prices** rooms L138,500-L270,000 with breakfast **Rooms** 38, all with bath, central heating, air-conditioning, phone, TV, minibar hairdrier **Credit cards** AE, DC, MC, V **Closed** never

---

Town hotel, Rome

Hotel Madrid

An elegant entrance of tubbed palms and a glimpse of classical statuary leads to a well-kept lobby and a friendly welcome. Bedrooms are inoffensively modern in style. From the white garden furniture on the roof terrace, guests can overlook the picturesque domes and pantiles of this historic central quarter.

■ Via Mario de Fiori 93-95, 00187 Rome **Tel** (06) 699 1510 **Fax** (06) 679 1653 **Meals** breakfast **Prices** rooms L160,000-L220,000 **Rooms** 24, all with bath or shower, central heating; most have air-conditioning, TV, phone **Credit cards** AE, DC, MC, V **Closed** never

Lazio and Abruzzi

Town hotel, Rome

Margutta

Shabby from the outside, but inside it is spick and span and recently renovated. A dark, functional breakfast room with marble-look tables and modern seating lies behind reception; upstairs, rooms are unexpectedly clean, light and airy, several with pleasing rooftop views of old Rome.

■ Via Laurina 34, 00187 Rome **Tel** (06) 679 8440 **Meals** breakfast **Prices** rooms L105,000 with breakfast **Rooms** 21, all with bath or shower, central heating; most rooms have phone **Credit cards** AE, DC, MC, V **Closed** never

---

Town hotel, Rome

Mozart

An unassuming location on a narrow side-street near the Spanish Steps. Inside, the lobby is a calm expanse of cool, creamy archways and stylish parlour palms. Bedrooms are traditionally furnished but well equipped, with many mod cons.

■ Via dei Greci 23b, 00187 Rome **Tel** (06) 678 7422 **Fax** (06) 678 4271 **Meals** breakfast **Prices** rooms L148,000-L203,000 **Rooms** 31, all with bath or shower, air-conditioning, TV, phone, minibar **Credit cards** AE, DC, MC, V **Closed** never

---

Town guest-house, Rome

Pensione Parlamento

From the entrance up shabby stairs, few would guess that many a well-known politician stays here, conveniently near the parliament building. The rooms are very simple, but the atmosphere is civilized and friendly. Breakfast is served in a pleasant, personally furnished room with a terrace.

■ Via delle Convertite 5, 00187 Rome **Tel** (06) 684 1697 **Meals** breakfast (on request only) **Prices** rooms L59,000-L102,000 **Rooms** 22, all with phone, hairdrier; all double rooms have bath or shower **Credit cards** not accepted **Closed** never

---

Town hotel, Rome

Teatro di Pompeo

This small hotel is tucked away in a little-frequented corner off the Campo di Fiori. The rough-cast barrel vaulting of bar and breakfast room impart more flavour of antiquity than its matching modern furnishings, but the interior is spotless and in excellent condition. Periodically hosts small conferences.

■ Largo del Pallaro 8, 00186 Rome **Tel** (06) 687 2566 **Fax** (06) 654 5531 **Meals** breakfast **Prices** rooms L180,000-L210,000 with breakfast **Rooms** 12, all with bath or shower, air-conditioning, radio, TV, phone, minibar **Credit cards** AE, DC, MC, V **Closed** never

Lazio and Abruzzi

Town hotel, Rome

Portoghesi

Common in Venice or Florence but rare in Rome: a central hotel that is unpretentious, attractively old-fashioned and fairly priced. The delightful Piazza Navona and stunning Pantheon are only yards away. Furnishings are simple, service helpful if not notably warm. Pleasant breakfast room with little terrace.

■ Via dei Portoghesi 1, 00186 Rome **Tel** (05) 686 4231 **Fax** (05) 687 6976 **Meals** breakfast **Prices** rooms L110,000-L180,000 with breakfast **Rooms** 27, all with bath or shower, phone, air-conditioning, TV; most with bath or shower **Credit cards** MC, V **Closed** never

---

Town villa, Rome

Villa delle Rose

This calm old villa near the railway station is energetically managed by its Swiss owner, and steadily being upgraded. It boasts an unexpectedly grand bar-lounge of marbled columns and ceiling frescos, though most bedrooms are more practical than elegant. It has a small, pretty garden.

■ Via Vicenza 5, 00185 Rome **Tel** (06) 445 1788 **Fax** (06) 445 1639 **Meals** breakfast **Prices** rooms L110,000-L177,000 **Rooms** 37, all with bath or shower, central heating, phone, TV **Credit cards** AE, DC, MC, V **Closed** never

---

Mountain chalet, Scanno

Mille Pini

'A very friendly place indeed', says a reader, confirming our recommendation of this simple, neat chalet at the foot of the chairlift up to Monte Rotondo, in the highest part of the Apennine chain. For less energetic tourists, the Lago di Scanno is not far away.

■ Via Pescara 2, 67038 Scanno (L'Aquila) **Tel** (0864) 74387 **Meals** breakfast, lunch, dinner **Prices** rooms L105,000-L135,000 with breakfast; DB&B L110,000; FB L120,000 **Rooms** 21, all with bath, central heating, phone **Credit cards** not accepted **Closed** restaurant only, Tue

Campania

Area introduction

Hotels in Campania

Campania has three components: the frantic city of Naples (where, somewhat to our surprise, we have succeeded in finding one attractive small hotel – the Miramare, page 195); the extremely popular seaside resorts to the south of Naples on the Sorrento peninsula and the islands of Capri and Ischia (where there is a super-abundance of such hotels); and the coast and countryside away from Naples, where we have drawn a complete blank – though you could try the Hermitage, just outside Avellino, a peaceful and comfortable hotel 50 km inland from Naples (Tel (0825) 674788, fax 674772, 30 rooms, swimming-pool).

Ischia is hard work for the seeker of small hotels. Tourism there was originally, and is still, closely linked with the island's thermal springs, and large hotels with spa facilities are the norm – accounting partly for the island's domination by German visitors. One of the most popular excursions is to Sant'Angelo on the south coast – a tiny fishing village on a narrow isthmus. Sant'Angelo would be a pleasant place to stay for longer than an hour or two – indeed, it is at its best before the daily coaches arrive or after they depart – and apart from the San Michele (page 195) it has a couple of other hotels which make acceptable bases. The Miramare (Tel (081) 999219, fax 999325) is almost at sea level on the east side of the village, with a big terrace on the waterside which gets the morning sun. Just behind it up the steep hillside, with views over the rooftops from its little terraces, is La Palma (Tel (081) 999215, fax 999526).

On Capri, in addition to those descibed in more detail on pages 194 and 195, we can recommend the Pazziella (Tel (081) 837 0044, fax 0085), a smart ex-private villa with flowery terraces and gardens, or the luxurious and secluded Punta Tragara (Tel (081) 837 0844, fax 7790), built into rock high above the sea and offering magnificent views of the coast. At the other end of the scale, the simple, family-run Quattro Stagioni (Tel (081) 837 0041, 12 rooms) offers excellent value in an expensive area. Back on the mainland coast, and with excellent views of Capri, is the Delfino (Tel (081) 878 9261, fax 808 9074), peacefully set on an inlet near Massa Lubrense.

Hotels on the Sorrento peninsula are well represented in the pages which follow. It is more difficult to find hotels to recommend further south near Paestum (the site of the best preserved Greek temples on mainland Italy), but one possibility is the Schuhmann (Tel (0828) 851151, fax 851183), a modern, well-equipped hotel with glorious views along the coast.

This page acts as an introduction to the features and hotels of Campania, and gives brief recommendations of reasonable hotels that for one reason or another have not made a full entry. The long entries for this region – covering the hotels we are most enthusiastic about – start on the next page. But do not neglect the shorter entries starting on page 194: these are all hotels that we would happily stay at.

Campania

Converted monastery, Amalfi

Cappuccini Convento

A rickety-seeming elevator from the roadside is your unimpressive introduction to this extraordinary hotel, perched in an apparently impossible position on the cliff face above Amalfi; not surprisingly, one of its great attractions is the superb views of the rugged Amalfi coast, shared by the flowery, creeper-covered terraces and many of the rooms.

But the other merits of this 12thC monastery soon become clear, too. The public areas are light and airy, with a striking sense of space, many original features retained, and antiques lining the wide hallways. The salon/bar has Oriental rugs on tiled floors, with comfortable pink-covered armchairs and sofas, a newly built brick fireplace and a piano adding to the clubby atmosphere. The large dining-room is a delight, with superb vaulting and columns, crisp white tablecloths and bentwood and cane chairs on a tiled floor. The bedrooms are mostly large and charmingly furnished with antiques; most have tiled floors with rugs, and quite a few have both a sea view and a balcony.

The recently restored cloisters are the cool, dignified venue for occasional piano and other recitals.

Nearby Grotta dello Smeraldo (4 km); Ravello (7 km).

Amalfi 84011 Salerno
Tel (089) 871877 **Fax** 871886
Location 300 m from middle of Amalfi, high up on cliffs, reached by lift/elevator up from main road; garden and private car parking at road level
Food & drink breakfast, lunch, dinner
Prices rooms L120,000-L200,000; DB&B L140,000-L180,000
Rooms 46 double, 7 single, all with bath or shower; all rooms have phone
Facilities dining-room, sitting-rooms, bar, solarium, conference facilities; beach
Credit cards AE, DC, V
Children accepted
Disabled no special facilities
Pets accepted
Closed never
Proprietor Alfredo Aielli

Campania

Luna Convento

The middle of Amalfi is crowded and bustling, and the most desirable hotels lie just outside it or well above it up on the rockface. The Luna Convento is one of the former – about five minutes' walk uphill from the cathedral. It occupies two separate buildings, separated by the winding coast road – one of them an old Saracen tower perched right on the sea.

The hotel opened in 1825 (it is one of the oldest in Amalfi), and has been in the same family for five generations. But you only have to step inside to see that the building's history goes back much further than the 19th century. The unique feature is the Byzantine cloister enclosing a garden and ancient well. The arcade serves as a quiet and civilized sitting area and breakfasts are served within the actual cloister – a delightful spot to start the day. You have the choice of modern or traditional bedrooms, and for a premium you can have your own private sitting-room. Lunch and dinner are taken either in the vaulted restaurant in the main building, where large arched windows give beautiful views of the bay, or better still across the road where the terrace and parasols of the tower restaurant extend to the water's edge. The swimming-pool forms part of the same complex – as does the somewhat incongruous disco.

Nearby cathedral of Sant'Andrea and cloisters of Paradise (in Amalfi); Valle dei Mulini (1 hr walk); Ravello (6 km).

Via P Comite 19, Amalfi 84011 Salerno
Tel (089) 871002 **Fax** 871333
Location short walk from middle of resort, overlooking sea, with private garage
Food & drink breakfast, lunch, dinner
Prices rooms L100,000-L160,000; FB L150,000-L170,000; 20% reduction for children under 6, sharing parents' room
Rooms 45 double, 5 single, 5 family rooms; all with bath; all rooms have minibar, phone, TV
Facilities 2 dining-rooms, 2 bars, Byzantine cloister; swimming-pool, disco
Credit cards AE, DC, MC, V
Children welcome
Disabled 2 lifts/elevators
Pets not accepted
Closed never
Manager A Milone

Campania

Seaside villa, Baia Domizia

Hotel della Baia

Baia Domizia is a modern and quite sophisticated seaside resort, stretching along a splendid, broad, sandy beach north of Naples. But at the Hotel della Baia you are unaware of being in a resort at all. It is a low-lying white building, standing well away from the main development, and its lush gardens lead straight past the tennis-court to the beach.

The hotel was opened about 25 years ago by the three Sello sisters from Venice, who have successfully reproduced the peaceful atmosphere of a stylish, if rather large, private villa. Spotless white stucco walls, cool quarry-tiled floors and white sofas are offset by bowls of fresh flowers and potted plants, and the antique and modern furnishings blend well together. The house feels lived-in, with books and magazines around, and an interesting range of pictures on the walls.

Bedrooms are no less attractive; all have balconies. A smartly furnished verandah links the house to the garden, and deck-chairs and extravagant white parasols are set out on the lawn.

The hotel has traditionally aimed high with its food, but we lack recent reports on the accuracy of that aim.

Nearby Gaeta (29 km); Naples within reach.

Via dell'Erica, Baia Domizia
81030 Caserta
Tel (0823) 721344 **Fax** 721566
Location in S part of resort, with gardens leading down to long sandy beach; ample car parking
Food & drink breakfast, lunch, dinner
Prices rooms L95,000-L170,000, FB L122,000-L145,000; reductions for children
Rooms 54 double, 18 with bath, 36 with shower; 2 single, one with bath, one with shower; all rooms have central heating, balcony, phone
Facilities 2 sitting-rooms, TV room, bar, terrace, dining-room; tennis, bowls, beach
Credit cards AE, DC, MC, V
Children welcome
Disabled no special facilities
Pets small, well-behaved ones accepted **Closed** Oct to mid-May **Proprietors** Elsa, Velia and Imelde Sello

Campania

Scalinatella

The little town of Capri is a ritzy, glossy place, full of boutiques selling denims encrusted with false gems. Those who feel at home in this scene may well head for the deluxe Grand Hotel Quisisana, or, if they want something smaller-scale, the Scalinatelli, run by the son of the owner of the Quisisana.

No expense has been spared in the creation of this exclusive small hotel. A spotless white building with a profusion of arches and oriental ornamentation, it feels distinctly Moorish. Inside a world of cool luxury awaits you. Every corner is air-conditioned and the rooms have all the trimmings that you might expect for the very high price you will be paying – telephones in the bathroom, private terraces and beds that disappear into alcoves, converting your rooms into a sitting-room by day. Furnishings vary from the simple and refined to the extravagant and perhaps over-rich. But there are few other flaws. Its location, with beautiful views to the Carthusian monastery of San Giacomo, leaves little to be desired; the garden and pool (where buffet lunches are served) are immaculate. The hotel was refurbished in 1989.
Nearby Monastery of San Giacomo (overlooked by hotel).

Via Tragara 10, Capri 80073 Napoli
Tel (081) 837 0633 **Fax** 8291
Location on Punta Tragara road; with garden and ample car parking
Food & drink breakfast, buffet lunch by pool
Prices rooms L160,000-L440,000 with breakfast
Rooms 30 double, all with bath and jacuzzi; all rooms have air-conditioning, phone, TV, minibar

Facilities sitting-rooms, breakfast room, bar; swimming-pool, tennis
Credit cards not accepted
Disabled no special facilities
Pets accepted
Closed Nov to mid-Mar
Proprietors Morgano family

Campania

Seaside hotel, Capri

Villa Brunella

The Villa Brunella was built in 1970 and its modern façade is of no great distinction – but, since the building is almost submerged in greenery, that is of little account. What really makes the place is its exceptional setting, perched on terraced slopes in the south-east of the island, with superb views of rugged cliffs and azure waters. You can admire the views from the balcony of your room, from the terrace dining-room where a buffet lunch is served, or from the pool which lies below the hotel (with a newly-improved surrounding terrace). The atmosphere is relaxed and the bedrooms are spacious, light and modern. Last year some reconstruction took place, increasing the number of suites and greatly reducing the number of rooms.

All in all, Villa Brunella is a very attractive place to stay; but we have two caveats. First, access is down a series of steep steps – estimates vary between 150 and 185 steps in all. Secondly, Sg Ruggiero has the reputation of dishonouring reservations when it suits him. One reader who has suffered in this way demands that we omit the hotel; we continue to include it for the benefit of low-season travellers for whom it may be an option.

Nearby beach of Faraglioni, monastery of San Giacomo.

Via Tragara 24, Capri 80073
Tel (081) 837 0122
Fax 837 0430
Location on terraced slopes, overlooking sea and cliffs, a few minutes' walk from Capri town; no proper road or car parking
Food & drink breakfast, lunch, dinner
Prices rooms L280,000; suites L350,000 with breakfast; meals about L35,000
Rooms 10 double, 8 suites, all with bath; all rooms have central heating, air-conditioning, phone, TV
Facilities 2 sitting-rooms, 2 bars; swimming-pool, panoramic terrace
Credit cards AE, V
Children accepted
Disabled no special facilities
Pets not accepted
Closed Nov to mid-Mar
Proprietor Vincenzo and Brunella Ruggiero

Campania

Il Monastero

Ischia Ponte gets its name from the low bridge giving access from the 'mainland' of Ischia to the precipitous islet on top of which stands the original settlement of Ischia, known collectively as the Castello although it consists of several buildings. One of these is an old monastery which is now run as a simple but entirely captivating *pensione*.

A lift reached by a tunnel into the rock of the island takes you up to the Castello (though there are steps as an alternative). Discreet signs bring you to the locked door of the *pensione*, and a ring on the bell summons the amiable *padrone*. Up a final flight of stairs and at last you are there. Many paintings hang on the plain walls of the hallway and the neat little sitting-room. The dining-room, recently redecorated, has satisfyingly solid wooden furniture. Bedrooms are monastically simple; some are reached from inside, some from the outside terrace, which gives a breath-taking view of the town and island of Ischia. We have no first-hand experience of the food, and half-board is inescapable; but we know that the cooking is good enough to keep the Monastero full in spring and autumn when other hotels are half-empty.
Nearby Castello d'Ischia.

Castello Aragonese 3, Ischia
Ponte 80070 Napoli
Tel (081) 992435
Location on island E of Ischia
town, linked by causeway
Food & drink breakfast,
dinner
Prices DB&B L58,000-
L73,000
Rooms 21 double, one single;
21 rooms have bath or shower
Facilities dining-room, bar, TV
room, large terrace
Credit cards not accepted

Children accepted
Disabled not suitable
Pets not accepted
Closed mid-Oct to mid-Mar
Proprietor Ciro Eletto

Campania

La Villarosa

This is a sharp contrast to the Monastero in every way: it is immersed in a jungle of a garden right in the heart of the little town of Ischia, and its great attraction – apart from the garden and pleasant thermal pool (which was greatly enlarged in 1991) – is its series of delectable sitting-rooms, beautifully furnished with comfortable armchairs and ornate antiques. The bedrooms are, by comparison, rather plainly furnished, but perfectly acceptable.

The light, welcoming restaurant upstairs leads out on to a terrace overlooking the garden and the roof-tops of Ischia, and meals are served there in summer. At one time only full board terms were offered, but we are pleased to report that Sg Amalfitano now offers 'room only' and half-pension terms as we have no evidence about the standard of cooking.

Like many hotels on the island, the Villarosa offers thermal treatments of various sorts – though the atmosphere is far removed from that of the traditional spa hotel, and visitors not seeking a *kur* will not feel out of place.

Nearby port of Ischia (500 m); Castello d'Ischia (2 km).

Via Giacinto Gigante 5, Porto d'Ischia 80077 Napoli
Tel (081) 991316
Location 200 m from lido; with limited car parking
Food & drink breakfast, lunch, dinner
Prices rooms L100,000-L200,000 with breakfast; DB&B L115,000-L155,000; FB L130,000-L170,000
Rooms 34 double, 20 with bath, 14 with shower; 6 single, all with shower; all rooms have

central heating, phone
Facilities sitting-room, bar, dining-room, TV room, terrace; swimming-pool, sauna
Credit cards AE, DC, MC, V
Children not suitable
Disabled access possible – lift/elevator to bedrooms
Pets not accepted in public rooms or dining-room
Closed Nov to Mar
Proprietor Paolo Amalfitano

Campania

Seaside hotel, Positano

Miramare

Whatever bedroom you are given at the Miramare, it will have a private sea-facing terrace, shaded by vine or bougainvillea and furnished with table and deck chairs. The rooms are simply but elegantly furnished, with white walls and prettily tiled floors. Bathrooms (some with sea views themselves) are spacious, and decorated with hand-painted tiles.

The sitting-room is an attractive area with a vaulted ceiling, Oriental rugs, antique furniture and plenty of plants and flowers. The dining-room – where the food is prepared and presented with flair – is a delight: a glassed-in terrace with bougainvillaea hanging from the ceiling in great swathes, and views to the beach far below.

Set on the steep hill to the west of Positano's beach and the fishing boats, the Miramare is a series of old fishermen's houses joined to make a charming and thoroughly comfortable hotel, close to the centre yet away from most of the noise. Arriving by car, park at the 'Miramare Parking' sign, then walk back up the hill to a corner where the hotel is signposted down a long flight of steps. More steps lead from the hotel to the seafront.

Nearby Amalfi (17 km); Ravello (23 km).

Via Trara Genoino 25-27, Positano 84017 Salerno
Tel (089) 875002
Location 3 minutes W of main beach; with private parking for 10 cars
Food & drink breakfast, lunch, dinner
Prices rooms L100,000-L300,000 with breakfast; dinner L50,000
Rooms 30 double, 3 single, 12 suites; all with bath and shower, central heating

Facilities dining-room, bar, 3 sitting-rooms
Credit cards AE, MC, V
Children not encouraged
Disabled not suitable
Pets not allowed in dining-room
Closed never; restaurant Nov to mid-Mar
Proprietor Sg Attanasio

Campania

Seaside hotel, Positano

Palazzo Murat

Most hotels in Positano are ranged up the steep hills either side of the ravine leading down to the sea. The Palazzo Murat, in contrast, is right in the heart of things – just inland of the *duomo*, and on a pedestrian alley lined with trendy boutiques.

The main building is a grand L-shaped 18thC *palazzo*. Within the L is a charming courtyard – a well in the middle, bougainvillea trained up the surrounding walls, palms and other exotic vegetation dotted around – where you can take breakfast (though in spring early risers will find it sunless). Along one side of this courtyard run the interconnecting sitting-rooms, which are beautifully furnished with antiques.

Bedrooms in the *palazzo* itself are attractively traditional in style – some painted furniture, some polished hardwood – and have doors opening on to token balconies (standing room only). Rooms in the more modern extension on the seaward side of the main building have the attraction of bigger balconies.

Positano's many restaurants are mainly congregated behind the beach, a short stroll away. 'Excellent value, stunning location', was one visitor's verdict.

Nearby tour of Amalfi coast and Sorrento peninsula.

Via dei Mulini 23, Positano
84017 Salerno
Tel (089) 875177 **Fax** 811419
Location in heart of resort;
paying car park nearby
Food & drink breakfast
Prices rooms L135,000-
L210,000 with breakfast
Rooms 28 double, all with
bath and shower, phone,
balcony, radio, minibar
Facilities sitting-room, TV
room, terrace, bar
Credit cards AE, DC, MC, V

Children accepted
Disabled access difficult
Pets small ones only accepted
Closed Nov to Easter week,
but open for Christmas week
Proprietor Carmela Cinque

Campania

Seaside hotel, Positano

Villa Franca

Provided you are not worried by heights, or by remoteness from the centre of things, this smartly traditional hotel has much to commend it. The position, high on the western side of the Positano ravine, gives an excellent view of the resort and the coast beyond from the windows and terraces – but does mean that the walk down to the resort centre and beach takes a few minutes and that the walk back up is exhausting. Happily, there is a private bus to and from the beach at certain times.

If the hotel's panoramic position is its first attraction, the second is its smart, cool sitting area – a series of interconnecting spaces with white-tiled floors and white-painted walls, linked by arched doorways. Comfortable armchairs with vivid blue covers are grouped around low tables, with enormous potted plants dotted around. The dining-room has the same decorative style.

The bedrooms are spacious and comfortable, and the best have their own sea-view terraces. The small pool also shares the view. We lack recent reports, but the visitor who originally recommended Villa Franca found the proprietors and staff welcoming, and the food satisfying and freshly-prepared.

Nearby Amalfi (17 km); Sorrento (17 km); Ravello (23 km).

Via Pasitea 318, Positano
84017 Salerno
Tel (089) 875655
Fax 875735
Location on main road above middle of Positano, with fine sea views
Food & drink breakfast, snacks, dinner
Prices rooms L165,000-L240,000 with breakfast; meals about L40,000
Rooms 28 double, one single, all with bath or shower; all

rooms have central heating, radio, satellite TV, phone, air-conditioning
Facilities dining-room, bar/sitting-room; swimming-pool
Credit cards AE, DC, MC, V
Children welcome
Disabled not suitable
Pets accepted, but not allowed in dining-room
Closed never
Proprietor Mario Russo

Campania

Town hotel, Ravello

Caruso Belvedere

The Caruso Belvedere is one of several hotels in this justly popular beauty spot which have been converted from old *palazzi*. Ever since it opened in 1903 it has been in the hands of the Caruso family.

The grandeur may have faded somewhat and the rooms cannot be called luxurious – reporters confirm our impression that they are simpler than you might expect at these prices, with unreliable plumbing and electrics. But unaffected, informal charm is the key to its success.

Many of the original features, such as the Corinthian columns and marble pillars, still survive; the antiques, faded sofas and open fireplaces are entirely in keeping with the setting. The restaurant is simple, light and spacious, but its best feature is the summer terrace with sensational views of the rugged coast and the Gulf of Salerno. Food is reportedly 'pleasing but not consistent', the wines that come from the Caruso's own vineyards 'excellent'. Staff are 'without exception helpful and friendly'.

Perhaps the most romantic feature of all is the terraced garden, with its timeless views of the sea far below.

Nearby Villa Rufolo, Villa Cimbrone; Amalfi (7 km).

Via San Giovanni del Toro 52, Ravello 84010 Salerno
Tel (089) 857111 **Fax** 857372
Location 500 m from the main piazza, with garden; public car parking in front of hotel
Food & drink breakfast, lunch, dinner
Prices rooms L120,000-L165,000; DB&B L150,000-L205,000
Rooms 22 double, 2 single, all with shower; 2 family rooms, both with bath; all rooms have central heating, phone
Facilities dining-room, bar, TV room, solarium
Credit cards AE, DC, MC, V
Children welcome
Disabled no special facilities
Pets small ones only accepted, and not in public areas
Closed never
Proprietor Gino Caruso

Campania

Palumbo

A Moorish-inspired *palazzo*, built for a nobleman in the 12th century, the Palumbo was bought by a Swiss hotelier in the mid-19th century and is still run by his family. No expense has been spared in its conversion to a five-star hotel, but what distinguishes it from most other hotels of its category is its understated luxury and elegance.

Public rooms focus on a 13thC inner courtyard where Corinthian-topped columns, oriental arches and a profusion of flowing plants provide a cool, civilized sitting-area. The restaurant is equally elegant, though more French than Moorish, with its peach tablecloths, gilt mirrors, mouldings and bentwood chairs. But on fine days the choice location is the balcony, where you look down over terraced vineyards to dazzling blue seas below. Various other balconies and terraces (hung with vines and roses) share this same stunning panorama. Throughout the hotel there are beautiful antiques and paintings – including what is purported to be a Caravaggio. Bedrooms are light and airy and tastefully furnished with antiques, tiled floors and rugs. Those in the annexe are more modern in style, but much cheaper.

Nearby Villa Cimbrone, Villa Rufolo; Amalfi (7 km).

Via San Giovanni del Toro 28, Ravello 84010 Salerno
Tel (089) 857244 **Fax** 858133
Location perched on cliffs; with garden, sun terrace and private car parking
Food & drink breakfast, lunch, dinner
Prices rooms L320,000-L500,000; DB&B L225,000-L315,000
Rooms 21 double, 3 suites; all with bath; 7 rooms are in annexe close to main building; all rooms have phone, TV, minibar
Facilities sitting-rooms, bar, dining-room
Credit cards AE, DC, MC, V
Children accepted
Disabled not suitable
Pets dogs not allowed in dining-room
Closed never
Proprietors Vuilleumier family

Campania

Seaside hotel, Amalfi

Hotel Lido Mare

This recently opened little hotel off Amalfi's Piazza del Duomo is in the same family as the Parsifal up in Ravello (page 197). Its arched, white-walled rooms are prettily furnished with antiques, and some of the bedrooms have views over the sea, only a few yards below.

■ Largo Ducci Piccolomene 9, 84011 Amalfi (Salerno) **Tel** (089) 871332 **Fax** (089) 857972 **Meals** breakfast **Prices** rooms L46,000-L75,000; breakfast L10,000 **Rooms** 13, all with bath or shower, air-conditioning **Credit cards** AE, DC, MC, V **Closed** never

---

Seaside hotel, Capri

Flora

On the edge of the fashionable little town of Capri, the Flora is immersed in greenery and flowers. It is a very well cared-for hotel, with calm and spacious bedrooms, many with balconies giving sea views, and an attractive terrace. A new restaurant and other facilities were added a couple of years ago.

■ Via Federico Serena 26, 80073 Capri (Napoli) **Tel** (081) 837 0211 **Fax** (081) 837 8949 **Meals** breakfast, lunch, dinner **Prices** rooms L250,000-L360,000 **Rooms** 24, all with bath, TV, minibar, air-conditioning; most rooms have terrace, phone **Credit cards** AE, DC, MC, V **Closed** Feb

---

Seaside hotel, Capri

Luna

A refreshing contrast to the ritzier hotels on Capri – a somewhat old-fashioned hotel in one of the island's most desirable locations, perched on the cliffs of the south coast. Bedrooms are spacious and comfortable, the pool is large by local standards.

■ Viale Matteotti 3, 80073 Capri (Napoli) **Tel** (081) 837 0433 **Fax** (081) 837 7459 **Meals** breakfast, lunch, dinner **Prices** rooms L190,000-L410,000 with breakfast; meals L55,000 **Rooms** 48, all with bath, air-conditioning, phone, TV, minibar; most rooms have terrace **Credit cards** AE, DC, MC, V **Closed** Nov to Mar

---

Seaside villa, Capri

Villa Sarah

There is no access by road: you have to walk, luggage and all, to this whitewashed building among the vineyards; the reward is peace and simplicity, well away from the bustle and vulgarity of the town. Rooms are neat and well-kept, with fine gardens in which to take breakfast or just soak up the sun.

■ Via Tiberio 3a, 80073 Capri (Napoli) **Tel** (081) 837 7817 **Meals** breakfast **Prices** rooms L81,000-L185,000 with breakfast **Rooms** 20, all with bath or shower, phone, TV **Credit cards** AE **Closed** Nov to Mar

Campania

Seaside villa, Capri

Villa Krupp

A welcome retreat from the bustle of the town, this serene white villa, where both Lenin and Gorky once lived, is set on a gentle hillside above the sheer cliffs of Marina Piccola. Bedrooms are bright, clean and mainly spacious; there are no public rooms.

■ Via Matteotti 12, 80073 Capri (Napoli) **Tel** (081) 837 0362 **Meals** breakfast **Prices** rooms L90,000-L170,000 with breakfast **Rooms** 12, all with bath or shower, balcony **Credit cards** V **Closed** never

---

Seaside hotel, Conca dei Marini

Hotel Belvedere

There is more to the Belvedere than the belvedere; but in the end the setting is the thing – on the edge of a cliff with splendid views of the Amalfi coast. A lift takes you down to a fair-sized sea-water pool, and steps to a private rocky beach.

■ Strada Statale 163, 84010 Conca dei Marini (Salerno) **Tel** (089) 831282 **Fax** (089) 831439 **Meals** breakfast, lunch, dinner **Prices** rooms L80,000-L190,000 with breakfast; DB&B L115,000-L155,000; FB L135,000-L180,000 **Rooms** 36, all with bath, balcony, central heating, phone **Credit cards** AE, MC, V **Closed** mid-Oct to Apr

---

Seaside hotel, Ischia

San Michele

This villa-style building is perched peacefully on the hillside above the little car-free village of Sant'Angelo, in beautiful gardens that include a splendid pool, terraces and (of course) thermal facilities. Modern, neat furnishings predominate, though the dining-room is more traditional in style.

■ Sant'Angelo, 80070 Ischia (Napoli) **Tel** (081) 999276 **Fax** (081) 999149 **Meals** breakfast; lunch and dinner in season **Prices** FB L165,000-L175,000 **Rooms** 44, all with bath or shower, phone; some have minibar **Credit cards** not accepted **Closed** Nov to Mar

---

Town hotel, Naples

Miramare

An appealing little hotel in an excellent position, on the waterfront, handy for ferries to the islands and some of the major sights. Compact but comfortable bedrooms. Hearty breakfasts are served in a smart, light, penthouse room with views of the bay, surrounded by a roof terrace. Helpful staff.

■ Via Nazario Sauro 24, 80132 Naples **Tel** (081) 427388 **Fax** (081) 416775 **Meals** breakfast, dinner **Prices** rooms L195,000-L320,000 with breakfast **Rooms** 31, all with bath or shower, air-conditioning, phone, TV, minibar, trouser-press **Credit cards** AE, DC, MC, V **Closed** never

Campania

Seaside hotel, Positano

Albergo L'Ancora

Modern and unpretentious hotel, next door to the famous and
over-priced Syrenuse, with the same enviable views and proximity
to the heart of Positano. Spacious and simply furnished bedrooms, and a dining-room that opens on to a shaded terrace. Car
parking.

■ Via C Colombo 36, 84017 Positano (Salerno) **Tel** (089) 875318
Fax (089) 811784 **Meals** breakfast, dinner **Prices** rooms
L140,000-L180,000 with breakfast; DB&B L100,000-L120,000 **Rooms** 18,
all with bath, phone, minibar, TV, some air-conditioning **Credit cards** AE,
DC, MC, V **Closed** mid-Oct to Mar

Seaside hotel, Positano

Marincanto

The rooms in the main part of this modest hotel are surprisingly
spacious and well furnished, and the views of colourful Positano
from its flowery terraces (where you can take breakfast) are
memorable. The car park is an asset, but it is not free. Don't
worry about the lack of a restaurant – you'll enjoy eating out.

■ 84017 Positano (Salerno) **Tel** (089) 875130 **Fax** (089) 875760
Meals breakfast **Prices** rooms L127,000 with breakfast; parking L10,000
Rooms 26, all with bath or shower, phone, minibar **Credit cards** AE, DC,
MC, V **Closed** mid-Oct to week before Easter

Town villa, Ravello

Giordano Villa Maria

The shady garden restaurant of this charming old villa beside the
path to the Villa Cimbrone is understandably popular, and there
is a traditionally furnished dining-room for cooler days. Bedrooms are simple, but have newly equipped bathrooms. Guests
can use the pool at the nearby Hotel Giordano.

■ Via Santa Chiara 2, 84010 Ravello (Salerno) **Tel** (089) 857170
Fax (089) 857071 **Meals** breakfast, lunch, dinner **Prices** rooms
L75,000-L175,000 with breakfast; suites L230,000-L280,000 **Rooms** 17,
all with bath or shower, central heating, phone; TV and minibar on request
Credit cards AE, MC, V **Closed** never

Town hotel, Ravello

Graal

The great attraction of this hotel, unpretentious but entirely
renovated during the late 1980s, is its splendid swimming-pool,
sharing the stunning view that is at the core of Ravello's appeal.
Simple but satisfying food, starting with an impressive buffet
breakfast, and good-value rooms.

■ Via della Republica 8, 84010 Ravello (Salerno) **Tel** (089) 857222
Fax (089) 857551 **Meals** breakfast **Prices** rooms L35,000-L112,000
Rooms 35, all with bath, central heating, phone, air-conditioning, TV
Credit cards AE, DC, MC, V **Closed** never

Campania

Seaside hotel, Ravello

Marmorata

Despite the address, the Marmorata is not up in the hills but down on the shoreline. It is an old paper mill, converted to a smart hotel with a nautical design theme. Large windows make the most of the sea views, and the main terrace is perched directly above the water.

■ Strada Statale 163, Localita Marmorata, 84010 Ravello (Salerno) **Tel** (089) 877777 **Fax** (089) 851189 **Meals** breakfast, lunch, dinner **Prices** rooms L110,000-L325,000 with breakfast **Rooms** 41, all with bath or shower, central heating, satellite TV, radio, minibar, air-conditioning, phone **Credit cards** AE, DC, MC, V **Closed** never

---

Converted monastery, Ravello

Parsifal

This little hotel retains a certain monastic simplicity along with its 13thC cloister. Bedrooms are plainly furnished, and some are on the small side: ask for the one with the terrace and sea view – which is heart-stopping, and shared by the creeper-clad terrace where honest, plain food is served.

■ Via G d'Anna 5, 84010 Ravello (Salerno) **Tel** (089) 857144 **Fax** (089) 857972 **Meals** breakfast, lunch, dinner **Prices** room L100,000 with breakfast; DB&B L120,000 **Rooms** 19, all with central heating; most have bath or shower **Credit cards** AE, DC, MC, V **Closed** first week Oct to end Mar

---

Town hotel, Ravello

Hotel Rufolo

The view along the coast is the great attraction of this plain but 'wonderfully situated' hotel, which comes strongly recommended by a reader. The terraced gardens incorporate a narrow but adequately long pool. The buffet breakfast is 'plentiful', the staff 'friendly, and helpful when pressed'.

■ Via San Francesco 3, 84010 Ravello (Salerno) **Tel** (089) 857133 **Fax** (089) 857935 **Meals** breakfast, lunch, dinner, snacks **Prices** rooms L120,000-L210,000 with breakfast; DB&B L105,000-L150,000 **Rooms** 30, all with bath, central heating, phone **Credit cards** AE, DC, MC, V **Closed** 10 Jan to end Feb

---

Town villa, Ravello

Villa Cimbrone

The gardens and views of Villa Cimbrone, a 10-minute walk from the centre, are one the great tourist attractions of Ravello. The villa has long been open to guests and was listed in early editions of the guide, but closed for a period of renovation in 1990. We have good reports of the results.

■ 84010 Ravello (Salerno) **Tel** (089) 857459 **Fax** (089) 857777 **Meals** breakfast **Prices** rooms L200,000-L260,000 with breakfast **Rooms** 19, all with bath, phone **Credit cards** MC, V **Closed** Nov to April

Campania

Seaside hotel, Sorrento

Bellevue Syrene

One of the grand old hotels of Sorrento, with a splendid position perched on the cliffs, with a lift/elevator down to the beach and jetty. The bedrooms have been splendidly renovated recently, and one reader feels that the public areas need the treatment; we quite like their faded elegance. 'Ordinary' food, says a report.

■ Piazza della Vittoria 5, 80067 Sorrento (Napoli) **Tel** (081) 878 1024 **Fax** (081) 878 3963 **Meals** breakfast, lunch, dinner **Prices** rooms L140,000-L200,000 with breakfast; meals about L50,000 **Rooms** 59, all with bath, phone, TV, radio **Credit cards** AE, DC, MC, V **Closed** never

---

Restaurant-with-rooms, Sorrento

La Tonnarella

Superb sea views (best enjoyed from the flowery terraces) are a major attraction of this cliff-top restaurant-with-rooms; the food is another. A lift/elevator takes you down the cliffs to a small private beach far below.

■ Via Capo 31, 80067 Sorrento (Napoli) **Tel** (081) 878 1153 **Meals** breafast, lunch, dinner **Prices** rooms 85,000-L100,000; meals L30,000 **Rooms** 18, all with bath, central heating **Credit cards** AE, DC, MC, V **Closed** 30 Nov to 25 Mar

---

Seaside hotel, Vico Equense

Capo la Gala Hotel

Squeezed into the limited space below the Sorrento coast road, this is a neat modern hotel arranged in terraces stepping down from the reception level to the sea (and the restaurant). Rooms are uniformly done out with tiled floors, plain walls and pretty cane furniture. Fair-sized pool.

■ Via Luigi Serio 7, Capo la Gala, 80069 Vico Equense (Napoli) **Tel** (081) 801 5758 **Fax** (081) 879 8747 **Meals** breakfast, lunch, dinner **Prices** rooms L155,000-L220,000 with breakfast; DB&B L170,000-L215,000; FB L220-L265,000 **Rooms** 18, all with bath, phone, minibar, balcony with sea-view **Credit cards** AE, MC, V **Closed** Nov to Mar

The heel and toe

Area introduction

Hotels in the heel and toe

To say that charming small hotels in the heel and toe of Italy are difficult to find is a wild understatement. It would be nearer the truth to say that they don't exist. The hotels which have full entries in the following pages are the best you will find, but some alternative recommendations may be helpful, particularly in the heel.

Lecce is a city of baroque architecture, which is well worth exploring; the Risorgimento (Tel (0832) 42125, fax 45571) is in a splendid central building, but way overdue for refurbishment. If your ambition is to make it right to the southern tip of the heel, you could aim for the Terminal (Tel and fax (0833) 753242), a well-run seaside holiday hotel at Marina di Léuca.

None of the major cities of the area is particularly alluring; each has a handful of routine big hotels. But if circumstances dictate a night in Foggia the place to head for is the Cicolella (Tel (0881) 3890, fax 78984), which has an attractive restaurant. To the north at Peschici, on the other side of the Gargano peninsula from our Mattinata recommendation, are the Paradiso (Tel (0884) 964201, fax 964203, 50 rooms) and the Solemar (Tel (0884) 964186, fax 964188, 45 rooms), both peaceful beach hotels set amidst pine trees.

For travellers in the 'toe' heading south with time to spare, the SS18 makes a slow-paced alternative to the A3 motorway, sticking to the eastern coast south of Lagonegro where the motorway takes a long detour inland. Two of our recommended hotels are at the northern end of this stretch of coast, and there are a few places further south that are worth bearing in mind. At Diamante is the Mediterranean-style Ferretti (Tel (0985) 81428, fax 81114), with terraces overlooking the sea and a highly reputed restaurant. The 65-room Grand Hotel San Michele (Tel (0982) 91012, fax 91430) at Cetraro is rather more swish – a well–restored old house in an attractive informal garden on cliffs above the beach. 90 km inland is the Barbieri (Tel (0981) 948072, fax 948073), worth a stop for excellent Calabrian fare and views of the medieval village of Altomonté.

The main tourist attraction of the toe, however, is on the other side of the A3 – the magnificently wild landscape of the Sila mountains east of Cosenza and north of Catanzaro. Each of these towns has a handful of acceptable hotels.

This page acts as an introduction to the features and hotels of Italy's 'heel' and 'toe', and gives brief recommendations of reasonable hotels that for one reason or another have not made a full entry. The long entries for this region – covering the hotels we are most enthusiastic about – start on the next page. But do not neglect the shorter entries starting on page 202: these are all hotels that we would happily stay at.

The heel and toe

Trulli **hotel, Alberobello**

Dei Trulli

The 'heel' of Italy has only one major tourist attraction: *trulli* – tiny stone buildings with conical, pointed roofs, usually joined in jolly little groups to make up multi-roomed houses. In Alberobello, a whole sector of the town consists of *trulli*, making it the natural goal of most visitors to the heel – though there are plenty of *trulli* dotted around the countryside, too. The Dei Trulli offers *trulli* enthusiasts the irresistible opportunity to go the whole hog – not just to peer at these quaint dwellings but actually to stay in one. The hotel is a sort of refined holiday camp – it consists of little bungalows, each partly contained in a *trullo*, set among pines and neat flower beds. You get a small living-room as well as a spacious bedroom and compact bathroom, plus seats outside your front door. There is a rather plain restaurant staffed by waiters whose charming demeanour quickly evaporates when problems arise. The cooking is competent, and the price for half-board now (in contrast to a couple of years ago) seems quite reasonable in comparison with the bed-and-breakfast rate. But for more variety there are restaurants in the town (within walking distance, through Alberobello's main *trulli* zone).
Nearby coast (15-20 minutes by car).

Via Cadore 28, Alberobello 70011 Bari
Tel (080) 932 3555 **Fax** 3560
Location 5 minutes' walk from middle of Alberobello; with private car parking
Food & drink breakfast, lunch, dinner
Prices rooms L150,000-L220,000; DB&B L175,000
Rooms 28 double apartments, 11 with bath, 17 with shower; 11 family apartments all with bath and shower; all have TV, phone, sitting-room, minibar
Facilities dining-room, bar; swimming-pool, playground
Credit cards AE, V
Children welcome
Disabled no special facilities
Pets small ones only accepted
Closed never
Manager Riccardo Cottino

The heel and toe

Villa Cheta Elite

The remote and mountainous region of Basilicata does not possess much coastline. But the tiny stretch of shore on the west side, where a corniche cuts through wild and beautiful cliffs, is one of the most spectacular parts of Italy's deep south. Villa Cheta Elite is set high up on this precipitous coastline, with splendid views. If the villa enjoyed no other distinction, its position would be enough to attract many travellers to the south. But this gracious art nouveau building has other attractions.

The villa is a pleasure to behold: a confection of ochre and cream stucco, decorated with ornate mouldings that would look at home in a grand Edwardian living-room. It lies among lush, flowery terraces, one of which is set out with café-style chairs and smartly laid dining tables. Inside, lace table-cloths, chintz sofas, carefully-chosen period pieces and abundant pictures create the air of a private home.

The beaches in the area are not wonderful, but the waters are clear, and reached in only a few minutes from the villa. The Aquadros are relaxed and charming hosts, who take great care over every aspect of their hotel, including the food.

Nearby Maratea (8 km); spectacular corniche road.

Via Nazionale, Acquafredda di Maratea 85041 Potenza
Tel (0973) 878134
Location 1.5 km S of Acquafredda, in gardens overlooking sea; private car parking
Food & drink breakfast, lunch, dinner
Prices rooms L90,000-L135,000; DB&B L105,000-L165,000
Rooms 16 double, one with bath, 15 with shower; 2 family rooms, both with shower; all have central heating, phone
Facilities dining-room with sea-view terrace, TV and reading-room, bar
Credit cards AE, DC, MC, V
Children welcome if well behaved **Disabled** access difficult **Pets** small ones only accepted; allowed in dining-room in low season only
Closed mid-Oct to Mar
Proprietors Marisa and Lamberto Aquadro

The heel and toe

Seaside hotel, Castro Marina

Orsa Maggiore

A straightforward place, thin on charm but certainly recommendable in this area: a modern building, high above the sea on the bottom of Italy's heel, run amiably and competently by the five Ciccarese brothers. Well kept, with a high local reputation for its food.

■ Litoranea per Santa Cesarea 303, 73030 Castro Marina (Lecce) **Tel** (0836) 97029 **Fax** (0836) 97766 **Meals** breakfast, lunch, dinner **Prices** DB&B L95,000; FB L115,000 **Rooms** 30, all with bath or shower, central heating, phone **Credit cards** AE, DC, MC, V **Closed** never

---

Country villa, Cisternino

Villa Cenci

A peaceful, out-of-the-way alternative to the dei Trulli (page 200), with the common feature of accommodation in simply furnished trulli. There are also rooms in the main house, along with a stylishly furnished restaurant. The pleasant gardens include a fine swimming-pool.

■ Via per Ceglie Messapica, 72014 Cisternino (Brindisi) **Tel** (080) 718208 **Fax** (080) 718208 **Meals** breakfast, lunch, dinner **Prices** rooms L52,000-L140,000; DB&B L75,000-L93,000 **Rooms** 22, all with bath or shower, central heating, TV **Credit cards** V **Closed** Oct to Apr

---

Country hotel, Fasano

La Silvana

A useful and economical base from which to explore *trulli* country – modern, clean and spacious, with plainly furnished rooms (some with views), and run by a welcoming and helpful family. Their efforts attract many non-residents to the large restaurant. Not to be confused with the much larger Sierra Silvana, nearby.

■ Viale de Pini 87, Selva di Fasano, 72010 Fasano (Brindisi) **Tel** (080) 933 1161 **Meals** breakfast, lunch, dinner **Prices** rooms L55,000-L85,000 with breakfast; DB&B L75,000 (minimum stay 3 days) **Rooms** 18, all with central heating; most have bath or shower **Credit cards** V **Closed** restaurant only, Fri in winter

---

Seaside hotel, Maratea

Santavenere

One of the most refined hotels of the deep south, in a splendid position close to the rocky shore, just outside the charming old town. The low-lying, arcaded building is set amid lawns and surrounded by trees, and furnished with taste and restraint. Spacious rooms, many with sea views from their terraces.

■ Fiumicello di Santa Venere, 85040 Maratea (Potenza) **Tel** (0973) 876910 **Fax** (0973) 876985 **Meals** breakfast, lunch, dinner **Prices** DB&B L220,000-L290,000 **Rooms** 44, all with bath, phone, terrace or balcony, TV, minibar **Credit cards** AE, DC, V, MC **Closed** Oct to Apr

The heel and toe

Seaside hotel, Mattinata

Alba del Gargano

Low-rise modern hotel in the middle of a lively little town (a short, free bus-ride from the beach), built around a courtyard where meals are served – fresh fish in particular. Simple but quite stylish furnishings.

■ Corso Matino 102, 71030 Mattinata (Foggia) **Tel** (0884) 4771 **Fax** (0884) 4772 **Meals** breakfast, lunch, dinner **Prices** rooms L48,000-L78,000 with breakfast; air-conditioning L15,000; FB L75,000-L145,000; reductions for children under 6 **Rooms** 39, all with shower, phone; 9 rooms have air-conditioning **Credit cards** V **Closed** restaurant only, Nov to 1 Apr

---

Country villa, Monópoli

Il Melograno

'The Pomegranate' was a working farm until quite recently. It now has conference and banqueting facilities, but retains its charm – secluded behind white walls, the grounds dotted with quiet courtyards, the rooms beautifully decorated and furnished with antiques.

■ Contrada Torricella 345, 70043 Monópoli (Bari) **Tel** (080) 690 9030 **Fax** (080) 747908 **Meals** breakfast, lunch, dinner **Prices** rooms L190,000-L440,000 with breakfast; lunch/dinner L50,000 **Rooms** 37, all with bath, central heating, air-conditioning, phone, satellite TV, hairdrier, radio, minibar, safe **Credit cards** AE, DC, MC, V **Closed** Feb

---

Town hotel, Otranto

Albania

Not so much charming as stylish and spotless – a modern hotel run with Swiss efficiency, at the extremity of the Adriatic coast, where any attractive hotel is worth noting. Public areas and bedrooms alike are spacious, light and calm. Seafood specialities.

■ Via S Francesco di Paola 10, 73028 Otranto (Lecce) **Tel** (0836) 801183 **Meals** breakfast, lunch, dinner, snacks **Prices** rooms L50,000-L80,000 with breakfast **Rooms** 10, all with bath or shower, central heating, air-conditioning, phone, radio, TV **Credit cards** DC, MC, V **Closed** never

---

Resort village, Parghelia

Baia Paraelios

An unusual hotel, with 72 bungalows built on a wooded hillside from the sea. The setting is superb, overlooking a bay of white sands washed by blue seas. Communal areas consist of three pools and open-air bar, and a dining-room/terrace by the sea.

■ Fornaci, 88035 Parghelia (Catanzaro) **Tel** (0963) 600300 **Fax** (0963) 600074 **Meals** breakfast, lunch, dinner **Prices** FB L100,000-L315,000; reductions for children **Rooms** 72, all with bath, sitting-room, terrace, phone, ceiling fan; some rooms have heating **Credit cards** AE, DC, MC, V **Closed** never

The heel and toe

Village hotel, Stilo

San Giorgio

This little hotel has been formed in a handsome stone-built 17thC house that was once a cardinal's palace, set in a pretty village in a scenic part of Calabria. The interior does not disappoint, and the theatrical friends of owner Francesco Careri ensure an animated atmosphere.

■ Via Citarelli 8, 89049 Stilo (Reggio di Calabria) **Tel** (0964) 775047 **Fax** (0964) 629306 **Meals** breakfast, lunch, dinner, snacks **Prices** rooms L55,000-L75,000 with breakfast; DB&B 70,000-L85,000 **Rooms** 14, all with bath or shower, central heating **Credit cards** not accepted **Closed** never

---

Seaside hotel, Vieste del Gargano

Seggio

At the tip of the Gargano peninsula, Vieste is a tight little town, perched on cliffs; the Seggio is right on the edge, with resultant views, and a tiny terrace down on the shoreline. The hotel is mainly done out in a smart, uniform, modern style; the vaulted restaurant is more traditional.

■ Via Veste 7, 71019 Vieste del Gargano (Foggia) **Tel** (0884) 708123 **Fax** (0884) 708727 **Meals** breakfast, lunch, dinner **Prices** rooms L55,000-L110,000 with breakfast **Rooms** 22, all with bath, central heating, phone **Credit cards** AE, MC, V **Closed** mid-Oct to mid-Mar

The islands

Hotels in the islands

Sicily, the largest and most populous island in the Mediterranean, has an extraordinary mix of sightseeing interest – spectacular scenery, ancient Greek ruins, medieval towns, splendid cathedrals, busy street markets, not to mention an active volcano – and therefore attracts hordes of visitors in the summer months. Taormina is the main resort and is well represented by hotels on the following pages. We have yet to find a sufficiently small and charming hotel to include for either Palermo or Siracusa, the two main cities. To see the sights of Palermo, you could stay in Cefalu, a pretty fishing port 60 km to the East. The Riva del Sole (Tel (0921) 21230, fax 21984) is a comfortable hotel close to the beach and the port, or the Baia del Capitano (Tel (0921) 20003, fax 20163)is a 39-room hotel 5 km out of town.

If you plan a more peaceful holiday, you might do best to choose one of the Aeolian (or Lipari) Islands, seven beautiful volcanic islands to the North of Sicily. We have an entry for the Villa Diana on Lipari (see page 213); in addition we suggest the Villa Meligunis (Tel (090) 981 2426, fax 988 0149), the Giardino sul Mare (Tel (090) 981 1004, fax 988 0150) and the Oriente (Tel (090) 981 1493, fax 988 0198), as other possibilities on Lipari. On the neighbouring island of Salina, try a cliff-top hotel, Punta Scario (Tel (090) 984 4139), or a restaurant-with-rooms, L'Ariana (Tel (090) 980 9075).

Although about the same size as Sicily, Sardinia is completely different: its population is sparse; there are few major sightseeing attractions and no very large towns or resorts; and there are no crowds, even in the most developed area for tourists, the Costa Smeralda – which is where most of our recommendations are located. Development is gradually spreading along the coastline from there in both directions. On the north coast, in addition to the Shardana (page 214), the Li Nabbari, also at Santa Teresa Gallura (Tel (0789) 754453, 38 rooms), is a possibility, as is the Albergo Corallo (Tel (079) 694055), a modern, 37-room hotel at Trinita d'Agultu.

On the east coast, the Pensione l'Oasi (Tel (0784) 93111, fax 93444) at Dorgali is a well-equipped hotel set on a hill overlooking the sea, amidst gardens and pinewoods. But if you really want to 'get away from it all', two small islands just off the south-west coast of Sardinia may appeal: Sant'Antioco — try the Club Ibisco Farm (Tel (0781) 809 003, fax 809003) — and the Isola San Pietro — try the Hieracon (Tel (0781) 854028, 24 rooms).

This page acts as an introduction to the features and hotels of Sicily and Sardinia, and the Aeolian islands, and gives brief recommendations of reasonable hotels that for one reason or another have not made a full entry. The long entries for this region – covering the hotels we are most enthusiastic about – start on the next page. But do not neglect the shorter entries starting on page 212: these are all hotels that we would happily stay at.

The islands

Villa Athena

Agrigento was one of the richest cities of the ancient world, and the Valley of the Temples, where the ruins rise in isolated splendour, is one of Europe's most compelling ancient sites (and sights). Since this is undoubtedly what you will be visiting Agrigento to see, the argument for staying at the Villa Athena is a powerful one: it is set right in the Valley, with the Temple of Concord directly in view.

From an 18thC villa it has been converted into a smart four-star hotel. The handsome, classical façade is in part a fair replica of a Greek temple, with outcrops of Doric columns in one or two places. Sadly, the interior is relatively modern in style – but it is comfortable enough, and you are not likely to be settling here for long. The view of the Temple of Concord is enjoyed by some of the bedrooms.

Another drawback is that there is no proper sitting-room; but such reservations are outweighed by the beauty of the site – the grounds, the pool, the palms and the terraces, where you can eat looking across to the timeless temples. It is particularly compelling at night, when the temples are illuminated.

Nearby Valley of the Temples.

Via dei Templi 33, Agrigento 92100
Tel (0922) 596288
Fax 402180
Location 3 km south of Agrigento, in the Valley of the Temples; with own garden and ample car parking (supervised)
Food & drink breakfast, lunch, dinner
Prices rooms L130,000-L210,000; DB&B L140,000-L160,000

Rooms 34 double, 6 single; all with shower; all have central heating, air-conditioning, radio, TV, phone
Facilities dining-room, bars, terrace, swimming-pool
Credit cards AE, MC, V
Children accepted; baby-sitting available
Disabled no special facilities
Pets accepted
Closed never
Proprietor Francesco d'Alessandro

The islands

Country hotel, Oliena, Sardinia

Su Gologone

The Barbagia is a mountainous inland region where the landscape is wild, the villages remote and bandits still thrive – though tourists are unlikely to encounter them. The hotel is a low-lying white villa, covered in creepers, surrounded by flowing shrubs and set in a landscape of rural splendour: wooded ravines, fields of olives, pinewoods and the craggy peaks of the Supramonte mountains. It feels isolated, and it is; but the Su Gologonne is far from undiscovered. Once, only a few adventurous foreign travellers found their way here; now, they come for the peace, or indeed for the food alone, which is typically Sard: cuts of local meats, roast lamb and the speciality of roast suckling pig – you can watch it being cooked on a spit in front of a huge fireplace. The wines are produced in the local vineyards. The dining-room spreads in all directions – into the vine-clad courtyard, the terrace and other rooms, all in suitably rustic style. The bedrooms are light and simple, again in rustic style, in keeping with the surroundings. Walls are whitewashed, floors are tiled and there are lovely views. Despite its size, the Su Gologone still feels small and friendly, and in most respects still typically Sard.
Nearby Gennargentu mountains; Monte Ortobene (21-km).

Oliena 08025 Nuoro
Tel (0784) 287512 **Fax** 287668
Location 8 km NE of Oliena, in remote mountain setting with private parking
Food & drink breakfast, lunch, dinner
Prices rooms L70,000-L95,000 DB&B L87,500-L101,500; FB L99,500-L129,500
Rooms 61 double, 4 family rooms, all with bath; all have central heating, phone, air-conditioning, colour TV; 15 rooms have minibar
Facilities 5 dining-rooms, 2 bars, conference room; disco, swimming-pool, tennis, bowls, riding, mini golf
Credit cards AE, MC, V
Children accepted
Disabled no special facilities
Pets accepted
Closed Nov to Feb
Proprietor Giuseppe Palimodde

The islands

Pitrizza

The smart playground of the Costa Smeralda is liberally endowed with luxury hotels, but there is one that stands out from the rest: the Pitrizza. What distinguishes it (apart from its small size) is its exclusive, intimate, club-like atmosphere. No shops, disco or ritzy touches here. Small private villas are scattered discreetly among the rocks and flowering gardens, overlooking a private beach. Rooms are furnished throughout with immaculate taste, some of them amazingly simple. The style is predominantly rustic, with white stucco walls, beams and locally crafted furniture and fabrics. Each villa has four to six rooms, and most have a private terrace, garden or patio. The core of the hotel is the club-house, with a small sitting-room, bar, restaurant and spacious terrace where you can sit, enjoying the company of other guests or simply watching the sunset. A path leads down to the golden sands of a small beach and a private jetty where you can moor your yacht. Equally desirable is the sea-water pool, which has been carved out of the rocky shoreline.

There is of course a hitch to the Pitrizza. The rooms here are among the most expensive on the entire Italian coastline.
Nearby beaches of the Costa Smeralda; Maddalena archipelago.

Porto Cervo 07020 Sassari
Tel (0789) 91500 **Fax** 92060
Location 4 km from Porto Cervo, at Liscia di Vacca; ample car parking
Food & drink breakfast, lunch, dinner
Prices DB&B L335,000-L480,000; reductions for children sharing parents' room
Rooms 38 double, 13 suites; all with bath; all rooms have air-conditioning, minibar, phone, TV, radio; most rooms have terrace or patio
Facilities bar, dining-room, terrace; sea-water swimming-pool; beach, water skiing, boat hire, windsurfing, private mooring
Credit cards AE, DC, MC, V
Children accepted
Disabled no special facilities
Pets not accepted
Closed Oct to mid-May
Manager Sg. P Tondina

The islands

Villa Belvedere

The Belvedere is a simple but stylish hotel which has been in the same family since 1902, with each generation making its changes without altering the inherent charm of the place. Currently in charge is Frenchman Claude Pécaut and his Italian wife, both of them friendly and helpful. One of the villa's great assets is its location. It is close to the middle of Taormina, commanding a spectacular panorama of the bay and the slopes of Etna to the south. Ask for a room at the front, and preferably one with a terrace. Not only do the few rooms at the back of the hotel lack these superb views – they are also noisy and gloomy by comparison. Flowery gardens lead down to a small pool where the setting and poolside bar (snacks and light lunches) tempt guests to linger all day and postpone the more serious business of sightseeing. There is no proper restaurant, but this can scarcely be considered a drawback given the choice down the road in central Taormina. And the hotel does have two prettily furnished drawing-rooms, an indoor bar and a spacious breakfast room. All in all, a sound choice for a reasonably priced family hotel when you don't want to be tied down by meals.

Nearby Greek theatre, Corso Umberto, public gardens.

Via Bagnoli Croce 79, Taormina 98039 Messina
Tel (0942) 23791 **Fax** 625830
Location close to public gardens and old town, with garden and parking for 15 cars
Food & drink breakfast
Prices rooms L91,000-L176,000 with breakfast
Rooms 43 double, 5 single, 15 with bath, 33 with shower; all have central heating, phone; 14 have air-conditioning
Facilities 2 sitting-areas, 2 bars, breakfast room, TV room; swimming-pool
Credit cards MC, V
Children accepted if well behaved **Disabled** no special facilities **Pets** welcome if well-behaved
Closed Nov to mid-Mar
Proprietor Claude and Silvia Pécaut

The islands

Seaside villa, Taormina, Sicily

Villa Sant'Andrea

The Villa Sant'Andrea was originally built and furnished by an aristocratic English family. It was converted to a hotel in 1950, but even after modernization it still has the stamp of a rather elegant turn-of-the-century English home. Flowery fabrics (largely Sanderson), cool colours and a few carefully chosen antiques combine to create a light and inviting interior – helped by the big windows that overlook the bay. Some of the guest rooms are a little old-fashioned in comparison with the rest of the hotel, but the front rooms with terraces are hard to beat for views. The bars and dining-rooms, in contrast, are crisply Continental.

The hotel stands among luxuriant sub-tropical terraces just above the pebbly beach of the bay of Mazzaro (deck-chairs and parasols are provided for guests). One of the restaurants is right on the beach, and you can lunch or dine here in the shade of palm trees overlooking the bay – an inviting spot both by day and night, when you can watch the fishing boats glide silently out to sea. The main restaurant is kept fresh by sea breezes wafting through the white arches which frame the bay.

Nearby Greek theatre, Corso Umberto and public gardens of Taormina, all reached by cable car; excursions to Etna.

Via Nazionale 137, Mazzaro, Taormina-mare 98030 Messina
Tel (0942) 23125 **Fax** 24838
Location on NE side of town, in gardens overlooking private beach; parking for 30 cars
Food & drink breakfast, lunch, dinner
Prices rooms L140,000-L380,000 with breakfast; FB L190,000-L350,000; reductions for children under 12
Rooms 56 double, 44 with bath, 12 with shower; 3 single, one with bath, 2 with shower; all rooms have central heating, air-conditioning, phone; TV, minibar on request
Facilities 2 dining-rooms, 2 bars, sitting-room; windsurfing, rowing-boats
Credit cards AE, DC, MC, V
Children accepted
Disabled no special facilities
Pets not accepted
Closed mid-Jan to late Mar
Manager Francesco Moschella

The islands

Seaside hotel, Taormina, Sicily

Villa Paradiso

Next to the public gardens and close to the heart of historic Taormina, the Villa Paradiso also has the advantage of a glorious panorama along the coast and across to the hazy cone of Etna. The only drawback to the location is that it is on a main road, which means some noise for back rooms and major problems with parking in high season.

The hotel is a well-maintained white building, and the public rooms have all the style and atmosphere of a private villa: white arches, patterned carpets on tiled floors, stylish sofas and an imaginative collection of prints, paintings and watercolours. The restaurant makes the most of the views, and the food is distinctly above average. Every bedroom has a balcony, and inevitably the most sought-after are those at the front with sea views. The majority are larger than you would expect from a *pensione;* some have attractive painted furniture. You can reach the beaches by cable-car or – more conveniently – the hotel minibus, which takes you to the Paradise Beach Club in Letojanni (free facilities for guests from the beginning of June).

Nearby Greek theatre, Corso Umberto and public gardens; excursions to Etna.

Via Roma 2, Taormina 98039 Messina
Tel (0942) 23922 **Fax** 625800
Location on SE edge of town; small public car park next door, paying garage nearby
Food & drink breakfast, dinner
Prices DB&B L90,000-L250,000
Rooms 33 double, 19 with bath, 2 with shower; 3 single, all with shower; 9 suites, all with bath; all rooms have central heating, air-conditioning, phone, TV, radio, hairdrier
Facilities 2 sitting-rooms, bar, dining-room, terrace
Credit cards AE, DC, MC, V
Children welcome; special meals and baby-sitting on request
Disabled access possible
Pets small cats and dogs only accepted **Closed** early Nov to Mar **Proprietor** Salvatore Martorana

The islands

Seaside villa, Alghero, Sardinia

Villa las Tronas

Originally the holiday home of the former royal family of Italy, this villa is furnished in suitably palatial style. Gardens surround the hotel and you can swim off the rocks below.

■ Via Lungomare Valencia 1, 07041 Alghero (Sassari) **Tel** (079) 981818 **Fax** (079) 981044 **Meals** breakfast, lunch, dinner **Prices** DB&B L145,000-L250,000; FB L170,000-L230,000; 20% reduction for children under 7 sharing parents' room **Rooms** 30, all with bath or shower, central heating, minibar, colour TV, phone **Credit cards** AE, DC, MC, V **Closed** restaurant only, winter

---

Town hotel, Erice, Sicily

Elimo

An extraordinary hotel, opened in the late 1980s: each of the rooms has been given an individual character – some traditional, some modern, some local, some exotic – followed through to the last detail. Public areas, too, have been meticulously done out.

■ Via Vittorio Emanuele 75, 91016 Erice (Trapani) **Tel** (0923) 869377 **Fax** (0923) 869252 **Meals** breakfast, lunch, dinner **Prices** rooms L150,000 with breakfast; DB&B L130,000; FB L150,000 **Rooms** 21, all with bath or shower, central heating, phone, TV, minibar **Credit cards** AE, DC, V **Closed** never

---

Town hotel, Erice, Sicily

Moderno

As the name suggests, some parts of this central hotel – notably the split-level sitting-room – are smartly modern. But some bedrooms are elegantly traditional, and there are pictures, ornaments and plants everywhere. Fine views from the sunny terrace. Warm welcome from the Catalano family.

■ Via Vittorio Emanuele 63, 91016 Erice (Trapani) **Tel** (0923) 869300 **Fax** (0923) 869139 **Meals** breakfast, lunch, dinner **Prices** rooms L80,000-L160,000 with breakfast; DB&B L110,000-L130,000; FB L120,000-L160,000; single person supplement L15,000 **Rooms** 40, all with bath or shower, central heating, phone **Credit cards** AE, DC, MC, V **Closed** never

---

Seaside hotel, Giardini-Naxos, Sicily

Arathena Rocks

An attractive alternative to the busy sands of Giardini-Naxos (not one of Sicily's most peaceful resorts), with swimming in the sea from rocks or from a man-made beach, as well as the pool. Light, cheerful rooms, some with views over the sea and hotel gardens. Run by a friendly family.

■ Via Calcide Eubea 55, 98035 Giardini-Naxos (Messina) **Tel** (0942) 51349 **Fax** (0942) 51690 **Meals** breakfast, lunch, dinner **Prices** rooms L99,000-L187,000 **Rooms** 45, all with bath or shower, phone **Credit cards** MC, V **Closed** Nov to Mar

The islands

Town guest-house, Lipari, Aeolian islands

Villa Diana

This skilfully restored villa, with ample terraces and quiet gardens overlooking Lipari and the surrounding bays, is still very much a family home, furnished and looked after with care. Dinners include a variety of local dishes, served with wines made on the island.

■ Via Tufo, Isole Eolie, 98055 Lipari (Messina) **Tel** (090) 981 1403
Meals breakfast **Prices** rooms L65,000-L105,000 with breakfast
Rooms 12, all with bath or shower **Credit cards** V **Closed** Nov to Mar

---

Seaside hotel, Porto Cervo, Sardinia

Hotel Balocco

A more modest (though by no means cheap) alternative to the five-star luxury of the Costa Smeralda: a stylishly rustic modern hotel in lush gardens, only a short walk from the shops and chic harbour of Porto Cervo. Fine views, pleasant pool.

■ Via Liscia di Vacca, 07020 Porto Cervo (Sassari) **Tel** (0789) 91555
Fax (0789) 91510 **Meals** breakfast **Prices** rooms L160,000-L350,000 with
breakfast (1992) **Rooms** 34, all with bath or shower, phone, TV,
air-conditioning, balcony or terrace **Credit cards** AE, DC, MC, V
Closed mid-Oct to Apr

Seaside hotel, Porto Cervo, Sardinia

Hotel Cappricioli

You don't have to spend a fortune to stay on the rugged Costa Smeralda: the Cappricioli is a simple family-run hotel standing among windswept *macchia* close to a pretty beach. The Azara family started their restaurant here 30 years ago, and Ristorante Il Pirata is still the focus of the rustic, villa-style hotel.

■ Cappricioli, 07020 Porto Cervo (Sassari) **Tel** (0789) 96004 **Fax** (0789)
96422 **Meals** breakfast, lunch, dinner **Prices** DB&B 120,000-L243,000
Rooms 27, all with bath or shower, central heating **Credit cards** AE, MC,
V **Closed** Oct to Apr

Seaside hotel, Porto Rotondo, Sardinia

Sporting

An oasis of luxury, consisting of neo-rustic villas scattered around a promontory, with sea views all around, particularly from their terraces. Everything is tastefully simple – beams, tiled floors, white walls, plain fabrics. The atmosphere is quite clubby, with a strong yachting contingent.

■ Olbia, 07026 Porto Rotondo (Sassari) **Tel** (0789) 34005 **Fax** (0789)
34383 **Meals** breakfast, lunch, dinner **Prices** FB L280,000-L460,000
Rooms 27, all with bath, minibar, phone, balcony **Credit cards** AE, DC,
MC, V **Closed** end Sep to mid-Apr

Seaside hotel, Santa Teresa Gallura, Sardinia

Shardana

Another affordable alternative to the Costa Smeralda norm, isolated near a sandy beach on the northern tip of Sardinia. Accommodation is mainly in separate, stylish little villas, some in the central clubhouse along with the restaurant and bar. Small, pretty pool, watersports.

■ Capo Testa, 07028 Santa Teresa Gallura (Sassari) **Tel** (0789) 754031 **Fax** (0789) 754129 **Meals** breakfast, lunch, dinner **Prices** rooms L107,000-L214,000; FB L89,000-L204,000 **Rooms** 51, all with bath or shower, phone, TV, air-conditioning, minibar **Credit cards** AE, V **Closed** Oct to May

Seaside hotel, Taormina, Sicily

Villa Fiorita

A small, clean bed-and-breakfast hotel built into the rock high on a mountain terrace and with a grand panorama of the bay below Taormina. There is a swimming-pool but the funicular down to the beach is only a couple of minutes' walk away.

■ Via L Pirandello 39, 98039 Taormina (Messina) **Tel** (0942) 24122 **Fax** (0942) 625967 **Meals** breakfast **Prices** rooms L125,000; suites L177,000 **Rooms** 26, all with bath or shower, air-conditioning, phone, colour TV, radio, minibar **Credit cards** AE, MC, V **Closed** never

Resort village, Vaccileddi, Sardinia

Don Diego

Despite a reader's report critical of cleanliness of the pool and beach, the Don Diego keeps its place here on the grounds of sheer charm. It consists of comfortable, stylish cottages scattered among *macchia* and flowery gardens, each with a terrace. The dining-room and sitting-room are tastefully rustic.

■ Porto San Paolo, Costa Dorata, 07020 Vaccileddi (Sassari) **Tel** (0789) 40007 **Fax** (0789) 40026 **Meals** breakfast, lunch, dinner **Prices** DB&B L150,000-L270,000 **Rooms** 60, all with bath or shower, phone **Credit cards** AE **Closed** never

Index of hotel names

In this index, hotels are arranged in order of the first distinctive part of their names. Very common prefixes such as 'Hotel', 'Albergo', 'Il', 'La', 'Dei' and 'Delle' are omitted. More descriptive words such as 'Casa', 'Castello' and 'Villa' are included.

Index of hotel names

Index of hotel names

Index of hotel names

Index of hotel locations

In this index, hotels are arranged in order of the names of the cities, towns or villages they are in or near. Hotels located in a very small village may be indexed under a larger place nearby. An index by hotel name precedes this one, on page 000.

Index of hotel locations

Index of hotel locations

Index of hotel locations